Books are to be returned on or before
the last date below.

IBREX–

D1494555

Child Well-Being
Understanding Children's Lives

EDITED BY COLETTE MCAULEY AND WENDY ROSE

FOREWORD BY DAME GILLIAN PUGH

Jessica Kingsley *Publishers*
London and Philadelphia

Figure 1.1, Box 3.1, Box 3.2 and Table 4.3 all reprinted with the permission
of the Controller of HMSO and the Queen's Printer for Scotland
Table 8.1 reprinted with permission from the Annie E. Casey Foundation
Table 8.2 reprinted with permission from the US Department of Health and Human Services
Table 8.3 reprinted with permission from Child Trends
Table 8.4, Table 8.5 and Table 8.6 are all from *What Works in Family Foster Care?* by Peter J. Pecora
et al. © 2010 Oxford University Press, reprinted with permission from Oxford University Press

First published in 2010
by Jessica Kingsley Publishers
116 Pentonville Road
London N1 9JB, UK
and
400 Market Street, Suite 400
Philadelphia, PA 19106, USA

www.jkp.com

Library of Congress Cataloging in Publication Data

Child well-being : understanding children's lives / edited by Colette
McAuley and Wendy Rose ; foreword by Dame Gillian Pugh.
p. cm.
Includes bibliographical references and index.
ISBN 978-1-84310-925-9 (alk. paper)
1. Child welfare. 2. Family policy. I. McAuley, Colette. II. Rose, Wendy, 1944-
HV713.C38284 2010
362.7--dc22

2010007470

British Library Cataloguing in Publication Data
A CIP catalogue record for this book is available from the British Library

ISBN 978 1 84310 925 9

Printed and bound in Great Britain by
MPG Books Group

Contents

List of figures, tables and boxes

FIGURES

TABLES

BOXES

Preface

Jonathan Bradshaw, one of our authors in this volume, wrote in 1990 that, 'In any society, the state of children should be of primary concern – their well-being is not only an indication of a society's moral worth, they are human capital, the most important resource for its national future' (Bradshaw 1990, p.3). In the past two decades there has been a burgeoning interest in the idea of 'child well-being', which has spread from the world of children's campaigners, academics and psychologists to incorporate a vast array of politicians, policy makers, planners and professionals. The language about children in social policy has changed from focusing on the most vulnerable in our society and notions of child rescue and child welfare to a much broader and holistic view of child development within an ecological perspective. Policy aspirations for children are now couched in terms of what we would want for all our nation's children, and government has incorporated child well-being into legislation. However, it has become clear that the term child well-being is not well understood – indeed, it is defined and used in very different ways. Yet, despite this, it is beginning to be perceived as useful in providing a shared language for all the different disciplines working with children and families.

As the result of exchange with colleagues in the UK and internationally through their joint membership of the International Association for Outcome-Based Evaluation and Research for Family and Children's Services (iaOBERfcs), the editors of this book were convinced that the time had come to shed some light on what was known about child well-being from the world of research, policy and practice across the disciplines – not least being the editors' commitment to obtaining the views and experiences of children and young people themselves concerning their well-being, and also to hearing from the adults in their lives. The editors set about this by inviting colleagues from the UK and other countries with whom they had collaborated over a number of years to join with them in exploring some of the features and issues surrounding child well-being and to produce this volume with them.

The book is presented in three parts. The first part explores how child well-being can give us a better understanding of children's lives in those environments where they will spend most time and that will have a profound influence in shaping their lives as they grow up – at home, in school and in the community. In Chapter 1, Jane Aldgate starts by looking at some contemporary approaches to well-being, including the contribution of thinking in areas of child development such as ecology, wellness and attachment. Most importantly, she considers how children *themselves* can contribute to our understanding of well-being, how they are agents in shaping their own well-being and what can be learnt from the ways in which they spend their time. The chapter ends with a case study from Scotland describing how well-being indicators can be used in practice to improve outcomes for children.

Chapter 2, by the editors and Roger Morgan, the Children's Rights Director for England, specifically examines what we do already know from children about their understanding of well-being. Drawing upon a range of research studies that directly interviewed children and a body of consultative work, the views of children from different family types and circumstances, as well as disabled children and those in care, are explored in relation to the most significant relationships in their lives and their emotional worlds. Wider issues about how children think about consultation and the importance of the notion of safety to them are also explored.

Chapter 3 tells the story of how child well-being came to be incorporated into government policy, demonstrating how the idea of outcomes for *all* children developed and how the framework was modified as different circumstances and interests influenced its journey through the policy machine. This chapter is written by one of the editors (Wendy Rose) and John Rowlands, both former civil servants who worked on children's policy in England.

Pamela Munn, in Chapter 4, examines how schools can use the current policy aspirations for children to contribute to the promotion of the well-being of pupils. She demonstrates how a 'whole-school approach' can be used, which addresses how the school functions to support children's well-being, through the formal, informal and hidden dimensions of curriculum. She also then looks more closely at how a well-being approach can assist in targeted work with individual children.

In the final chapter of the first part, Pat Dolan, who has recently been appointed as UNESCO Chair, begins with a brief overview of how well-being is conceptualised, measured and valued within an international agenda. The chapter then focuses on the central value of social support and its connection to well-being. The role and benefit of social-civic engagement of young people is described and a case example of youth peer-mentoring programmes is illustrated. Finally, a new conceptual model is proposed that relates well-being, social support and civic engagement for young people.

In the second part of the book, we attempt to capture some of the most interesting international developments around how different nations measure and monitor children's well-being. In the first of these chapters (Chapter 6), Asher Ben-Arieh provides a useful overview of the child indicators movement and its response to the changing context of increasing demand for indicators, and methodological and measurement advances as well as normative and theoretical changes. The chapter concludes with a discussion on future directions.

Chapter 7, by Anne Marie Brooks, Sinéad Hanafin and Sylda Langford, provides a rich illustration of how the Republic of Ireland has taken forward many of the ideas contained in Chapter 6 and applied them in their own country. The authors take us through the detailed processes involved in producing their first two State of the Nation reports on the well-being of children – of particular interest being the fact that they consulted children about their views during the process.

In Chapter 8, Peter Pecora and Markell Harrison-Jackson describe how child well-being is measured in the United States and address some of the methodological challenges that are inherent in this work. There is a special focus on the advances and challenges in measuring child well-being in the field of child and family services. The authors also present some of the rich US data that has recently become available on the well-being of children currently or formerly living in foster care.

Internationally, there has been a recent realisation among those concerned with developing indicators of child well-being that we need to include measures of subjective well-being. However, this is a very new area, with many challenges emerging. In Chapter 9, Jonathan Bradshaw and his colleagues share with us his latest work in trying to advance this area in collaboration with the Children's Society in England.

The final part of the book, containing the editors' closing chapter, addresses issues such as the lack of clarity about the concept of child well-being and questions the extent to which children and parents have been engaged by government in shaping this concept, in the light of the fact that it has become the dominant discourse nowadays in relation to policy regarding children in England. However, there does appear to be consensus that the well-being of children needs to be considered in the wider environmental context. And whilst there remain concerns about the meaning of the concept, there is evidence that it has been used by policy makers, professionals and a variety of disciplines to bring about constructive change in the lives of children and families. The involvement of children in shaping the concept, and possibly in measuring and monitoring their own well-being, are some of the most interesting future developments discussed at the close of the chapter.

PART I

CHILD WELL-BEING: UNDERSTANDING CHILDREN'S LIVES AT HOME, SCHOOL AND IN THE COMMUNITY

threads' are attended to. These include the need for a clear and unremitting focus on the well-being of the most vulnerable, good leadership, effective data and commissioning of services, collaborative working, listening to and responding to the views and needs of individual children and young people, and working with their parents and within communities (C4EO and LGA 2008, 2009).

As this book shows, there have been considerable steps forward in the extent to which children are seen as active agents in contributing to their own sense of well-being. Children's right to participate in key decisions about their lives, and to contribute their views and to be listened to, are not only much more common practice now than they were even a decade ago, but are also increasingly embedded in legislation. As is clear from the chapters that follow, priorities for children are a loving family, good friends, a safe environment, feeling in control of their lives and being taken seriously – listened to and receiving feedback. These are also important themes from major inquiries such as the Good Childhood Inquiry (Layard and Dunn 2009) and the Cambridge Primary Review, the most comprehensive review of primary education for over 40 years and the first one to embed a consideration of primary education within the context of children's lives and the changing world in which they are living (Alexander 2009). The concept of well-being was central to this important study, the first aim of primary education being:

> to attend to children's capabilities, needs, hopes and anxieties here and now, and promote their mental emotional and physical well-being and welfare. Happiness, a strong sense of self and a positive outlook on life are not desirable in themselves; they are also conducive to engagement and learning. (Alexander 2009, p.197)

Both Narrowing the Gap and the review of primary education provide evidence of the role that schools can play in improving children's well-being. Although there has been a degree of resistance on the part of some head teachers who felt that a focus on well-being could detract from the pressure to raise standards, there is increasing evidence that the broader welfare agenda – networks of multi-professional services in local areas, linked into schools, and requiring schools to provide for children's needs in a broader way, through the provision of extended services such as out-of-school activities and support for parents – is leading to improved educational outcomes as well as improved behaviour and school attendance. Not surprisingly, attending to the needs of the child in a broader context – awareness of difficult issues in the family, bullying or particular health issues, for example – leads to overall improvements across all outcomes at school.

The themes that emerge from the work on reducing inequalities and narrowing the gap reflect those that are highlighted in the chapters that follow: the importance of listening to how children and young people view their lives, of working in partnership with children and their parents within the context of the communities that they live in and the schools that they attend, and of working together across professional boundaries. And above all of seeing children as individuals, about whose needs we have relevant and up-to-date data, so that we can respond in an effective and timely manner.

Although a focus on improving outcomes in general and well-being in particular has led to criticisms that we are becoming increasingly target driven and obsessed by indicators, this is to underestimate the importance of understanding more about how well individual children and groups of children are doing, and of knowing whether the services that we are providing for them are both meeting their needs as they identify them and are having the impact that we wish them to – so that no child is let down or left behind.

The challenges of improving children's well-being, however, go beyond the provision of more effective public services, important though these are. The bigger questions are, how can we create a society in which children are better valued and parents better supported in bringing up their children? And what can be done to reduce the inequalities which impact on every aspect of children's well-being? More unequal societies are bad for almost everyone within them, the well-off as well as the poor, as Wilkinson and Pickett's recent book *The Spirit Level* (2009) shows. The authors present a damning indictment of the degree of inequality in countries such as the UK and the USA where the extent of social malaise and consequent stress associated with inequality leads to poorer social and mental health for all citizens, by comparison to more equal societies such as Scandinavia. These findings have also been reflected in two government-funded reviews, one on the degree of income inequality (Hills *et al.* 2010) and one on health inequalities (Marmot 2010).

The research and policy initiatives explored in this book are crucial to continuing improvements in children's well-being. But it is only the creation of a more equal society that will bring equal benefit to all children.

Dame Gillian Pugh
Chair, National Children's Bureau

Acknowledgements

Producing this book has been a learning experience for the editors. Authors have contributed new knowledge, insights and perspectives which have caused us to rethink and review some of the assumptions we have held. Authors have also opened up exciting possibilities for future development as well as facing us with challenges we all need to address in the interests of children. The rich material from the views of children, young people and parents represents one of these challenges – how do we ensure children and their families are engaged as equal partners in the journey to improve the well-being of all children, whatever their circumstances?

We are indebted to our colleagues who have contributed to this volume and enriched us in the process. We are also grateful to many other people who have provided valuable information and insights into specific issues and, in particular, we would like to thank Anne Jackson, Bill Alexander and Andy Pithouse. Such a book takes some time from gestation to final production. We have had tremendous support and encouragement throughout from the editorial staff of Jessica Kingsley Publishers. We particularly appreciated the wise counsel of Stephen Jones, Senior Commissioning Editor, and the efficient support provided by Caroline Walton and Victoria Peters. We would like to thank Tricia Keilthy for administrative support in the later stages of the process. We are also indebted to Dame Gillian Pugh for providing such a reflective Foreword.

At the conclusion of working on this book, however, the lasting memories are of the inspirational children and young people we have encountered and consulted with over recent years in the course of research studies, conferences and consultation events, as well as, of course, the children who are an integral part of our own family lives. Understanding their lives and promoting their well-being has to be the greatest challenge.

Colette McAuley and Wendy Rose
Editors

Foreword

There has been a growing interest over the past decade in the concept of child well-being – amongst policy makers, practitioners and academics – in both the UK and internationally. But what does this concept mean, and does it mean the same thing to children and families as it does to policy makers? How can it be measured? And if it has begun to impact on government policy, has it made any difference to children's lives?

During the course of this book the concept of well-being is defined in many different ways, including the quotation in Chapter 1 from UNICEF:

> The true measure of a nation's standing is how well it attends to its children – their health and safety, their material security, their education and socialization, and their sense of being loved, valued, and included in the families and societies into which they are born. (UNICEF 2007, p.4)

But as the editors conclude, more important than agreement on a definitive definition is the fact that the discussion has led to a widespread debate in many countries across the world about how to improve outcomes for all children. Critically, this debate has its roots in an ecological perspective of children's development, seeing children's lives as a whole and their development in the round, and in the context of their families and of the communities that they live in.

In many respects, children and young people today have never been better off – the health, living standards, educational opportunity and access to information and entertainment for the majority have never been so good. But amidst this increasing prosperity, there are anxieties for many about family breakdown, about pressures to conform, about personal safety, drugs and alcohol, about global issues such as climate change and – perhaps above all – about financial difficulties.

For, despite a commitment from the UK Government to eliminate child poverty, the UK is still one of the most unequal societies in the world and there are strong links between the socio-economic group into which a child is born and their adult outcomes. Children from lower socio-economic groups have the greatest chance of poor outcomes on a whole range of measures, including physical health, emotional health, educational attainment, school attendance and employment opportunities. They are also more likely to commit offences, to be taken into care, to become very young parents and to fail to continue into further education or employment. Moreover, the social class gap opens early and widens swiftly. More able children from poor homes are, by the time they are six years old, doing less well in reading and maths tests than less able children from well-off homes. Thus, while the overall well-being of children is improving, there is a long tail of children who are failing to thrive and prosper.

A response to improving the life chances of the most vulnerable children in the countries featured in this book has been to move away from a deficit model of children and young people with problems, to one of entitlement – what should we expect for all our children across all areas of their lives, to what should they be entitled, what are the obstacles that prevent some children doing as well as they should, and how can they be overcome? In England this approach has led to the *Every Child Matters* agenda which, over the past seven years, has aimed to transform the way in which public services are planned and delivered. This co-ordinated approach has had a strong focus on improving outcomes for *all* children, not just the most vulnerable (though with a particular focus on those who are falling behind), and with a concern for children's lives in the here and now, as well as with an eye to the future. This better-co-ordinated approach to strategic planning, to governance, to assessment and commissioning, and to the delivery of services themselves has created a new framework for thinking about children's well-being.

By focusing on improving outcomes for all children, across all areas of their development, we know from a range of interventions that we can narrow the gap and give vulnerable and disadvantaged children the extra help that they need. The recent Narrowing the Gap project, which has been working with over 100 local authorities across England, aimed to answer a fundamental question – what is it that, if applied universally and pursued relentlessly, would make a significant impact on the outcomes of vulnerable groups of children and young people? The project, which continues with the work of the Centre for Excellence and Outcomes in Children's Services (C4EO), shows what can be achieved if the 12 key messages or 'golden

CHAPTER 1

Child Well-Being, Child Development and Family Life

JANE ALDGATE

Introduction

The idea of children's well-being is increasingly at the heart of current policy and practice in many disciplines, and 'well-being' is a term now used by a wide range of practitioners, researchers and policy makers. There are many ways of approaching and measuring child well-being. This chapter looks at some contemporary approaches to well-being, including the contribution of thinking in areas of child development such as ecology, wellness and attachment. Most importantly, it explores how children themselves can contribute to our understanding of well-being. The chapter ends with a case study from Scotland of how well-being indicators can be used in practice to improve outcomes for children.

Well-being and well-becoming

Promoting the well-being of children is seen as important because it lays the foundations for adult functioning. Cynics might, therefore, argue that the central purpose of paying attention to child well-being is to make an investment in the future, in what Ben-Arieh has called 'children's well-becoming' (Ben-Arieh 2002, p.150). Certainly, there is evidence that policy makers believe that investing in children's well-being as they grow up is likely to influence their contribution to their countries as adult citizens, as this example from Scotland shows:

> We want our children and young people to be successful learners, confident individuals, effective contributors and responsible citizens. (Scottish Government 2008, p.5)

A child's ecology and well-being

The evidence for using well-being to shape policy and practice comes from increasing interest in what has become known as the 'ecological approach to children's development'. First developed by Bronfenbrenner in the 1970s (Bronfenbrenner 1979), the ecological approach recognises that all the experiences children have will contribute to their overall well-being and that what is happening in one part of a child's life will affect what is going on elsewhere:

> Ecological theory suggests that children are surrounded by layers of successively larger and more complex social groupings which have an influence on them. These include family and extended family, friendship networks, school, neighbourhood and work influences, and the family's place within the community. Still wider is the influence of the culture within which children live. Children across the world will experience childhood in many different ways. (Aldgate 2006, p.23)

The interaction between the main ecological factors influencing a child's well-being have been used by UK governments in varying frameworks for the assessment and planning for children in need of services (Department of Health, Department for Education and Skills and Home Office 2000; Scottish Government 2008). The ecological knowledge base underpinning the Assessment Framework used in England and Wales is described by Rose and Aldgate (2000). As well as considering children's relationships with others and their family's circumstances, the Assessment Framework includes the impact on children's well-being of structural factors such as poverty and the safety of communities (Rose and Aldgate 2000). Jack and Gill (2003) also provide an excellent analysis of the impact of structural factors on children's well-being, while the research of Aldgate and McIntosh on kinship care (2006a) and the daily activities of children looked after by local authorities in Scotland (2006b) support the view that poverty can inhibit opportunities for children to develop their talents.

The UNICEF definition of well-being

The ecological approach to children's well-being is embedded in the UNICEF definition of well-being. This takes a broad view of well-being that can serve as a foundation for policy and support the development of services for children:

> The true measure of a nation's standing is how well it attends to
> its children – their health and safety, their material security, their
> education and socialization, and their sense of being loved, valued,
> and included in the families and societies into which they are born.
> (UNICEF 2007, p.4)

The UN Convention on the Rights of the Child places the responsibility
for implementing this broad ecological approach on both the family and
the State. The principles of the UN Convention on the Rights of the Child
(United Nations 1989) state that both family and State should give attention
to various aspects of children's lives, including education, care, recreation,
culture and health, and children's social behaviour.

Ecology, wellness and well-being

The broad ecological view of how to approach well-being is complemented
by the approach to children's development taken by developmentalists who
link children's well-being to wellness, recognising that well-being will be
influenced by many factors that are part of the physical and psychological
wellness of children, irrespective of their circumstances. As Prilleltensky
and Nelson have suggested:

> Child wellness is predicated on the satisfaction of material, physical,
> affective, and psychological needs. Wellness is an ecological
> concept: a child's wellness is determined by the level of parental,
> familial, communal, and social wellness. (Prilleltensky and Nelson
> 2000, p.87)

A strengths approach to well-being

A further important strand in the wellness and well-being debate is the view
that it is important to look at an individual's strengths and achievements as
well as the deficits they experience. Practitioners in all areas of children's
services have begun to move away from looking at deficits to stressing
strengths and achievements. Such an approach is equally applicable to
adults and children, as is suggested in Lorion (2000):

> The work of psychologists is moving from an emphasis upon the
> troubles, the anxieties, the sickness of people, to an interest in how
> we acquire positive qualities, and how social influences contribute
> to perceptions of well-being, personal effectiveness and even joy.
> (Kelly 1974, quoted in Lorion 2000, p.5)

Schaffer, writing about how children can overcome adversity, supports the strengths approach:

> The optimism about growth and development has permeated research on children's development and well-being. There is a growing understanding that children can change their behaviour and[,] equally, that children can recover from negative experiences of adversity, including the impact of rejection, separation and loss, provided they have subsequent experiences that help to build their resilience. (Schaffer 1996, p.8)

Schaffer's optimism is reinforced by the work done in recent years on resilience as a protective factor in children's well-being. Resilience is defined as 'normal development under difficult conditions' (Fonagy *et al.* 1994). In the UK, Rutter's work on outcomes for young people who have become resilient in spite of growing up in adverse circumstances has given insights into experiences that are likely to protect children.

Rutter (1985) cites three factors associated with resilience:

- a sense of self-esteem and confidence

- a belief in own self-efficacy and ability to deal with change and adaptation

- a repertoire of problem-solving approaches.

(Rutter 1985, p.598)

The importance of children's attachments and well-being

One of the major contributing factors to the development of strengths and resilience is the part played by those close to the child in relation to developing their emotional and social well-being. In this part of the chapter we will now look in more depth at the significance of a child's attachment to adults in supporting his or her well-being.

It would be too simplistic to say that it is parents or primary carers who are mainly responsible for children's well-being. Children are influenced by relationships with *many* others in their ecology – including other family and significant adults outside the family, such as teachers. Children's attachments to adults and other children are significant in building the social and emotional aspects of children's well-being. This is why attachment theory has been seen as a significant contributor to understanding children's well-being and development.

Attachment theory grew out of the work of John Bowlby in the 1950s (Bowlby 1958), and it has retained a major place in child-development literature. Contemporary writers such as Howe, Brandon and Schofield (1999) and Aldgate and Jones (2006) have looked at the relevance of attachment to contemporary thinking on child development, while researchers such as Howes (1999) have shown the relevance of attachment to modern family circumstances. Owusu-Bempah (2006) has also added a new dimension of socio-genealogical connections to the application of attachment to children who are separated from their parents. There is much more awareness of different cultural patterns of rearing children (Quinton 1994), but, nevertheless, attachment remains a valid global construct (Van Ijzendoorn and Sagi 1999).

'Attachment behaviour' is activated when children are stressed and fearful and seek the proximity of an adult whom they know well, who is seen as stronger and wiser, and becomes an 'attachment figure'. It is suggested that attachment behaviour develops around six months in children (see Aldgate and Jones 2006), although clearly children show signs of fear and being comforted much earlier. When attachment behaviour is activated in children through anxiety, their natural curiosity and desire to explore the world around them are suppressed. The response of their caregiver or attachment figure to this anxiety will influence how a child internalises mechanisms for overcoming fear. If responses to a frightened child are positive and consistent, the child learns that this response can be expected. Loss and change will affect attachment but not necessarily permanently provided the right help is put in place (see Schaffer above).

Attachments are only one aspect of a child's relationships with adults. However, these are especially significant to children's well-being because the way children learn to develop attachments will influence their emotional and social behaviour, including the perception they have of how far they can trust and build positive relationships with others in later life.

Contemporary commentators have found it helpful to look at attachment both from the point of view of the child and from the point of view of the adults who provide the response to the child's attachment behaviour – the caregivers. Early, sensitive reactions to children's behaviour are likely to produce in the child an internal working model that helps them to see the world as reliable. Children who have been unable to rely on a consistent and positive response from attachment figures are likely to develop problems in their emotional and social development (see Aldgate and Jones 2006; Howe et al. 1999).

Attachment theory has usually suggested that children have a hierarchy of attachment figures (Bowlby 1958; Howe *et al.* 1999), a model developed from a Westernised version of a traditional nuclear family. However, in Western countries today, children often have a network of caregivers, for example, to accommodate different cultural approaches to child rearing or parental working patterns. Research within the past decade from the USA (Howes 1999) has suggested that children may integrate *all* their attachment relationships into their internal working model of attachment. Their attachment behaviour will therefore be based on the quality of all the relationships in a child's network: one relationship will not dominate but children will benefit from an aggregate of positive relationships. Howes (1999) has developed her thinking further to suggest that different caregivers may contribute to different domains of development with, for example, mothers influencing children's competence or children learning from their attachment to fathers about how to resolve conflicts (see Aldgate and Jones 2006; Howes 1999). Although research on this new broader approach to attachment figures is in its infancy, it does offer a plausible and relevant model for this important aspect of a child's well-being within the ecology of the 21st-century child.

Howes suggests that, in the network approach, attachment figures can be identified by asking the following questions:

- Does the person provide physical and emotional care?

- Is this person a consistent presence in the child's social network?

- Is this person emotionally invested in the child?

- What about the child who is living away from the parental home – in the care system or with extended family, for example?

(Howes 1999, p.674)

As mentioned above, Owusu-Bempah has developed an important new take on attachment theory in relation to children separated from their families.

Socio-genealogical connectedness refers to the extent to which children integrate into their inner world their birth parents' biological and social backgrounds: the extent to which a child sees her or himself as an offshoot of his or her parents' backgrounds, biologically as well as socially. (Owusu-Bempah 2006, p.114)

Owusu-Bempah argues that the quality and amount of information children receive about themselves will influence integration, and that chidren with more favourable information will have a deeper sense of conectedness (Owusu-Bempah 2006).

Finally, it is now known that although attachment patterns develop early on in a child's life these patterns can be modified by sensitive caregiving. In other words, attachment patterns are dynamic. Not only can modifications happen in childhood but also throughout the life-cycle. So as Rutter and Schaffer, quoted earlier, have suggested, children's emotional well-being is not fixed. Aldgate and Jones report that studies of adoption and fostering of children placed when they were aged between 4 and 8 (see Steele 2003) suggest that children *can improve* their internal working models – albeit with the caveat that younger children show more change than older children and that children who have experienced serious deficits in developing good attachment relationships will need extra-special and persistently sensitive caregiving. (Indeed, the critical factor in bringing about change will be the sensitivity of the caregiver (Aldgate and Jones 2006).)

Studies of adults suggest that life events and partnership relationships can also act as mediating factors on adults (see Aldgate and Jones 2006). Aldgate and Jones conclude that:

> Even if internal working models do not change substantially, there can be protective factors within adult partnerships that improve caregiving to children. A partner who has a secure sense of attachment may act as a buffer for a parent who has an insecure internal representation of attachment. (Aldgate and Jones 2006, p.94)

The implications of the research on attachment for children's well-being is that there is scope for change at any stage. This has implications for practitioners, who thus have the opportunity to use professional intervention at any stage to both improve children's internal working models and those of their caregivers – and improvements in the emotional and social elements of children's development will have an impact on their overall well-being.

Children shaping their own lives

Apart from the influences on children's well-being from important figures in the network within their ecology, there has been a growing recognition that children can influence their own well-being through their participation and input into factors that affect their childhood (Clark and Moss 2001). It is increasingly being argued that children have a right to participate in decisions and events that affect them directly. The mandate for children's participation comes from section 12 of the UN Convention on the Rights of the Child 1989, which states that children should be seen as competent individuals who can be consulted and involved in decision-making that affects their individual lives. This principle is enshrined in various sections of UK legislation governing the upbringing of children, such as the Children Act 1989, Children (Scotland) Act 1995 and Children (Northern Ireland) Order 1995.

As well as helping children to be fully part of decisions that shape their lives, there is also a growing movement that recognises children are able to provide both a competent commentary on their own experiences and the lives of children in general, and thus contribute to both policy and practice. This idea is exemplified by writers who have described children as 'social actors' (Clark and Moss 2001; Sinclair 2004). It has been put into practice by policy makers, with an example from Scotland being the development of a Children's Charter for child protection services (Scottish Executive 2004) and by children having an input into how they would like to see services organised for the Scottish policy development *Getting It Right for Every Child* (Scottish Executive 2006).

Such an approach means that children should have full participation in any policies and plans for services, and should be empowered to put forward their own agendas. In other words, children should be seen as:

> Fellow citizens with rights, participating members of the social groups in which they find themselves, agents of their own lives but also interdependent with others, co-constructors of knowledge, identity and culture, who co-exist with others in society on the basis of who they are, rather than who they will become. (Moss 2002, p.6)

Moss has proposed using the concept of 'children's spaces' as part of children's services to translate this idea into practice. A good example of taking into account 'children's spaces' in Scotland comes from the consultation exercise carried out by Children in Scotland, as part of the Scottish Executive's policy review of special educational needs of children in 2001. This consultation involved over 100 young people who employed a variety of different styles of communication, including disabled children and those for whom English was not their first language. The project showed that children have a great deal of knowledge and information that can help policy makers.

It also showed, however, that translating children's views into action can be problematic if they do not fit into the pre-existing adult agenda (Tisdall and Davis 2004). Indeed, one criticism of children's participation has been that children are often asked to respond to the adult agenda rather than set their own (Prout 2003). Consequently, it has been argued by commentators, such as Holloway and Valentine (2000) and Hill *et al.* (2004), that unless adults are willing to try to understand how children themselves see their daily lives, there will be shortcomings in any attempts to promote a child-centred approach to children's well-being:

> It is important that adults, thinking about children's lives, needs and education embraces not only the spaces to be found in formal provision by adults, but also those territories and pathways claimed by children for their own purposes in myriad locations within the areas they inhabit and visit. (Hill *et al.* 2004, p.84)

Combining children's rights with children's perspectives is a feature of Ben-Arieh's research on how children spend their time (Ben-Arieh 2002). Ben-Arieh believes that children's experience of childhood, as reported by them, should be counted alongside adult indicators of positive well-being in children and suggests:

> A re-defined concept of children's well-being, therefore, can be guided by two underlying assumptions: that children are entitled to dignity and basic human rights, and that their childhood is also a stage deserving our attention and respect. (Ben-Arieh 2002, p.153)

He goes on to argue that, in order to study children's own perspectives on their well-being, measures need to be developed that take a child-centred approach:

> To better understand what children are doing and how they feel about their lives and activities from a child-centred perspective and to promote their self-fulfilment, empowerment, and life satisfaction, measures must be developed to assess their activities. (Ben-Arieh 2002, p.155; see also Andrews and Ben-Arieh 1999)

In a small qualitative study of 24 children (which formed part of the 2006 Social Work Inspection Agency's review of looked-after children in Scotland), Aldgate and McIntosh (2006b) adapted Ben-Arieh's ideas (Ben-Arieh 2002) to explore children's experiences of well-being. Eight dimensions of activities were developed:

- sleep
- productive activities: schoolwork, personal creative work, paid work, care of others and domestic/household work

- other activities that contribute to the community
- spiritual activities
- travel time
- personal care: eating, getting ready
- social interaction: interacting socially with others not for explicitly productive purposes (such as hanging out, listening to music and talking)
- leisure/recreation: such as play, sports, reading, watching television, arts and crafts.

(Aldgate and McIntosh 2006b, p.10)

Semi-structured interviews and time diaries over 48 hours were used to gain an insight into children's perspectives on their daily activities.

Many of these activities are controlled by adults, especially productive activities, such as going to school or travel time. School can be a source of stress to children (Aldgate and McIntosh 2006a), but can also provide opportunities for children to achieve. Gilligan has written of the importance of school in building resilience (Gilligan 2000). Group activities, such as sport and being in an orchestra, provided positive experiences for some children in the Aldgate and McIntosh study.

Additionally, Ben-Arieh has argued that, if children are involved in activities within their communities, this will increase their efficacy and self-esteem. Within this study, children were clearly benefiting from responsibility within their school communities. One example was the 10-year-old appointed as a school monitor: 'I stop dogs and cats coming into the playground or people who aren't welcome to the school. I protect all the wee yins' (Aldgate and McIntosh 2006b, p.18).

When they are playing in the playground, children can, to a large extent, choose what activities they engage in. Children who are bullied clearly will experience these times as stressful but for many children peer relations are both important to them and a means of exercising choice as well as engaging in social learning. It is argued that rejection by friends may be a factor contributing to anti-social behaviour (Daniel and Wassell 2002).

In the Aldgate and McIntosh study, meeting up with friends was an important part of daily activities. On most days, every child spent some time with at least one friend. From their diaries, children indicated how they valued this time. Children saw their lunchbreak as a chance to meet up with friends again and they spent their lunchtimes in a variety of ways.

The older children tended to 'sit in a café and talk with friends' or 'grab a bite to eat at the chippie' (Aldgate and McIntosh 2006b, p.25).

Friendships after school were dictated by travel and distance but half the children spent time regularly talking to friends outside school hours:

> The most popular activity undertaken with friends, cited by 11 children, was to play computer games. Nine children played sports with their peers which included ice skating, swimming, football, rugby, skateboarding, bowling and hill walking. Less active 'hanging out' was also popular with nine children. Watching the television or videos at each other's homes was cited by six children. The remaining activities included window shopping, clubbing, talking on the phone, eating out and going to activity clubs. Three young people told us they 'went to the pub'. (Aldgate and McIntosh 2006b, p.27)

In the increasingly structured world that children inhabit, choosing to be alone can be an important time for children's emotional health and well-being (Scott and Hill 2006). Twenty-two of the 24 children in the Aldgate and McIntosh study said they enjoyed time 'chilling out', mostly listening to music or watching the television on their own, and, on average, children spent six hours a day alone, excluding time for sleep.

Jack and Gill (2003) have suggested that adolescents place great importance on their appearance and choice of clothes. Where young people neglect their self-care, this has thus been seen as a sign of low self-esteem (Parker *et al.* 1991), so it was no surprise that self-presentation and self-care were included in the Department of Health's *Looking After Children* assessment and action records used by social workers in the 1990s (Ward 1995). In the Aldgate and McIntosh study, there were also indications from both younger and older children that self-presentation was indeed an important part of activities, especially preparation to go out with peers in leisure time:

> There were examples of some children who had developed a very distinctive presentation of themselves. For example, there was one young person who spent a lot of time in the skate park and specially dressed in the appropriate fashionable attire of baggy trousers and trendy t-shirts. Another young person, who was fond of rap and heavy metal music, presented herself as a 'Goth', where clothes, hair and make-up were meticulously put together in order to present a very definite self-image. As in the kinship care study (Aldgate and McIntosh 2006a), children drew attention to the importance of

trainers as part of their self-image. Hairstyles were also significant. There were some spectacular examples of spiky hairstyles in the boys, which were held together with copious amounts of hair gel and one child was eager to end the interview so that he could go off to the hairdresser. (Aldgate and McIntosh 2006b, pp.21–22)

Other aspects of children's choice influencing their leisure activities in the study of children's well-being and daily activities (Aldgate and McIntosh 2006b) revealed a range of activities, from group sports to using the computer, especially to play games. Although 23 of the 24 children said they engaged in some sporting activities each week, it was clear that adult intervention and encouragement played an important part in getting them to their sporting destination. Given the emphasis on encouraging children to be more active (see, e.g. Scottish Executive 2003), it was noticeable that the children who were in foster and residential homes had more opportunities to build their self-esteem by testing their physical agility through dancing classes, hill walking and learning to climb. Several children from adverse circumstances said they relished the opportunity being 'in care' gave them for achievement and new experiences.

In the spirit of conducting a child-centred study that recognised children's ability to be competent commentators, children were asked to evaluate their involvement as research participants. The comments reveal a sense of self-worth and insights that leave no doubt about children's ability to shape their own well-being, as these examples from the study show:

- I've learnt how important the time I spend with people is.

- I was quite astonished at all the things I do all day.

- It made me think that I don't do much with my time. I don't get out enough, I sit around and watch TV and should get out more.

- Yes, I have learnt I am a boring person and I do the same routine over again. But then I am not boring because I keep myself busy.

- I do a lot of interesting things.

(Aldgate and McIntosh 2006b, p.50)

Applying well-being in practice in children's services

Although definitions and indicators of well-being are well established in research (see, e.g. Andrews and Ben-Arieh 1999; Ben-Arieh 2002; Bradshaw and Richardson 2009; Bradshaw *et al.* 2009), it is only fairly recently that policy makers have attempted to use well-being indicators as a practical application to assess, plan and provide help for children. All the governments in the UK have developed models for assessment of children, which incorporate the idea of well-being indicators (see Rose and Rowlands, Chapter 3 in this volume, for England's approach). In this current chapter Scotland's approach is used as a case study of applying well-being in practice.

In 2001, the Scottish Executive published its blueprint for an integrated approach to children's services, *For Scotland's Children*, which set out a policy base to give every child in Scotland 'the best possible start in life' (Scottish Executive 2001, p.7). In 2005, a co-ordinated integrated assessment framework for all agencies working with children and families, *Getting It Right for Every Child*, was launched as part of the review of the Scottish juvenile justice system, the children's hearings (Scottish Executive 2005). The application of *Getting It Right for Every Child* was subsequently widened to be used in practice with all children. The context of the approach was the Government's aspiration to promote the best possible outcomes for children. These can be described, in Ben-Arieh's terms, as 'children's well-becoming'. The Government wanted all children to become 'confident individuals, effective contributors, successful learners and responsible citizens' (Scottish Executive 2005, p.4).

The Scottish Government's aspirations for children reflected the consensus among those interested in children's development: that it is important for children to reach all their well-being indicators at every stage of childhood if they are to flourish (Aldgate *et al.* 2006). Therefore, in order to achieve their well-becoming, every child not only required a good start in their early years but also needed their family and the State to give attention to all aspects of children's well-being throughout childhood. One major problem was the absence of a working ecological, multi-agency approach to helping children. It was a priority of the Scottish Government that this should be addressed (Scottish Executive 2001). Apart from making sure that each branch of policy for children was linked to others, there was also a need for a conceptual base that could be used to encourage agencies to work more closely together and to cut down on duplication.

So *Getting It Right for Every Child* began to evolve. It had a shared concept of children's well-being, using a common language and tools based on well-being across all agencies to translate that concept into practice. The concept of well-being in *Getting It Right for Every Child* has much in common with UNICEF's broad definition of well-being, quoted earlier in this chapter. This translates into a working practical definition of eight well-being indicators: that children should be 'safe, healthy, active, nurtured, achieving, respected, responsible and included' (Scottish Government 2008, p.12), thus covering all the core aspects of children's development (see Figure 1.1). These link to children's well-becoming cited earlier.

Figure 1.1 The Getting It Right for Every Child *well-being indicators*

Source: Scottish Government 2010, p.14, published by kind permission of the Scottish Government

In order to ensure this practical definition of well-being could be used in practice in all agencies, *Getting It Right for Every Child* introduced a common co-ordinated framework, based on a set of values and principles rooted in an ecological approach to child development, and emphasising strengths and resilience. The approach also recognised children's competence to comment on decisions that affect them. It was stressed that children and families should get the services they need in the way that is most helpful to them, even if this means changing the ways in which services are organised and presented. It is an evidence-based approach to practice, reflecting knowledge both of child development and research on the participation of children and families in services (Scottish Government 2008).

These elements have helped to shape the ten core components, and these core components can be applied in any setting and any circumstances. They are at the heart of *Getting It Right for Every Child* and provide a benchmark from which practitioners can apply the approach to their own area of work:

1. A focus on improving outcomes for children, young people and their families based on a shared understanding of well-being.

2. A common approach to gaining consent and sharing information where appropriate.

3. An integral role for children, young people and families in assessment, planning and intervention.

4. A co-ordinated and unified approach to identifying concerns, assessing needs, agreeing actions and outcomes, based on the well-being indicators.

5. Streamlined planning, assessment and decision-making processes that lead to the right help at the right time.

6. Consistent high standards of co-operation, joint working and communication where more than one agency needs to be involved, locally and across Scotland.

7. A Lead Professional to co-ordinate and monitor multi-agency activity where necessary.

8. Maximising the skilled workforce within universal services to address needs and risks at the earliest possible time.

9. A competent and confident workforce across all services for children, young people and their families.

10. The capacity to share demographic, assessment and planning information electronically and within and across agency boundaries through the national eCare programme where appropriate.

(Scottish Government 2008, p.14)

Getting It Right for Every Child draws together the Scottish Government's focus on children's rights, social justice and early intervention. It gives all practitioners across Scotland a common set of values and principles that can apply in any circumstances. Its overarching aim is to provide help for children and families that is timely (early intervention), proportionate (as much or as little assessment and help as is needed), and puts children and families at the centre (by seeking their views and accommodating their circumstances). It begins in the universal services of health and education but also applies to targeted services, such as social work and specialist health services.

To improve practice to match the new ways of working, the *Getting It Right for Every Child* programme has concentrated on bringing about transformational change in practice and culture, as well as urging local agencies to streamline their systems, but it has left alone the organisational structures of each local authority that provide the governance for implementing *Getting It Right for Every Child.*

Working closely with the Pathfinder in Highland, the *Getting It Right for Every Child* development team evolved a practice model that all practitioners can use, either on a single agency or multi-agency basis, to assess, plan, take action and review a child's progress. For more details, see *A Guide to Getting It Right for Every Child* (Scottish Government 2008).

As described earlier, the practice model is based around the eight areas of well-being, that children should be: safe, healthy, achieving, nurtured, active, respected, responsible and included. Any practitioner, as well as children and their families, can use the well-being indicators for several purposes at different stages of assessment planning and review: as an *aide-mémoire* to identify concerns, to help formulate a child's plan (either in a single agency or on a multi-agency basis) and to measure outcomes at the end of the period of treatment or intervention. The Scottish system expects every practitioner to take responsibility for providing help, reprising the title of the 2002 Child Protection Audit and Review *It's Everyone's Job to Make Sure I'm Alright* (Scottish Executive 2002).

There are five questions every practitioner should ask if they have concerns about a child:

- What is getting in the way of this child's well-being?

- Do I have all the information I need to help this child or young person?

- What can I do now to help this child or young person?

- What can my agency do to help this child or young person?

- What additional help, if any, may be needed from others?

(Scottish Government 2008, p.24)

There are no fixed templates for professionals to use and it is left to individual agencies to decide if they want to use a form format. Neither are there timescales set by government for completion of assessment, which is indicative of the emphasis the Scottish Government places on recognising and valuing the skills and judgement of professionals.

If practitioners think they need further information beyond that gathered through using the well-being indicators, they can refer to the 'My World Triangle', an ecological assessment tool that approaches assessment from a child's-eye view, placing the child at the centre of thinking (see Scottish Government 2008). They also have a 'Resilience Matrix', adapted from the work of Daniel and Wassell (2002), to help make sense of large amounts of information they may have gathered. In cases where there are two or more agencies involved a lead professional will co-ordinate a Child's Plan. To streamline matters, there is only one Child's Plan – although, in complex cases, it will include many different aspects of well-being.

In many cases, where needs are straightforward, a plan can be put in place using the well-being indicators, and it is expected that agencies will co-operate on a basis of trust without elaborate referral systems.

A significant feature of the Pathfinder in Highland that has been developing multi-agency systems and practice using the *Getting It Right for Every Child* approach has been to implement the recommendation in *For Scotland's Children* (Scottish Executive 2001) that every child should have a named professional (now called a 'named person') in health or education who is a contact point for early intervention. Highland has developed comprehensive systems for making transitions between lead professionals and named persons (see Highland Council 2007).

Computer systems are being developed nationally to help in the sharing of information, but this will be on a need to know basis, and each agency will keep its own records of the child. Scotland has learnt much from being behind England in the implementation of computer systems and has decided to go for systems that are as simple as possible.

An evaluation of implementation in Highland of *Getting It Right for Every Child* by Stradling, MacNeil and Berry (2009) shows transformational change has taken place in the first year of implementation. There are fewer meetings, fewer children on the child-protection register and fewer inappropriate referrals to the children's hearings. There is also an increase in plans for individuals, which suggests early intervention is beginning to have an effect and that help is more targeted. The practice model is being implemented, and changes in culture, systems and practice are evident. Practitioners across all agencies report favourably on the use of the well-being indicators in practice. The new ways of working have also improved trust and collaboration. Children and families are reporting they feel more equal and more included.

This is, of course, just the beginning and there is a long way to go, but there is now enough confidence on the part of ministers, policy makers and local authorities to move forward with the goal of implementing *Getting It Right for Every Child* across Scotland by 2011. In the field of health care, the *Getting It Right for Every Child* well-being indicators are now included in every copy of the 'red book' given to parents to chart infants' progress.

The concept of children's well-being has become a realistic and workable approach to improving practice for children and families. Nonetheless, it remains to be seen if applying well-being in this way can have an impact on children's well-becoming in the long term.

CHAPTER 2

Children's Views on Child Well-Being

COLETTE MCAULEY, ROGER MORGAN
AND WENDY ROSE

Introduction

There is a growing recognition that, if we are to further develop our knowledge about child well-being, we need to ask children directly about their understanding of well-being (Ben-Arieh 2005; Ben-Arieh, Chapter 6, this volume). This realisation has been reached through a number of key influences.

The United Nations Convention on the Rights of the Child (UNCRC) clearly offers a normative framework for understanding child well-being with its emphasis on: establishing basic rights for all children; seeing children as citizens in their own right; giving equal weight to a range of interrelated rights; and having their views taken into account on matters directly affecting them. It has been argued that it is these ideas that have led to current conceptualisations of well-being, which are inclusive of all children, start from the child as the focus of analysis, adopt an ecological model of development (Bronfenbrenner 1979), recognise the many dimensions of children's lives, and see children as acting and interacting with multiple influences in their environment (Ben-Arieh 2008).

Alongside this, for some time now, proponents of the 'sociology of childhood' (James and Prout 1990; James, Jencks and Prout 1998) view children as social actors, contributing to and influencing relationships and the environment around them. Children are seen as subjects with unique perspectives rather than objects of interest. Childhood and children's experiences of it are seen as valid areas for exploration. And our interest is both about children's current experiences of childhood as well as what it can tell us about their future life as adults. Current thinking on child well-being draws upon this thinking, and the child indicators movement is keen to understand the views of children on their current lives as an end in itself (well-being) as well as in relation to future outcomes (well-becoming) (Ben-Arieh, Chapter 6, this volume).

The shift in focus from child welfare to child well-being also deserves mention, albeit briefly, in the introduction to this chapter. The late Alfred Kahn spoke of the shift from 'child saving to child development', having reached the conclusion that striving to raise conditions for all children was likely to be the most effective way of protecting the vulnerable (Kahn 2010). The policy shift from child welfare to child well-being is currently the subject of international debate (Kamerman, Phipps and Ben-Arieh 2010). Alongside this, attempts are being made by governments to identify the positive outcomes we hope to achieve for all children and equating these with indicators of child well-being in their own countries (see Rose and Rowlands, Chapter 3, this volume).

A related important point is that much of the global and national child-indicators data traditionally collated has been based solely upon objective measures. Complementing this with subjective perspectives on childhood has been one of the most important recent developments, although this move has not been uncontested (see Bradshaw *et al.,* Chapter 9, this volume). As our understanding of children as active contributors to the world around them develops, it becomes important that we move to include their views about well-being. Whilst objective measures of well-being may be appropriate in some areas, it is now recognised that there are areas of well-being where we particularly need to capture children's accounts, such as in relation to their emotional and social relationships (Ben-Arieh 2008).

The concept of child well-being itself remains contested and elusive (Ereaut and Whiting 2008; see also Rose and Rowlands, Chapter 3, this volume). In an effort to consult with parents/carers and children/young people about what they are thinking about when they use the terms 'well-being' and 'happiness', the Department for Children, Schools and Families commissioned a consultative research study for the purpose (Counterpoint 2008). Interestingly, there was a high degree of consensus among the adults and children about the factors that determine a good, or content, childhood as well as those that undermine it. All were agreed that family was of the paramount importance in determining the well-being of children. Friends, schools/teachers and other outside factors (such as activities outside school, television and the wider community) were the other three categories identified. The lack of a safe environment, due to the degree of violence and aggression experienced by the child, was seen to be a major undermining factor. Pressure to earn more money, limited family time, pressure to buy things, political correctness and the UK not being a child- or family-friendly culture were the other undermining factors identified.

Recent developments in measuring subjective well-being through the use and refinement of standardised questionnaires are reviewed in detail by Jonathan Bradshaw and his colleagues in Chapter 9 in this volume. A separate strand of work has arisen from advocates of 'standpoint theory', who argue that, by using such measures devised by adults, we are presuming we know how children conceptualise well-being. Standpoint theory emphasises the importance of the 'knower' as the framer of knowledge (Fraser 2004).

Jan Mason and colleagues at the University of New South Wales are attempting to advance this work with children in the general school population (Fattore, Mason and Watson 2009). Their recent qualitative study aimed to explore children's views of what constitutes well-being, what meaning they ascribe to the concept and whether distinct dimensions of well-being could be identified. It involved 123 children aged between 8 and 15. The authors concluded that: 'The underlying mediums through which children understood experiences of well-being are children's significant relationships and emotional life' (Fattore *et al.* 2009, p.61).

The purpose of this chapter is to examine available evidence on children's views of their well-being. So far, however, studies have concentrated on particular aspects of their lives rather than addressing the wider concept. In the light of the growing consensus of the centrality of family to children's well-being, we have decided to devote the greater part of this chapter to examining what we do know about children's views on families, significant others and their wider emotional life from a range of studies and consultations that have directly asked children about these matters. Initially, we look at children living in different family types and the family life of disabled children, and then we move on to examine what we know from studies where children are living in difficult family circumstances. Finally, we reflect on what children who have experienced care have shared with us through consultations and research studies. Wider issues about how children think about their role in consultation and decision-making and the notion of safety are then explored. In the final section, we also reflect upon the emergent issues from the evidence and consider the implications for policy, practice and research.

In compiling this chapter, we have used two sources: selected UK research studies that have interviewed children directly on their emotional and social relationships and the body of consultative work with children and young people in care or living away from home in schools or colleges that has been carried out by the Office of the Children's Rights Director (CRD) in England.[1] The children consulted were aged between 6 and 23 (with usually a median age of 13 or 14 years), unless otherwise specified. We begin by looking at what children consulted have told us about what well-being meant to them.

How children and young people see well-being

In England, well-being is measured by the Government using the five *Every Child Matters* outcomes for children: being safe; being healthy; enjoying and achieving; making a contribution; and economic well-being. In 2005, children under 12 were consulted on these outcomes (Morgan 2005). While confirming the view that these were all important to children, the children added seven more outcomes that they thought important for all children, making a dozen well-being outcomes in all. Their seven additions were:

- having family

- having friends

- having enough food and drink

- having fun

- being loved

- being respected

- being happy.

More recently, for the report *Children on Rights and Responsibilities* (Morgan 2010), children and young people were asked the more general question of what, in their view, constituted well-being for people of their own age. The top ten components of well-being for children and young people, according to the 1,193 who contributed their views, were as follows:

- being healthy

- feeling loved

- having a home

- enjoying activities and having fun

- feeling happy

- being cared for
- being safe
- having a family
- having friends
- being supported.

They also thought that children experiencing well-being would 'be able to relax and enjoy themselves rather than being constantly afraid or nervous about the situation they are in'. One child added an important dimension of continuity to well-being: 'being able to know that there will be more nice things to come'.

Children on families and significant relationships

In an effort to understand more about children's views on families, we looked at the following: children in different family types; disabled children and their families; children in families experiencing considerable difficulties; and children in care.

Children living in different family types

Brannen, Heptinstall and Bhopal (2000) surveyed the views of 941 schoolchildren (aged 10 to 12) in two local education authorities in South London and later interviewed 63 of these children. They asked the children to reflect on family life both in terms of what it meant to them but also what they thought it *should* be. Children who were interviewed were drawn from two-parent, lone-mother, step-parent and foster families. The overarching finding was of the importance of family for the children, although far more important than family structure was the way in which family life was lived.

> That's something like in fairytale land when they show the happy couple walking and they're going with their children and their dog to this place. But I don't think there's any such thing as a happy family – or a perfect family. There is happy families but not perfect families…
>
> …say you're on your own and one parent, you still get love, that's still a family. Because family's all about love…
>
> *(Inderpal, South Asian origin boy in a lone-mother family)*

Love and care provided consistently and every day were the most crucial factors in helping the children to develop a good sense of self and to feel secure and safe. No matter which of the family types they lived in, the children considered their birth parents to be very important (in their inner circle of significant relationships). Whether the foster children were in contact with their birth parents or not, they too included them in this way. For the children generally, they identified birth siblings as second only in relative importance to the birth parents. Again, the foster children followed the same pattern whether they were in contact with their birth siblings or not. Beyond that, the children identified as of importance to them extended family members and friends, and some included figures such as teachers, doctors and social workers. The study particularly emphasised that these children were pragmatic actors accepting different family forms as long as parents provided them with love and affection. They were also active contributors to family life, able to sense the feelings of parents and siblings and to convey empathy as well as give and receive support.

> If I had a job I would look after my mum… If she needs help with her bills or anything like that, I would be glad to help.
>
> *(Elliott, a black boy in a lone-mother household)*

> It's not fair. They go out and work all day, then they have to come home and do everything for you.
>
> *(Anna, a white girl living in a step-family)*

> If she [mother] finds she has any problems, she'll talk to me a little.
>
> *(Latasha, a black girl living with two parents)*

> I love her. I'll be there when she's old and that's it.
>
> *(Lee, a white boy living with two parents)*

The children used wide definitions of family, including a wide range of kin beyond those they lived with as well as friends, pets and professionals. The authors concluded that the children's relationships with their family and siblings were particularly important at transition points, such as the move to secondary school when friendships are often subject to change.

Disabled children and their families

Connors and Stalker (2003, 2007) interviewed 26 disabled children aged between 7 and 15 in Scotland about their daily lived experiences. The

15 boys and 11 girls included one black child. Thirteen children were described as having learning disabilities, five had sensory impairments and six had physical impairments. Two of the children had profound/multiple impairment. They attended a range of schools: special (segregated), mainstream (inclusive) and integrated (segregrated units within mainstream schools). Their parents were also interviewed.

The majority of children appeared to be happy within themselves. Most of them appeared to have a practical, pragmatic attitude to their impairment even though they talked about repeated infections, being tired easily and suffering pain. They seemed to have learned to manage these things. Most focused on the similarities of their lives to those of their peers. This was in contrast to the parental accounts, which emphasised the differences.

The children described having a say and influencing others in their family life. In many ways, the tensions were similar to those in families without disabled children. For example, some of the adolescents were seeking more independence:

> She's [her mother] got to understand that she can't rule my life any more... I just want to make up my own mind now because she's always deciding for me, like, what's best for me and sometimes I get angry. She just doesn't realise that I'm grown up now but soon I'm going to be 14 and I won't be a wee girl any more.

Whilst all young people may strive for independence, a child with a significant impairment may face more challenges in persuading their parents to be less protective.

The researchers found that the children tended to focus on issues in the here and now that were preoccupying them. An important one for many of them was not having friends living nearby. The fact that they attended special schools some distance away from their homes meant that they had few friends living nearby. Consequently, they spoke of being bored much of the time outside school periods. In contrast, their parents' concern surrounded past incidences of discrimination and difficulties that had happened to their children. There was a sense that parental anxiety about the reaction of others might well be restricting their children's social activities and opportunities.

There were grounds, though, for such anxiety. Whilst some children encountered many material barriers (e.g. access, transport) that restricted their activities, it was the reactions of other people to their impairment that upset the children the worst. The children gave examples of being stared at, talked down to, having to deal with inappropriate comments or behaviour, or overt sympathy. Accounts were even given of harassment by neighbours of them and their families.

Almost half of the disabled children had experienced bullying, either at school or in the local neighbourhood. And at least one of the children appeared to be exposed to such difficulties on a daily basis. They expressed their hurt at such behaviour. Some reported it to parents or teachers and others took matters into their own hands and turned on the bullies. In their research, the authors drew on the work of Thomas (1999) on the social–relational model of disability to understand the children's experiences. Where non-impaired people behave in a hurtful, hostile or inappropriate manner that has a negative effect on an individual's sense of self – affecting what they feel they can be or become – that is referred to as a 'barrier to being'.

Examples were given where this occurred also in school, one instance being a special school where teachers labelled the children as 'wheelchairs' and 'walkers'. As one child commented:

> It's sad because we're just the same. We just can't walk, that's all the difference.

The researchers also interviewed their siblings (24 children aged between 6 and 19) (Stalker and Connors 2004). Although aware of their siblings' impairments, the majority of children did not see their disabled brother or sister as being very different to them and spoke with affection about them. Their accounts indicated normal sibling rivalry:

> He's just like a normal brother.

> We are friends. She's always pleased to see me.

> I play with her sometimes. She is fun having around. We don't get along with each other all of the time. We argue, nag and sometimes fight. The most annoying time is when we have our breakfast when she has the whole of [the] tomato ketchup.

However, these siblings were obviously also aware of the negative reactions of some other children and adults outside of the home. Some showed considerable empathy:

> It must make him feel like dirt, must make him feel as if 'What are you looking at me for?' It must get him upset sometimes.
>
> *(12-year-old girl commenting about her brother*
> *being stared at in public places)*

Examples of physical attacks were reported by siblings. Most reacted with anger and attempted to protect their siblings or turn on the bullies. Five reported having been the target of bullies themselves for having a disabled sibling. They were very conscious of their parents' anxieties, deciding sometimes not to tell them as it might add to their worries. Overall, the researchers felt that the siblings' perceptions of disablism were clearly affected by other people's reactions and the impact on the psycho-emotional well-being of their disabled sibling.

Children living in families experiencing difficulties
We have also learned more recently about children's views on living in families where there is domestic violence, parental mental health problem or substance abuse. Gorin's (2004) review of UK studies in the period 1990 to 2003 again emphasises that children in these situations actively participate in negotiating roles and responsibilities in their families. At times, though, in these circumstances they may have little or no choice about providing emotional and physical support to their parents. However, some indicate that they do not resent this as they feel needed and want to do this for them.

They are often more aware of the problems than their parents realise, even if they do not fully understand the reasons for the problems. Some behaviours do, however, make these children frightened and confused, the most distressing being violence and conflict. This is often compounded by the unpredictability of the parents' moods and behaviour.

> I'm frightened to leave her in case she goes into a fit or something. When we were little…she got really down and started taking overdoses and that really scared us… When she's really down she says I'm going to take an overdose… I'm frightened to leave her.
>
> *(Newton and Becker 1996, p.25)*

> It's not just the caring that affects you… In fact we're a close family and we all pull together. What really gets you is the worry of it all, having a parent who is ill and seeing them in such a state… Of course it's upsetting, you think about it a lot. Someone who is close to you and desperately ill is pretty hard to deal with.
>
> *(Frank 1995, p.42)*

Feelings of insecurity and living in an unsafe environment can impact on these children's school lives, with children often being unable to concentrate whilst in school. As a direct result of the parental difficulties, they may miss days at school or, indeed, experience a succession of house and school moves.

Friendships can be a source of support but making and maintaining these can be especially difficult for children in these circumstances, which may leave them increasingly isolated. The stigma and secrecy around their parents' problems can also perpetuate their sadness and isolation. They can experience bullying and, in the worst situations, some may become depressed. As we shall discuss later, children who stand out as different because of something about themselves or their families are likely to be the target of bullies. The stigma associated with the violent and addictive behaviours of their parents and the associated chaotic and impoverished lifestyles the children experience are also likely to affect how children see themselves.

> They [local youths] used to bully, they used to bully us, well they used to bully me. And hit, and punch me and everything…and they would go 'At least I haven't got a mental dad' or something.
>
> (Aldridge and Becker 2003, p.81)

Yet the studies convey that many of these children may have very close relationships with their parents. They can have a very strong sense of love and loyalty towards their parents, even if torn between that and feelings of anger, hurt, resentment and embarrassment.

> It can get difficult but it's good afterwards knowing I've helped my mum. I enjoy helping my mum, I only wish it could be a bit easier.
>
> (Bibby and Becker 2000, p.44)

> I can't bear it that he hits her. I feel so ashamed. I always worry that the neighbours will hear or that the teachers will find out at school… I felt really nervous about talking to you, and guilty about talking to you because my mum and dad are wonderful – they are really good people…really good parents and they love me a lot and they have done everything they can for me. It's not their fault, it's just the way it is with them.
>
> (Mullender et al. 2002, p.108)

These children may worry about their parents, both in relation to their parents' safety or ability to look after themselves. Often they are in a parental role with them – at least when their parents are less able to cope with family responsibilities.

These children use a range of coping strategies, the most common of which appears to be avoidance or distraction. Children in the same household, however, may react quite differently. Some take positive action using informal networks to seek confidential support and the opportunity to get away from the situation at home. From their accounts, few would seek help from professionals. However, they thought that confidential helplines might be useful.

Consultations carried out by the Office of the Children's Rights Director (Morgan 2006b) found that young carers, that is children taking on a caring role towards parents with physical or mental-health problems, report that they have prematurely to assume adult responsibilities for the well-being of adults, such as administering medication, supporting the adult through mental-health crises, and providing physical care including lifting and helping with mobility. The cost to themselves can be great, in terms of loss of the usual opportunities of childhood to socialise with peers or take part in spontaneous activities, in risk to their own physical or mental health, and in conflicts with educational requirements. Many young carers report missing vital school work deadlines because they had to deal with care crises at home, a situation many school staff are not sufficiently aware about to provide support and allowance.

> They have the disability – we're at risk.

> Because we can cope day to day they say we can manage – but we need help as well.

> [You] can miss out on so much and have to grow up so fast.

> *(Morgan 2006b)*

Children in care

From a series of consultations carried out by the Office of the Children's Rights Director, we know that, generally, children in care do not report that they are treated either better or worse than other children for being in care, and sometimes they have better support and more opportunities than other children. However, the most common way in which they are treated worse is being bullied for being in care, and the longer a child spends in care, the more likely they are to report experiences of being treated worse than their non-care peers (Morgan 2009a). Many children in care who were consulted on whether their care status led to prejudice reported being treated differently – sometimes better, sometimes worse – from those not in care, and around half said that being in care made them feel different from others, mainly because of their separation from families and different life experiences. Forty-five per cent were worried about other people finding out about their care status. Children in care perceive that the general public has a mainly negative view of children in care.

Children report two key consequences of being in care. One is that the longer a child spends in care, the higher is the risk of their losing contact with their birth parents, family and previous friends (Morgan 2009e). The other is that living in care very often separates brothers and sisters. Seventy-six per cent of children in care in the *Children's Care Monitor 2009* (Morgan 2009b) who had at least one brother or sister also in care reported living separately from a brother or sister.

A study by Skuse and Ward (2003, forthcoming) retrospectively interviewed 49 children and young people about their experiences of accommodation and care. The majority of children valued their time in accommodation or care for the experiences and opportunities offered to them, including self-development, and thought that their lives would have been worse had they remained at home:

> I think it was a good thing and I've come a long way… I just feel I am a better person. I don't think I would have gone back into school or done as well in school and wanted to go on to college, as what I would have if I had stayed at home.
>
> *(Girl speaking of her period in care when aged between 15 and 18)*

> I think at the time it was better… Now I think it is good because it was guaranteed that I was safe…because I came here because I was getting beaten at home. It is a good idea and it's not, because I miss my brothers and it upsets me for…the first few days after I've been to see them. But it is a good idea because it's a guarantee I have safety.
>
> *(Girl reflecting on her period in care when aged between 7 and 10)*

CHILDREN ON LIVING APART FROM THEIR FAMILIES

Although their home circumstances had been difficult, children put into care and living apart from their birth families, friends and the places they know found this experience very painful. McAuley (1996) interviewed a cohort of 19 primary-school-age children on three occasions during the first two years of their planned long-term foster placements. She found that most were thinking and dreaming about their birth families over time whilst in placement:

I dream about Daddy taking me out… I dream about all of them [his birth family] some nights… It's a happy dream…playing football in a field.

(Boy of 9 years)

In most cases, the parents of these children had had mental-health difficulties, addiction problems or been involved in domestic violence, and their consequent neglect of the children had precipitated the latter's need for care. As in Gorin's review, these children were often very loyal and loved their birth parents, irrespective of their behaviours. Most wanted contact with birth parents and siblings. Many were placed apart from siblings or had siblings still living at home. In some cases, these young children appeared to sense the vulnerability of their parents with addictions and wanted contact to reassure themselves about their safety. Where children were in a parental role with younger siblings, they sought contact for the same reasons.

Every night in bed…how she is getting on… I worry about her…same for brothers and sisters… I worry about them too… I worry most about Mum…feel sad.

(Girl of 8 years speaking of her birth mother and siblings)

In the follow-up study a decade later, McAuley (2005, 2006) asked these children, now young adults, to reflect on their care experience. Most had had regular contact with their birth family over time and they emphasised the importance of this contact to them, some thinking that it should have been more frequent. On the whole, contact was sought by, and was a positive experience for, this group. The young people also conveyed their feelings about the respect shown by their foster carers for their birth family and birth identity. Where there was such respect, the young people deeply appreciated this and felt more secure in their placements. Other studies have found that looked-after children generally seek contact with their birth families and often want it more frequently than it actually happens (Cleaver 2000; Shaw 1998; Sinclair, Wilson and Gibbs 2005).

However, for the more troubled young people, contact with birth parents at times brought further rejection and/or abuse, and the re-enactment of earlier dysfunctional family patterns. For them, contact brought the realisation that their birth parents continued to blame them for disclosures of abuse and had still not accepted responsibility for their own behaviour. Evidence from other studies suggests that contact with specific family members may be harmful particularly where there has been serious dysfunction (Sinclair 2005; Sinclair *et al.* 2005). Questions have been raised about the evidence base for the presumption that contact is associated with positive outcomes for children. In particular, the need for evidence about the long-term outcomes of contact has been emphasised (Quinton *et al.* 1997). We learn from this that decisions about contact need to be made for each individual child, in consultation with them where possible, and be subject to regular review.

CHILDREN ON MULTIPLE PLACEMENT AND SCHOOL MOVES

For many years research studies have highlighted the multiple changes of placement experienced by children in care (Jackson 2001; Rowe and Lambert 1973). Of the 49 children interviewed in the Skuse and Ward study (2003, forthcoming), 13 had had six or more placements whilst being looked after and this included one young person with 27 moves.

Multiple changes of school have also been highlighted by many research studies (Bullock, Little and Millham 2001; Jackson 2001) and in most cases these are found to be related to placement moves. This means that children coming into care or moving within care may be moved from their home, school and community settings at the same time. As a result, all the positive, supportive relationships they have built up with family, friends, teachers, carers and neighbours are no longer there and will only be maintained with effort. From an ecological development viewpoint, these children were being removed from their familiar network of relationships and placed, usually on their own, in a totally new environment.

In the McAuley (1996) study 15 of the 17 children who had attended primary school previously had had to change school as a result of moving to the study placement. Over half of these children expressed sadness and/ or confusion about leaving their previous schools. Many of the children felt sad at the loss of contact with teachers and friends. A number had already moved school before for the same reason. The extent of the anxiety felt by some children about this was well illustrated by a boy aged ten years who had had multiple moves:

> I don't want to move foster home again cos I might have to move school.
>
> *(Boy who had multiple care and school placements)*

Shortage of available long-term placements meant that placements offered were often in completely different areas and considerable distances from where the child had already been living and attending school. In the follow-up study (McAuley 2006), we learnt that most children experienced a decade of stability in foster care and schooling. However, for the most troubled young people, instability in both continued throughout primary and secondary years.

The Skuse and Ward study (2003, forthcoming) points out that children being looked after may sometimes enter care with a history of interrupted schooling, and that this pattern may continue once they return to their families. They also made the useful distinction between routine moves when children move to secondary school with their peers and those when children move school on their own. The latter is often mid-term when friendships have developed and classes are well advanced for the year.

> ...I hate changing school. I've done it all my life...and I'm just sick of it... I have to make friends and everything... It was okay when I went to X [name of school] 'cause I'd made friends from my previous school and it was like we were all going there as a group. I just can't be bothered to make friends and I just don't like being the new kid. I've always been the new kid and I don't like it.
>
> *(Boy reflecting on care period when aged between 9 and 12)*

Alongside this, however, it is very important to acknowledge that some placement and school changes may be viewed positively by the children involved. In the *Children's Care Monitor 2009*, 81 per cent of the children in care consulted thought they were in the right placement for them. Importantly, 69 per cent considered the last change of placement had been in their best interests, with a further 16 per cent not being sure about this. Fifty-four per cent of children who had changed schools because of a change in living placement considered their last change of school to be in their best interests, either educationally or socially or both – as children when consulted often say, 'it depends', and a change of placement or school can be either right or wrong for the particular child at a particular time (Morgan 2009b).

In further CRD consultations, the young people indicated what they thought should be done to address the issue of multiple placements. Getting the right placement first time is the most important task for a child's social worker (Morgan 2006a). When being placed or moved, children consulted have said they want a choice of at least two alternative new placements each time, gradual introduction to a new placement with visits and plenty of information (including photographs), their social worker often checking how they are settling in, and a back-up placement to move to if the first one does not work out (Morgan 2006c). In children's reported experience, arguments are the most common trigger for placement breakdown, although it is usually assumed that the breakdown is the child's fault rather than that of adults involved.

CHILDREN ON SIGNIFICANT PEOPLE IN THEIR LIVES

Children generally see their birth-family members as being very significant to their well-being. Children in care, of course, also have considerable contact with foster carers, residential staff and social workers. CRD consultations have found that a child's direct carers are key people in the child's life. Foster children are the most likely of those in care to regard their carers as the best thing about being in care (Morgan 2009a). Residential staff caring for children are in a key position to determine the quality, or otherwise, of a child's experience of residential care. Most, though not all, are seen very positively by the children they care for: 'some bad staff, but the majority are all right' (Morgan 2009h). 'Staff' appear on lists of both the best and the worst features of living in children's homes or residential special schools – they make the difference as to whether life in residential care is positive or negative (Morgan 2009f, 2009g). For children in children's homes, good staff are kind, caring listeners, helpful with problems, fun, happy, easy to get along with, supportive, understanding and encouraging. The worst staff there are those who are moody. Overall, children in residential settings are much more positive than negative about the staff who care for them.

CRD consultations confirmed that social workers are key people for children in care. They are generally rated highly; in consultations for the report *About Social Workers* (Morgan 2006a), children overall rated their social workers 8 out of 10. A good social worker is easy for the child to get hold of and is powerful enough to be able to take action and deliver their promises for their child clients without being overruled by senior staff on financial grounds or losing actions in administrative delays. They keep children informed – even when nothing significant is happening – and take proper account of children's views and feelings. Social workers are variable in these things: 'social workers are like young people, you have your good and bad ones'.

Children in that consultation identified two main negative factors in their experience of social workers. The first was that their social workers were changed too often, breaking their support to, understanding of and relationship with the child. The second was that, on many visits to check a child's well-being, social workers did not speak alone to the child safely out of sight and hearing of others such as carers, making it impossible for the child to tell them some things they might otherwise have told them (Morgan 2006d).

Research also highlights how relationships with social workers and carers are crucially important and how disappointing it can be for children when they do not get to spend time with them or, indeed, have many changes of social worker. In the Skuse and Ward study (2003, forthcoming), many of the young people spoke positively about their social workers but a few also highlighted the number of changes of social worker and how unsettling that had been for them. They also resented new social workers who had been given files about their lives and assumed they knew how the child was feeling without meeting with them to get to know them:

> They don't really know, do they, how I have been feeling because they have not been to ask me… How can they know if they haven't developed a relationship with you?

> *(Girl on her period in care when aged between 12 and 13)*

In the follow-up study cited above (McAuley 2006), many of the young people described what a difference their foster carers had made to their lives. Seven of the young people had remained for the rest of their childhoods with the planned foster carers and two had chosen to remain living with them after leaving care. Others had established their separate homes but were in close contact with their former carers. Over the years they had become part of the family, their extended family and the community in which they lived. They described sensing that they were accepted, wanted and how they were treated as though they were the carer's own child.

> The last few years of my life have been happy… I've always had the feeling that I've been loved, always been wanted… Nobody would know what they [the foster carers] mean to me, what they have done for me. They took me out of something bad and gave me something good. They always make me feel special.

> *(Young adult referring to his foster carers)*

Children in these situations described the foster carers' sense of pride in the children's achievements at home, school and work. It was clear that these children really trusted these carers and welcomed their support during and following care. The children continued to be regarded as part of the family. One girl was delighted to be invited to be the flower girl at their daughter's wedding. She also shared how her foster carers had persuaded a local shopkeeper to give her work experience. Two young men described how their carers had helped them to decorate and furnish their first flat or their future marital home. There was a strong sense that these foster carers had made a huge and continuing commitment to them.

The small number of young people whose lives remained more troubled provided rich reflections on some key issues. Central for them was the ability to trust, which they found particularly difficult. They had all experienced severe rejection and/or abuse by their parents early in childhood and described how they had never, or only partly, been able to trust anyone since then. They displayed emotional and behavioural difficulties and mental-health problems. These young people expressed anger at the lack of access to and provision of appropriate therapeutic help for them during their lengthy periods in care. The first national prevalence study of looked-after children in England (Meltzer *et al.* 2003) found that 45 per cent of looked-after children and young people aged between 5 and 17 had a diagnosable mental-health disorder. (For a review and discussion of the evidence-based services being introduced to England to prevent or alleviate these problems, see McAuley and Davis 2009.) However, recent thinking on the impact of early experiences would suggest that there is room for more optimism about change over time in a responsive environment (Aldgate, Chapter 1, this volume; Aldgate and Jones 2006; Howes 1999). Indeed, in the McAuley (2006) study, one of these young women described how she had eventually developed trust in a subsequent foster carer, who remained as a key support figure to her now she was a young mother in adulthood.

On a more general note about the well-being of children in care, in 2009 members of local authorities newly established Children in Care Councils across England were consulted on how they thought their local authorities were performing on the original government outcomes: being safe; being healthy; enjoying and achieving; making a contribution; and economic well-being ('enjoying and achieving' was divided into two) (Morgan 2009c). Local authorities were rated best at keeping children in care safe, with 53 per cent of those consulted rating them as doing well or very well, and next best at making sure children in care achieve well in their learning, with 46 per cent rating them as doing well or very well. Next, in descending order of performance as rated by the young people, came: keeping children in care healthy, then making sure they enjoy good activities and leisure time, followed by helping children in care make a good contribution to the community. The lowest performance rating given was for helping children in care prepare to get good jobs, where 30 per cent rated local authorities as doing well or very well and 46 per cent as doing poorly or very poorly.

Children on consultation and decision-making

From consultation with children on children's rights (Morgan 2010), it can be reported that 'having a say' comes below rights such as 'the right not to be abused', 'to have an education' and 'to be alive and well'. However, 'having a say' came top of the list of rights that children and young people want to be increased from their present level. 'Asking what children's wishes, concerns and feelings are' also comes high on children's own proposed protections against abuse and the risks of running away from care settings.

From consultations on the process of consultation itself, children have been clear on three points:

1. Consultation with children does not need to be based on games and indirect methods; children have repeatedly said that they appreciate being asked direct questions. This is often equated with being taken seriously.

2. Children value having a choice of means of putting their views forward; as in any other group or age group of people, some enjoy the cut and thrust of discussion, some are more reticent, some are articulate, some prefer the written word and some are shy and need encouragement and a safe opportunity in order to venture putting their views forward.

3. Children value feedback on what is being done with what they have said, even if the message is that nothing can be done. Consultation that leads into an abyss puts people off involvement next time.

The issue of being taken seriously repeatedly arises in consultation work. Children and young people are very aware that, although it is becoming standard practice to ask children their views, this does not necessarily lead to any change or impact. Some children, particularly those who are regularly involved in consultation work, tell us that they are becoming tired of being asked the same thing repeatedly, giving the same views repeatedly, but apparently having little or no impact – a phenomenon that has been referred to as 'consultation fatigue'.

There is a varying relationship between how often children say their opinions are sought and how much difference they consider their opinions actually make. Foster children have said their opinions are relatively often sought, but are relatively less likely to make a difference, while children living in boarding schools are relatively less likely to be asked their opinions in the first place, but thought they had more impact once they had given them (Morgan 2009b).

Overall, 50 per cent of children in care or living in residential boarding schools or colleges have told us that they consider they are often, or always, asked for their opinions about things that matter to them, while, overall, only 48 per cent believe that their opinions 'usually or always' make a difference to their lives (Morgan 2009b). As mentioned, feedback on any impact of expressing their opinions, including feedback on reasons for rejection of children's proposals, is important.

To maximise consultation impact, the Office of the Children's Rights Director involved a government policy official in discussion with a focus group of children on the question of consent for sharing of personal information, in the course of production of government guidance on the matter. Having dismissed the official's initial proposal that children aged over 12 should be deemed old enough to give or withhold consent, but those under 12 should not, the official challenged the children to come up with a workable alternative to an age criterion. The children advised that the child's understanding should be assessed in relation to the issue under consideration, and they came up with the following guidance on assessing a child's understanding.

Once it's fully explained, does the young person understand:

- the question?

- the reasons behind it?

- what the alternatives are?

- what will happen if they decide one way or the other?

Can they:

- weigh things up for themselves?

- say what they want for themselves?

- keep the same view, not keep changing it?

The official adopted this guidance. It is also interesting to note how close the children's criteria are to those developed by health and social care professionals for assessing both 'Gillick competence' (competence to consent to medical treatment) and competence under mental-health legislation.

Understanding an issue may be related to age, but understanding and age are two very different concepts when applied to competence to make decisions. Use of the concept of understanding allows for a child of any age to demonstrate sufficient understanding on a particular issue, and takes into account the point made by one young person that a particular 10-year-old could show enough understanding of an issue while a particular 18-year-old could not. The United Nations Convention on the Rights of the Child grants children who are capable of forming views the right to express their views freely in all matters affecting them, the views of the child being given 'due weight in accordance with the age and maturity of the child' (United Nations 1989, Article 12).

The Children Act 1989 goes further than this, requiring local authorities making decisions with respect to children they are looking after to ascertain the child's wishes and feelings, and to give these due consideration 'having regard to his age and understanding'. That Act therefore includes the concept of understanding alongside age, and, importantly, includes the concept of 'feelings', which, vitally, a child of any age can have about an issue, even where they may lack competent understanding. Consultations with children argue for a more pure criterion for determining competence to contribute to and make decisions according to understanding alone – with the addition of feelings to the equation whatever the child's age or level of understanding.

Consultation with children in care (Morgan 2009b) has identified how children in care experienced participation in the planning of their own care. (In England, each child in care has a statutory care plan, and statute requires children to be involved in their care planning, and in reviews of their care plans, as far as is practicable.)

In 2009, 73 per cent of the children in care who were consulted reported that they knew they had a care plan. Of those, 76 per cent reported knowing what their care plan contained, and 68 per cent that they agreed with their care plan. A further 23 per cent agreed with some, but not all, of their care plan. Of those who knew what their care plans contained, 82 per cent reported that their care plans were fully being kept to. Boys were more likely than girls to report that their care plans were being kept to.

Related to being consulted and 'having a say' is the even more fundamental issue of being kept informed about what is happening and what is *about to* happen. Children and adults alike experience anxiety if events happen to them without warning and if they are given insufficient information about changes affecting their lives. For children in care, or living away from home in residential-education settings, major changes can occur and children have identified warning and information as being essential in coping with change. In the *Children's Care Monitor* consultations, 69 per cent of children said they were 'usually or always' told what was going on when major changes were to happen in their lives, while 11 per cent said they are 'not usually or never' told.

Finally, on decision-making, children in care have strongly argued that the key is for the right decision to be made about what is right for each individual child at the time concerned, taking their wishes and feelings into account. Decisions should not be determined or influenced by an authority aiming to meet particular targets or quotas (Morgan 2007a). One of the most frequent answers given by children to questions about policy or practice is 'it depends' – that is, what is right, best or most appropriate depends on assessment of the individual's circumstances, and what may be right or wrong for one child at one time may not be so for another child, or for the same child at a different point in their lives. Children have told us that they do not want their care determined by general assumptions of what is 'best for most', but on what is best for them, taking their views, wishes and feelings into account. A newly proposed fundamental children's right 'to be treated as an individual, not as one of a group of children', secured 49 per cent of 3,668 possible votes from 1,834 children recently consulted on children's rights (Morgan 2010).

Thomas and O'Kane (1999a) carried out a study of looked-after children's participation in decision-making processes. Following a survey in seven local-authority areas in England and Wales of all children aged 8 to 12 years, 47 children were interviewed. Almost 53 per cent of those interviewed had attended all, or part of, their last review meeting. Reasons for attending included 'it is my life'; 'to find out what is going on'; 'because I am expected to'; and 'to see my mum'. Reasons given for *not* attending included that adults did not listen to them; feeling exposed at the meetings; not knowing what the purpose of the meeting was; and not feeling confident. Less than a third had been consulted as to who should attend the meeting and only around a quarter had been given a choice about time or place.

When children did attend, many children were pleased with the support they had received from a range of people, including carers, parents, social workers, residential keyworkers and teachers. However, they wanted more information in advance about the meeting, who would be there and what would be discussed. The majority of children felt that adults *did* listen to them at the review meetings. However, they distinguished between being listened to and having influence. Only 28 per cent felt they had a lot of influence. Half of them expressed dislike of the meetings, and reasons given for this included the length of the meeting and the feeling of being 'put on the spot'. Although many children did not think they had much influence, they were more concerned with having the opportunity to have their say and not necessarily to determine the outcomes, as some adults thought. At times, they welcomed adults taking decisions that were hard for them:

> Well, I like them making the decisions about when I go to my Mum and Dad's, because I find that difficult.
>
> *(Boy aged 12 cited in Thomas and O'Kane 1999b)*

Many children felt that adults underestimated them because they were too young:

> I think they should have a say and be trusted… They shouldn't just say 'Oh, they are only nine.'
>
> *(Girl aged 10 cited in Thomas and O'Kane 1999b)*

Sometimes the issue is about *how* we ask children for their views. The same authors comment in a related article on the study that they used methods of communication with children (i.e. direct work with children) that had been developed in social work practice, whilst the social workers in these cases were often not actually using such methods. Often children had been excluded from decision-making processes because of a perceived lack of understanding of the issues or perceived lack of competence to cope with the processes involved. Often these judgements correlated with age. Yet the authors found that the younger children in their sample were well able to express their views and understand those of others. However, their views were not always sought in ways that enabled them to demonstrate their competence (Thomas and O'Kane 2000).

The study also included the perspectives of the carers and parents of the children. Although there were found to be significant differences within the adult and child accounts, the authors made the observation that parents' concerns were often about the future, whilst children tended to emphasise the present (Thomas and O'Kane 1999b).

Children on feeling safe

The *Children's Care Monitor 2009* (Morgan 2009b) reported that children consulted felt safest in the building they lived in, next safest in school or college, next safest in the countryside, and least safe when out in urban areas.

To define what safety means to children, those involved in that consultation were asked what they saw as the major risks to safety for their age group, and what they saw as the major likely causes of accidents to their age group. The ten highest risks to safety identified (unprompted) by those children, in descending order of frequency identified, were:

- drugs

- alcohol

- knives

- strangers and kidnappers

- bullying

- road accidents

- gangs

- violence

- rapists

- smoking.

There were significant age and gender differences in what children regarded as being the greatest risks to their safety – and, thus, what made the difference between being safe and being unsafe. Over twice as many girls than boys identified alcohol as a risk to safety. Those aged 14 and over were more likely than those under 14 to identify drugs and alcohol as safety risks, while those under 14 were more likely than over 14s to identify strangers, kidnappers and bullying as risks. Although children did identify sexual abuse as a risk, this was not perceived as being the most likely risk to their safety. 'Safeguarding' is far wider than that, and also needs to encompass issues of dangers from substance abuse, actual and perceived dangers from knives, risks of bullying, and injury on the road.

As well as perceived risk of actual danger, children reported worrying about safety. Forty-three per cent of those consulted within the Children's Rights Director's remit reported being worried 'a little' or 'a lot' about their safety, while 38 per cent reported being worried 'not much' or 'not at all'. Worrying about safety can be as important as actual levels of risk.

Perception of safety is vital. For many children in care, being moved to a new placement and finding oneself in a strange place with strange people can bring feelings of lack of safety, although this can be reduced by information and gradual introduction to new places and people – 'Don't dump us with strangers'. In consultations, children have underlined the role of adults in keeping children both safe and *feeling* safe. Being with adults you trust and feel safe with is vitally important. Six out of ten have said that the adults working with them made them feel safe (Morgan 2007b).

Another important issue for children was bullying. In the annual children's assessment of the state of social care in England in 2009 (Morgan 2009b), 9 per cent of children in the Children's Rights Director's remit said they were 'often' or 'always' being bullied, and 45 per cent that they were 'never' bullied. Eighty-one per cent of bullying incidents were reported as being verbal, involving teasing or name-calling, 38 per cent involved spreading rumours about someone, 35 per cent involved being excluded from things by other children, and 31 per cent involved being hit or physically hurt. Twenty per cent of bullying incidents involved taking or damaging property. Twenty-six per cent of girls, and 12 per cent of boys, reported being the victims of cyber-bullying, involving messages on mobile phones or social networking websites. Disabled children reported being more bullied than other children, and 20 per cent of children in care reported being bullied simply for being in care.

Consulting children in more depth about their experiences of bullying identified a number of key aspects of the phenomenon (Morgan 2008). Children defined bullying according to three main criteria:

1. Bullying is something that, regardless of exactly what is done, has a harmful effect on the victim.

2. The person being bullied is unable to defend themselves: 'Picking on someone that can't defend themselves'.

3. The person that is being bullied does not deserve to be treated the way they are being treated: 'Picking on a person who has done nothing', or picking on someone 'For no reason or for attention'.

Children identified particular characteristics of children that make them prone to being bullied. These, in order of likelihood according to the children consulted, were:

- being different in any way to the majority group

- being perceived as being unable to stand up for yourself

- being someone a bully finds annoying

- being someone who shows off to others

- being a quiet person

- being good at school and wanting to learn

- being without a protective group of friends.

Differences that could make a child vulnerable to bullying included anything that made a child stand out as different – including accents, being in care, having a disability, or having ginger hair. One young person told us that in every group of children 'There is a kind of prototype of what everyone should be', and that children who don't fit that prototype are vulnerable.

Children reported that most bullying was carried out by age peers, and that there was a 60 per cent chance that when someone was being bullied the same bully had bullied them before. The children reported that bullying can make the victim feel upset, angry and, in a few cases, suicidal. Bullying that involved a lot of perpetrators and that carried on for a long time was most likely to damage the victim's health.

Children also reported that the level of worrying about bullying is higher than the level of actual bullying experienced. In the *Children's Care Monitor 2009* (Morgan 2009b), although 9 per cent reported being 'often' or 'always' bullied, 15 per cent reported 'often' or 'always' *worrying about* getting bullied. Although 45 per cent reported that they were 'never' bullied, only 36 per cent reported never worrying about getting bullied.

Children's advice to adults is that there are two main ways to help to reduce the chances of any particular child getting bullied. One is to help the child 'fit in' and not to 'stand out' as different from the group. The other is to help children to form protective friendship groups.

Discussion and reflections

A number of wider points emerged from the material reviewed in this chapter. Where the studies included child and parent perspectives, it was clear that the children's view (or standpoint) was different from that of their parents. Repeatedly, the studies emphasised children's concern with the present, that is what was happening to them in the here and now. This was in contrast to their parents' preoccupation with what had happened or what might happen in the future. This emphasises the importance of asking children directly about their experiences of well-being and reinforces the distinction between child well-being and well-becoming (as discussed elsewhere in this volume by Aldgate, Chapter 1; Rose and Rowlands, Chapter 3; and Ben-Arieh, Chapter 6).

Throughout the studies and consultations, there was clear evidence of children wanting to have their say as well as actively shaping their lives. Their advice about at what age children understand issues sufficiently to be consulted was a direct example of this. It was also a very strong illustration of how much can be achieved when adults and children work together to find solutions to challenging issues such as these.

In recent work by Mason and colleagues (Fattore *et al.* 2009) the two underlying mediums through which children understood well-being were found to be children's significant relationships and their emotional life. The evidenced surveyed in this chapter clearly demonstrates children's views on the importance of family life and relationships with significant others. It also clearly demonstrated their sensitivity to the feelings of family members and others and the fact that they *gave* as well as received support within families.

In the study by Fattore *et al.*, three overarching dimensions of well-being were also identified by the children: having a positive sense of self; having a sense of agency (control in everyday life); and having a sense of security and safety. As we might have expected, these dimensions were found to be interrelated and influencing each other.

From the accounts of all the children reviewed here, these dimensions appear highly relevant. They seem particularly so in relation to children living in families experiencing difficulties and to children in care. Both have described feeling different or being treated differently by others, being subjected to bullying, feeling unsafe and insecure and having to deal with stigma. Whilst there is evidence of children in care together striving for a voice and some agency, children still living in troubled families come across as being much more isolated and with much less agency. Consulting children who have had these experiences about how we might begin to support children in these circumstances might well be a useful way forward.

We are clearly at the beginning of a journey of understanding children's views about their well-being. The fact that the child indicators movement has recognised that subjective well-being needs to be included when estimating well-being is a major development. It provides an exceptional opportunity for adults and children to work together to advance our understanding of this important, but complex, area.

Note

1   One of the independent statutory functions of the Children's Rights Director for England is to ascertain the views of children either in care or receiving children's social care services, or living away from home in residential or boarding schools or colleges. This chapter draws on his continuing consultation programme with these children and young people.

The consultation methods used have included secure web surveys (with a paper completion alternative option and usually a symbol translation where needed) and written 'question card surveys' either completed by post or at national children's conferences at child-friendly venues. They include focus-group discussions, sometimes combining group discussion with individual written views on the topics discussed, weekly mobile-phone text consultations and electronic voting on consultation questions projected onto a big screen.

The rigour of consultations is maximised by random sampling of the establishments, services and authorities to which invitations are to be sent, although representativeness is then affected by variable responses of managers in passing on information and invitations to children, or in arranging for children to attend discussion groups or events. These views come from consultation, not research, but the consultation is as rigorous and the views as representative as possible. Consultations have aimed to enable the 'quiet child' to take part, rather than securing the views of those in established consultation fora.

CHAPTER 3

Introducing the Concept of Child Well-Being into Government Policy

WENDY ROSE AND JOHN ROWLANDS

'Would you tell me, please,' said Alice, 'what that means?'[1]

Introduction

Whatever other legacies the New Labour Government leaves, one about which there can be no doubt is the addition of the term 'child well-being' to the lexicon of UK public policy. Now firmly embedded in legislation, government guidance and reports, this term marks a significant shift following the election of New Labour in 1997 in the language used to describe the English Government's aspirations for children, and a clear departure from past practices of framing policy in terms of 'child care' and 'the welfare of children'.

The reality of this change, however, is not quite so stark, involving as it has a more evolutionary process of discussion and development that has been going on between children's campaigners, academics and many others, both in the UK and internationally, for several decades. The debates have covered a number of different strands, as the authors of chapters in this book amply demonstrate: the knowledge and understanding of childhood and children's rights; the contribution of children in understanding and defining what is important to them; the role of the State in addressing society's responsibilities for children; the impact of poverty, social exclusion and inequality; the influence of economic factors and consequential changing patterns of family life on children; and how data can be gathered and used to inform policy makers of how well children are doing.

However, now that the concept of child well-being is firmly incorporated into the governmental policy machine, not just in England but also in other countries of the United Kingdom, there has been an explosion in its use in public debate about children. As Axford (2009, p.372) has observed, 'suddenly it seemed that everyone involved in children's services is talking the language of "outcomes" and "well-being".' But this contemporary currency does beg a number of questions (Ereaut and Whiting 2008). What does child well-being actually mean? How is it defined and by whom? Is there consistency about its definition and its use? Is its introduction into government policy making a difference?

This chapter sets out to tell the story of how a new government came to adopt child well-being as the unifying idea around which its policy aspirations for children and families across government would be fashioned and to explore some of the implications this has had – both intended and unintended. It is a story told from the perspective of the authors whose combined careers as civil servants working on children's policy covered the period 1986 to 2006 (New Labour having been elected in 1997 after 18 years of Conservative Government). The account does not claim to be comprehensive but does offer some insights into the policy process and how a set of issues came to be developed and modified as they travelled through the policy machine.

The chapter concludes that the term 'child well-being' remains conceptually elusive and its use within policy is marked by 'ambiguity and instability' (Ereaut and Whiting 2008, p.1). However, it also suggests that there are signs that its adoption has in fact been useful in changing the policy landscape in the interests of children and young people.

Translating policy ambitions into action

In 1997/1998 the key ambition of the new government for the system of social services in England was modernisation, in line with similar proposals being developed for the National Health Service. 'We are determined to have a system of health and social care which is convenient to use, can respond quickly to emergencies and provide top quality services', wrote the then Secretary of State, Frank Dobson, in *Modernising Social Services* (Cm 4169 1998, p.2). The priority areas for children's social services were identified as: ensuring children were protected, raising the quality of care of children in care, and improving their life chances – all issues of political, professional and public concern at the time of the change of government. These priorities, however, were set within a wider agenda for children generally, which started with the ambitious pledge to eradicate child poverty in 20 years and continued:

> The Government is committed to taking action through a broad range of initiatives to strengthen family life, to reduce social exclusion and anti-social behaviour among children, and to give every child the opportunity of a healthy, happy, successful life. (Cm 4169 1998, p.4)

The new government was quickly to discover the dissonance between high-level ambitions and the capacity of local communities to plan and deliver the changes required. One of the first tasks of a newly formed Social Exclusion Unit was to look into problems of truancy and report to the Prime Minister (Social Exclusion Unit 1998). The report stressed that issues of truancy were clearly not just the province of schools and that a joined-up solution was required. However, the Social Exclusion Unit was dismayed by the plethora of planning requirements it found that professionals working with children who might truant or be excluded were required by law to produce. The various plans included Children's Services Plans, Behaviour Support Plans, Education Development Plans, Youth Justice Plans and Drug Action Strategies. The report commented that 'the number of them runs the risk of duplication and lack of co-ordination' (Social Exclusion Unit 1998). The case for integrating the multiplicity of statutory plans affecting young people had been made and was included in the Social Exclusion Unit's work programme.

This did not prove easy and the Social Exclusion Unit in fact failed to achieve the intended rationalisation of children's planning. The problem was then passed to the Department of Health, which at the time held policy responsibility for children's social services. A cross-government letter to local authorities and the NHS was issued, *Consultation on New Guidance for Planning Children's Services* (Department of Health 2000), proposing that children's services plans should be the vehicle for rationalising planning requirements concerned with vulnerable children. Significantly, it added 'ensuring that the outcomes sought for such children are consistent with those sought for all children and are coherent across all services' (Department of Health 2000). In the meantime, a groundswell of support was growing for rationalising children's planning. A major children's organisation, the National Children's Bureau, was holding regular meetings on children's services planning where there was a positive response from health, education, social services and other agencies to the idea of working towards shared objectives and one local plan.

The responses to the consultation confirmed disquiet over the number of existing plans and the problem of achieving coherence. There was wide support for a broad approach to planning. One of the authors (Rowlands, a civil servant in the Department of Health) was asked to take on the task of drafting new guidance that responded to the consultation and in so doing took account of the emergence of local strategic partnerships and the work of the newly established Children and Young People's Unit.

Two key problems quickly became evident. First, each plan had a separate policy driver and its own legislative imperative, especially in education. Several plans would necessitate legislative change to remove or amend the requirement. Second, and perhaps more importantly, agencies at local authority level were working without an agreed common set of objectives. Rowlands came to the conclusion that agreement between agencies on shared objectives was an essential pre-requisite for the successful co-ordination of planning. Only then could agencies address the question of how different services both separately and in concert could contribute to the achievement of a shared objective. Wistow (2002) reinforces the importance of having shared values and principles in helping to clarify desirable directions and destinations in social care:

> In other words, it requires a minimal framework of principles and purposes to guide the consistent development of policy and practice as well as to provide reference points for scrutiny, review and revision. (Wistow 2002, p.40)

Developing an overarching strategy for children and young people

The Government set up the Children and Young People's Unit in 2000, as 'a visible symbol of the Government's continued commitment to improving the life chances of our children and young people' (Children and Young People's Unit 2001a, p.26). The newly created unit sat rather uncomfortably within the departmental civil service structure, as a multi-disciplinary, cross-departmental part of government, located in the Department for Education and Employment and reporting to the Minister for Young People in the Home Office (the recently appointed Paul Boateng). Made up of staff from a range of backgrounds from across the public, private and voluntary sectors, its purpose was to support Ministers in the articulation and development of an overarching strategy and to drive forward the Government's investment in services for children and young people, including implementing and managing the new Children's Fund of £450 million over three years. Its remit also included monitoring the impact of new planning guidance as part of its work programme. The unit was to be informed by the views and experiences of children, young people and local practitioners, and it was definitely not intended to 'become just another piece of Whitehall furniture' (Children and Young People's Unit 2001a, p.30). This was to prove a creative but short-lived development, lasting barely three years.

Three initial strands of work were identified for the unit (Children and Young People's Unit 2001a, p.31):

1. monitoring the impact of the new cross-Government guidance on local planning for children which aims to rationalise and improve the process of planning local services for children

2. leading the development of unified overarching objectives for the delivery of services to children, flowing from the first recommendation of the Policy Action Team on Young People… and embedding these into policy making across all Government departments

3. developing an overarching Government strategy for Children and Young People, focusing on the vulnerable but with a commitment to ensure coherence of approach for all.

The Children and Young People's Unit rapidly set about its work of developing overarching objectives for children and these were articulated in a radical outcomes framework put out for widespread consultation in *Building a Strategy for Children and Young People* in November 2001 (Children and Young People's Unit 2001b). Two reasons were given for taking an outcomes approach. First, 'to enable everyone with a concern for children and young people's well-being to judge how we are delivering tangible improvements in children and young people's lives' (p.15). Second, to enable local communities to begin to 'own' their children and young people, by holding local services to account and participating in policy delivery and development, and thereby ensuring their well-being (p.15).

The provisional key outcomes for children and young people were defined into six areas:

*   health and well-being

*   achievement and enjoyment

*   participation and citizenship

*   protection

- responsibility
- inclusion.

(Children and Young People's Unit 2001b, pp.22–23)

The outcomes were presented in terms of 'Our aspiration' and 'How we could measure success', so that 'Health and well-being' were described, for example, in the following terms:

- Our aspiration: children and young people should develop healthy lifestyles and opportunities to achieve optimum health and well-being, within the context of high quality preventive and treatment services – if and when they need them. Children and young people should have the resilience, capacity and emotional well-being that allows them to play, learn, relate to other people, and resolve problems in life.

- How we could measure success: the range of specific outcomes that are important could include: life expectancy; physical health (morbidity); mental health; nutrition; dental health; teenage pregnancy; sexual health; personal safety (injury/accidents); behaviour (e.g. smoking; alcohol, substance/drug abuse); and living in a health-enhancing environment.

(Children and Young People's Unit 2001b, p.22)

At this stage, the concept of child well-being was hovering in the policy wings and had not become central to the Government's discussions about its aspirations for children. In the policy arena, as can be seen in the above example, well-being was usually associated with health in some way, as in 'Health and well-being' or 'Health and emotional well-being', even though researchers such as Bradshaw had been using the term for some time in a more all-encompassing sense when writing about the state of the UK's children (Bradshaw 1990). However, the intention was announced in *Building a Strategy for Children and Young People* to produce a regular national State of the Nation's Children and Young People's Report that would identify progress in achieving improved outcomes for children and young people.

Guidance issued by the Government earlier in the year, *Co-ordinated Service Planning for Vulnerable Children in England* (Department of Health 2001), had suggested that a similar set of six outcomes could be used as a valuable aid for encouraging shared ownership of children's services planning by new local strategic children and young people's partnerships.

This guidance provides signposts for some important developments that would materialise in the next few years:

1. The architecture for local strategic planning; the new partnerships could only be recommended at this stage but would become statutory in the Children Act 2004. It was acknowledged that there were still statutory and funding requirements that imposed barriers on effective local partnerships, and means of overcoming them would be explored by the Children and Young People's Unit.

2. The focus of local planning remained on vulnerable children. Whereas the unit had a wider remit, local partnerships had responsibility for planning, which it was proposed could be 'unified within a consensus of shared objectives and agreed targets for improving the well-being of *vulnerable children*' (para.13; authors' italics). It would ultimately require primary legislation, the Children Act 2004, to extend local planning responsibilities to improving the well-being of all children in an authority's area.

Thus, by the end of 2001, children's policy had developed in a number of significant new directions:

- The Government had made a commitment to improving the life-chances of the nation's children and eliminating child poverty, child deprivation and youth social exclusion.

- There was recognition that achieving this required national and local joined-up action, and that local children's services planning required a coherent set of objectives, shared by all partner agencies.

- Outcomes sought for vulnerable children needed to be consistent with those sought for all children.

- A framework of outcomes for children and young people had been proposed that could provide the shared objectives for a whole community and for its service-providing agencies.

- Transparency and accountability for achieving improvement in outcomes and knowing how well children were doing had been acknowledged as essential at both a national and local level.

Finally, a further significant aspect (although perhaps not so visible formally) was the extent to which children and young people themselves were being engaged and participating in the policy process. For the first time, their perspectives on what was important in their lives would contribute to framing national outcomes. This was exemplified by the Government's consultation, which was designed to encourage and enable children and young people to 'have your say' by various means, including activity books, questionnaires and a series of commissioned focus groups (Children and Young People's Unit 2001b).

How the outcomes framework evolved

The consultative process adopted by the Children and Young People's Unit had aimed to be inclusive and, as reported to an international seminar of senior policy makers co-hosted by the Children and Young People's Unit, it had allowed 'literally thousands of people to have input' (International Initiative 2003) by:

- seeking consultation about a set of basic questions, both in writing and through face-to-face dialogues with children, young people, adults and organisations. The Unit received 2,500 responses to its basic questions

- qualitative research about a proposed outcomes framework. This work, too, involved children and young people, parents and care givers, practitioners and policy makers, and their input was used to reshape the outcomes framework several times

- targeted consultations with key academics

- internal consultation across government, thereby ensuring that multiple agency viewpoints, perspectives and mandates were considered.

Throughout this process, the key question posed to many audiences was 'What are the really important things we should be monitoring to know how well our children and young people are doing?'

(International Initiative 2003, p.16)

The feedback from the consultation exercise was important in informing the further development of the outcomes framework. Significantly, but perhaps not surprisingly, the perspectives of parents, children, service providers and academics resulted in rather different, although not opposing, responses. The majority of respondents thought adopting an outcomes-based approach was right and many respondents welcomed combining traditional 'achievement' outcomes with non-traditional outcomes such as 'enjoyment' and 'being happy'. Parents, however, wanted 'to protect children' and children talked about wanting 'to feel safe'. Parents, children and schools distinguished between the here and now and the future, so that children talked of 'having fun' and 'enjoying the experience of being at school' while teachers placed emphasis on 'progressing well' (see McAuley, Morgan and Rose, Chapter 2, this volume). The distinction between present well-being and future well-becoming was also drawn at the time by authors in this current volume, Jonathan Bradshaw and Asher Ben-Arieh (e.g. Ben-Arieh 2002). This was not a simple, water-tight divide between adults' and children's timeframes. Children were also very much concerned about their futures. Similarly, adults were keen that children should be happy, safe and healthy during their childhood, but at the same time were preoccupied with how children would turn out as their lives progressed. The question became whether these two perspectives could be integrated within the same framework.

Academics brought another dimension to the feedback. They argued strongly about the importance of poverty and the links with childhood malaise, and questioned how these issues were being incorporated into the proposed framework. They also reinforced doubts about 'inclusion' being described as a discrete outcome in the framework (inclusion interpreted in this context as meaning the absence of prejudicial discrimination). They considered that the outcomes should apply to all children irrespective of race, ethnicity, religion and other factors.

The outcomes framework was presented to an international audience of senior policy makers at a seminar held at Cumberland Lodge, Windsor, in 2002, *Achieving Results: Policies that Make a Difference for Children, Families and Communities* (International Initiative 2003), and some of the feedback to the consultation process was now reflected in a revised framework (see Table 3.1).

Table 3.1 Outcomes framework for children and young people (England)

Outcomes	Health and emotional well-being	Being safe	Fulfilment	Social engagement	Material well-being
Present well-being	How good is the present state of children and young people's health?	How safe from harm are our children and young people?	How enjoyable and satisfying are the lives of children and young people?	How well do children and young people engage with the formal and informal communities in which they live?	How good are the material circumstances in which children and young people are living?
Future well-being	How well are children and young people growing up so as to enjoy as healthy a life as possible?	How well are children growing up so as to be able to protect themselves from avoidable harm?	How well are children developing towards adulthood in terms of education, personal and social skills?	How well are children developing pro-social skills, knowledge and attitudes?	How far are improving material circumstances promoting improved opportunities and outcomes?

Source: International Initiative 2003, p.16

The main changes to the framework were that six outcomes had been reduced to five: 'Material well-being' had been added as a new outcome, which related the importance of material circumstances to improving opportunities and outcomes for children and young people; 'Inclusion' had been removed altogether and would be treated as an aspect of the analysis of all other outcomes; 'Achievement and enjoyment' had been combined as being two aspects of a broader concept of 'Fulfilment'; and, finally, 'Responsibility, participation and citizenship' had been brought together into one outcome and, in this version, replaced by an outcome called 'Social engagement', although still difficult to define. (Subsequently, 'Social engagement' went through various further metamorphoses and the struggle to define it continued.)

Two other modifications to official thinking were taking place at this time. It was acknowledged that there was a useful distinction to be made between the quality of childhood as experienced by children and young people in the here and now and the importance of childhood as preparation for the future. As a result, this distinction was accommodated within the revised framework and ensured that children's perspectives about their present experience were given at least equal weight as adult perspectives about the important outcomes for children as they grew older. The second modification was in the use of the term 'well-being'. It began to be used to describe the 'total universe of life domains', so that it encompassed health, protection, fulfilment, participation and material well-being. At this point, 'child well-being' became the overarching, unifying theme of children's policy.

Finding evidence of outcomes

Rowlands, who was by now seconded to the Children and Young People's Unit for part of his time, commented in an internal document (14 June 2003):

> Our purpose in constructing this framework is to make sure that we consider the full range of aspects of childhood that we should include in the outcomes framework. It is not intended to be a rigid classification.

Although important, gaining consensus to the outcomes framework and its constituent parts was not seen as an end in itself and Rowlands, with external advisers and other colleagues, was now also grappling with the relationship of the framework of outcomes to environmental and service measures. In order to be able to know which children were doing well and which children were not, it was suggested that there was a need to disaggregate each outcome by factors such as socio-economic characteristics. Age and gender were also important. Thus, for example, with the outcome of 'Participation, responsibility and citizenship', aspirations for children clearly had to be specific and age-appropriate – what might be expected for a child in infancy, such as basic socialisation, would be quite different for teenagers and would be likely to embrace voting intentions or law-abiding behaviour. It was clear that such ideas would make demands for information far beyond the capacity of existing data collections to deliver. In addition, it was acknowledged that the aim of measuring how well children were doing did not contain any expectation that there was a simple relationship between an outcome and what had determined that outcome. It was recognised that multiple factors might apply, including parenting effectiveness, genetic inheritance, economic circumstances, environmental conditions, the effectiveness of services and, not least, children's own characteristics and contribution to their development, as Aldgate discusses in Chapter 1 in this volume. It would be very difficult for any government to be able to say 'Because we have done this, that improvement has occurred.'

The search was on, therefore, for indicators that were sufficiently specific, sensitive and significant. An indicator (or benchmark) in this sense meant a measure that helped quantify the achievement of a result – as Friedman (2005, p.20) says, 'Indicators answer the question "How would we recognize this result if we fell over it?"' There was discussion about how the five broad categories of outcomes could be refined through a series of 'contributory outcomes' into a set of manageable, specific 'contributory indicators'. The contributory outcomes would need to be sufficiently specific in their definition to allow focused programmes of cross-government policy reform, plans and action to be devised around them. An example considered was in relation to health: a contributory outcome might be 'a child is within the normal weight range for their age'. It can be seen from the present concern over obesity in children that a series of mutually related initiatives would be required. Weight, diet and exercise would constitute some of the significant, specific and measurable contributory indicators of children's health. Information needed to be available where possible in current data collections in order to measure both the effectiveness of the delivery programme and the impact it was having on children's well-being. If not, then bespoke surveys and other measures would be required. Above all, the process had to be carefully managed so that contributory outcomes and their indicators did not become so extensive that they engulfed the whole endeavour, and targets subsequently set for service agencies needed to be used only sparingly.

Bradshaw pointed out in 1990 that, in many respects, the UK had an excellent relevant database but that 'children have not been the primary focus of attention' and:

> although there is a rich variety of primary research and official statistics covering child poverty, deprivation, health and well-being, it is often not population based, it is cross sectional in approach and does not allow the analysis of change over time. (Bradshaw 1990, pp.3–4)

Twelve years later, Bradshaw (2002, p.369) noted that the evidence base on child well-being had been improving but that there were still big gaps. This, then, was the challenge with which officials were grappling as child well-being became even more significant in government policy. This challenge continues nearly a decade further on.

Child well-being into legislation

Policy is never developed in a vacuum and the children's policy context continued to be very noisy and cluttered in 2003. There were multiple initiatives and developments under way, running in parallel, and, above all, crises crowding in from different directions. The contextual issues included pre-occupation with Sure Start (the early years programme), anti-social behaviour, truancy, exclusion and child protection. Pre-eminent among the crises in terms of public attention and political concern was the tragic death of Victoria Climbié (which had occurred in 2001) and the subsequent independent statutory inquiry set up by the Secretary of State for Health and the Home Secretary. In January 2003, Lord Laming delivered his report of *The Victoria Climbié Inquiry* (Cm 5730 2003) and, in September that year, the Government issued its response in the form of a Green Paper, *Every Child Matters* (Cm 5860 2003), and *Keeping Children Safe* (Cm 5861 2003). Commentators such as Parton regard the Green Paper as the Government seizing the opportunity to bring about wider system change (Parton 2009, p.71):

> While presented by the government as a response to the Laming Report (2003) into the death of Victoria Climbié, the Green Paper ECM was primarily concerned with bringing forward the government's proposals for changing the organization and rationale for the delivery of children's services... In effect, the government used the opportunity of needing to be seen to be responding to the Laming Report for introducing a series of wide-ranging changes that went far beyond responding to concerns about child abuse.

In the first section of the Green Paper, the Government set out its goals for every child as 'the outcomes which mattered most to children and young people' from the consultation of the previous year – although, in reality, they could be described as encapsulating a consensus of the views expressed by children, parents, academics and policy makers:

- being healthy: enjoying good physical and mental health and living a healthy life style
- staying safe: being protected from harm and neglect

- enjoying and achieving: getting the most out of life and developing the skills for adulthood

- making a positive contribution: being involved with the community and society and not engaging in anti-social or offending behaviour

- economic well-being: not being prevented by economic disadvantage from achieving their full potential in life.

(Cm 5860 2003, pp.6–7)

Notable is the blurring of the distinction between well-being *now* and well-becoming in the future (as appeared in the revised framework of the previous year; see Table 3.1 above), with 'well-becoming' subtly emphasised at the expense of well-being in the here and now. The framework can also be seen as fulfilling the desire often held by policy makers and politicians for simplicity – an easier set of messages to promote perhaps than the matrix presented at Windsor (Table 3.1). It still required, however, detailed and complex work to translate it into a set of grounded, realistic and achievable contributory outcomes, indicators and service targets for which evidence could be gathered of any improvement or deterioration. Progress on this front was published in the form of a chart a year later as an enclosure with *Every Child Matters: Change for Children* (Department for Education and Skills 2004a).

Subsequent sections of the Green Paper laid out intended government action that was framed around the idea that integrated service delivery would lead to better outcomes for children, with the focus on improving service delivery by a more joined-up approach. It was a policy direction that carried some risk. Strong theoretical arguments for increasing inter-agency collaboration could be made. However, evidence from a wide range of sources suggested that not only was effective joined-up working difficult to achieve in practice but that 'greater collaboration between services will not necessarily produce better outcomes for children and families' (Gardner 2003, p.156; see also Glisson and Hemmelgarn 1998; Hudson *et al.* 1999). Achieving integrated service delivery, acknowledged the Green Paper, would require structural changes – which, in turn, would require additional primary legislation in order to create clear accountability for a wide range of children's services, to enable better joint working and to secure a better focus on safeguarding children. Less clear in the second part of the Green Paper is through what mechanisms the outcomes in the first part would be achieved by the structural changes proposed.

The five outcomes articulated in the Green Paper were carried forward into legislation. The Children Act 2004 thus became the first piece of legislation in the UK to enshrine the concept of 'children's well-being', to define it and to require local co-operation between partner agencies to promote it. (Although this was not the first time 'well-being' had appeared in primary legislation as, four years earlier, the Local Government Act 2000 gave local authorities the power to do anything that they considered was likely to achieve promotion or improvement of economic, social and environmental well-being in their area (s2.1).) On the face of the Children Act 2004, children's well-being was now defined (s10.2), with the definition repeated in s38.1 of the Education and Inspections Act 2006, as:

- physical and mental health and emotional well-being

- protection from harm and neglect

- education, training and recreation

- the contribution made by them to society

- social and economic well-being.

Child well-being was now centre stage in the policy arena and providing the umbrella beneath which all child-related policies could be shown to nestle. By 2007, the Department for Education and Skills had been renamed the 'Department for Children, Schools and Families' to reflect the wider departmental responsibilities it had acquired for children's policy, and a 'Director of Child Well-Being' had been appointed to head a new directorate within the departmental structure. The Department for Children, Schools and Families has summarised the approach it took, and the action that followed up to 2010, as shown in Box 3.1.

Box 3.1 Every Child Matters

In 2003, the Government published a Green Paper called *Every Child Matters* (Cm 5860 2003). It proposed system-wide reform so that services worked together more effectively to achieve five outcomes for children. It prompted widespread discussion about services for children, young people and families, summarised in *Every Child Matters: Next Steps* (Department for Education and Skills 2004b). The Children Act 2004 subsequently provided the legislative spine for Children's Trusts – requiring local partners to co-operate to achieve the five outcomes, through planning and delivering more effective and accessible services to meet the needs of children, young people and families (DCSF 2009b). The *Every Child Matters* Framework, summarised below, set the conceptual and operational framework for local delivery.

The *Every Child Matters* outcomes

Be healthy	Physically healthy Mentally and emotionally healthy Sexually healthy Healthy lifestyles Choose not to take illegal drugs *Parents, carers and families promote healthy choices*
Stay safe	Safe from maltreatment, neglect, violence and sexual exploitation Safe from accidental injury and death Safe from bullying and discrimination Safe from crime and anti-social behaviour in and out of school Have security and stability, and are cared for *Parents, carers and families provide safe homes and stability*
Enjoy and achieve	Ready for school Attend and enjoy school Achieve stretching national educational standards at primary school Achieve personal and social development and enjoy recreation Achieve stretching national educational standards at secondary school *Parents, carers and families support learning*
Make a positive contribution	Engage in decision-making and support the community and environment Engage in law-abiding and positive behaviour in and out of school Develop positive relationships and choose not to bully and discriminate Develop self-confidence and successfully deal with significant life changes and challenges Develop enterprising behaviour *Parents, carers and families promote positive behaviour*
Achieve economic well-being	Engage in further education, employment or training on leaving school Ready for employment Live in decent homes and sustainable communities Access to transport and material goods Live in households free from low income *Parents, carers and families are supported to be economically active*

Every Child Matters (ECM) was followed by a suite of further policy documents and programmes that developed the approach. They included the Childcare Strategy and the universal roll-out of Sure Start Children's Centres, the development of extended services in schools and the introduction of a duty on schools to promote pupils' well-being (defined in terms of the five ECM outcomes), Youth Matters, the Staying Safe Action Plan and Care Matters (relating to children in the care system).

The Department for Children, Schools and Families was created in 2007 as 'the *Every Child Matters* Department'. Its remit was to champion policy for children, young people and families across government, sharing responsibility with other government departments for issues such as child health, child poverty, youth justice and play. *The Children's Plan* (Cm 7280 2007) was published later that year, setting out the Government's vision for children to 2020 and actions to deliver it. An Annex to the plan explained how it supported the UK's commitments under the UN Convention on the Rights of the Child.

Five principles underpinned the Children's Plan:

- government does not bring up children – parents do – so government needs to do more to back parents and families

- all children have the potential to succeed and should go as far as their talents can take them

- children and young people need to enjoy their childhood as well as grow up prepared for adult life

- services need to be shaped by and responsive to children, young people and families, not designed around professional boundaries

- it is always better to prevent failure than tackle a crisis later.

Commitments in the Children's Plan led to further policy and delivery programmes such as the Child Health Strategy, Ending Child Poverty: Everybody's Business, the National Play Strategy and the Youth Crime Action Plan. Safeguarding became a focus of particular attention following the death of Baby Peter, and Lord Laming undertook a further review and made recommendations in early 2009 for improving child-protection arrangements.

Delivery was underpinned through the 2007 set of Public Service Agreements (PSAs): PSAs 9–14 supported each of the ECM outcomes. PSA indicators formed part of the National Indicator Set for Local Government, giving local partnerships better information to analyse local needs, prioritise action and monitor progress. The Apprenticeship, Skills, Children and Learning Bill 2009 (which received Royal Assent on 12 November 2009) put Children's Trust Boards on a statutory footing, with a duty to draw up a jointly owned Children and Young People's Plan in each local area.

In 2009, *The Children's Plan: Two Years On* (Department for Children, Schools and Families 2009a) noted that progress in delivering improved services to children and families included:

- over 3,000 Sure Start Children's Centres, with a commitment to 3,500 by 2010

- free early education for 3- and 4-year-olds, and the introduction of free childcare places for disadvantaged 2-year-olds

- one-to-one tuition in schools

- more young people working towards an Apprenticeship

- 93 per cent of schools offering extended services

- over 2,000 families supported by Family Intervention Projects

- fewer young people entering the youth justice system.

Source: Department for Children, Schools and Families 2010, reprinted with kind permission

Child well-being in Scotland and Wales

In parallel, the developments in England were also being reflected in the activities of the devolved governments in two of its neighbouring countries in the UK, Scotland and Wales. Both those countries, however, followed rather different routes and with rather different results.

The Scottish Executive expressed its vision for Scotland's children in similar terms to England in *For Scotland's Children* (Scottish Executive 2001): 'a Scotland in which every child matters, where every child, regardless of his or her family background, has the best possible start in life'. The thinking about well-being and well-becoming, however, is clearly linked but separate in Scottish policy. The ambitions for well-becoming first emerged in national policy in 2005 (Scottish Executive 2005) and have been incorporated into the Concordat agreed between the Scottish Government and its local government partners in terms of Scotland's young people becoming 'successful learners, confident individuals, effective contributors and responsible citizens' (see Scottish Government 2008).

Indicators of well-being were developed in 2004 as part of work undertaken by government with Highland Council and a multi-disciplinary group to produce national children's planning guidance. The aim was to have a manageable, comprehensive and definitive set of what were called 'well-being indicators' (rather than outcomes), which would capture the aspirations for all children but could be applied to understanding the lives of individual children. Ideally, they needed to be relevant across the diverse needs of children and understandable to children and families as well as to the whole community's service agencies. There were a number of purposes – to provide coherence to local integrated services planning for children but also to find a set of indicators that would allow aggregation in order to assess the well-being of communities.

The parallels with the process of development in England are evident: the significance of local children's planning requirements acting as a catalyst and the modifications to the set of indicators that took place over time (discussions about whether 'included' should be a separate indicator and whether 'respected and responsible' should be regarded as related aspects of one indicator). The eight indicators that were finally agreed for national use were: safe, healthy, achieving, nurtured, active, respected, responsible and included. These well-being indicators have formed the foundation for Scotland's programme of whole-system change, *A Guide to Getting It Right for Every Child* (Scottish Government 2008), for meeting the needs of children and young people at both the level of practice and policy (described earlier in Chapter 1 in this volume).

In Wales, the approach has taken a different direction. The strategic policy and seven core aims (see Box 3.2) are outlined in *Children and Young People: Rights to Action* (Welsh Assembly Government 2004). Pithouse (forthcoming) has observed that:

> While similar to the ambitions articulated in the English *Every Child Matters* framework, Wales seeks to go further by linking its seven core aims for children to specific UNCRC articles, particularly around child poverty and child participation across key decision-making forums for services that affect them.

Box 3.2: The Welsh Assembly Government's seven core aims for children and young people

- *Core Aim 1:* Every child should have a flying start in life and the best possible basis for their future growth and development (UN Convention on the Rights of the Child, Articles 3, 6, 29 and 36).

- *Core Aim 2:* Every child and young person should have access to a comprehensive range of education, training and learning opportunities, including the acquisition of essential person and social skills (UN Convention on the Rights of the Child, Articles 3, 13, 22, 28, 29 and 30).

- *Core Aim 3:* Every child should enjoy the best possible physical and mental, social and emotional health, including freedom from abuse, victimisation and exploitation (UN Convention on the Rights of the Child, Articles 3, 6, 9, 11, 13, 19–25 and 32–40, and supported by entitlements 6 and 7).

- *Core Aim 4:* All children should have access to play, leisure, sporting and cultural activities (UN Convention on the Rights of the Child, Articles 15 and 31, and supported by entitlements 8 and 9).

- *Core Aim 5:* All children and young people should be listened to, treated with respect and have their race and cultural identity recognised (UN Convention on the Rights of the Child, Articles 12–15, 20, 22 and 30, and supported by entitlements 3 and 10).

- *Core Aim 6:* All children and young people should have a safe home and community which supports physical and emotional well-being (UN Convention on the Rights of the Child, Articles 9, 11, 16, 23 and 33).

- *Core Aim 7:* No child or young person should be disadvantaged by poverty (UN Convention on the Rights of the Child, Articles 26 and 27).

Source: Welsh Assembly Government 2004

The core aims feed through into a template of outcomes that inform the drafting of local integrated children's services plans in Wales (Welsh Assembly Government 2007) and there is also annual reporting on progress across the seven core aims, using multiple data sources, undertaken by the *Children's and Young People's Well-Being Monitor for Wales* (Welsh Assembly Government 2008). Pithouse (forthcoming) comments on the significance of the approach adopted in Wales:

> This monitor and this commitment to report to the UNCRC (under Article 44 of the Convention) is the first of its kind in Wales. The importance of such developments is by no means symbolic only, but reflects a determination to shift investment and organisational practices in order to generate a more integrated response to the multiple challenges that children and young people face in Wales, and which in a number of critical instances around health, education, housing and poverty, suggest that conditions in Wales while improving over the last decade have not kept pace with other parts of the UK.

These variations on a theme of child well-being in policy described above reflect the different contexts, circumstances and priorities of the three countries of the UK in which they were developed. They also indicate the rather different purposes for which child well-being outcomes will be used in professional practice, local planning and national policy. What they share, however, is probably greater than that which distinguishes them – a concern for how well each and every children of the nation is doing; a view that childhood is a critically important time for children now and in preparing for their future; the responsibility the State shares with parents for creating an environment in which children can flourish, for which it can be held accountable; and, not least, a common language that can be used by children, families, planners, service providers and policy makers.

Conclusions and reflections
It is evident from the story of its introduction into government policy in England that child well-being can, and will, be defined differently according to perspective, interest, agenda and circumstance. Because it is not a stable, unambiguous definition, it is also likely to be refined, modified and changed in some of its detail and emphasis over time.

One of the consequences of adopting the language of child well-being is that government can be seen to have opened up a much more robust and public debate about the type of society in which children are growing up, one that subjects the role and responsibilities of the State to closer questioning. Writers such as Wilkinson (2005) and James (2008) have raised profound and difficult questions about the impact of poverty, inequality and 'selfish' capitalism. Layard and Dunn (2009) have inquired with some concern into how children experience childhood in the context of multiple, and often negative, influences in contemporary Britain, concluding that 'the key is an ethic in which we care more for each other' (p.162). Jordan (2006, pp.41–42) argues that services for children should contribute positively to happiness, and makes the case for redirecting attention to the neglected features of relationships rather than technical expertise. He reminds policy makers and managers that 'research on well-being stems from psychology and economics; it is reshaping the assumptions and methods of economic analysis that have underpinned service "modernisation"' (p.48). Whilst the well-being agenda does not always make for a comfortable time for policy makers and service providers, it does logically force a much broader perspective to be taken politically and publicly than just that of the coverage and effectiveness of services.

It has been shown that there is increasingly a shared ambition across governments to secure and improve the well-being of all their children, particularly by those governments of economically advanced nations, urged on by UNICEF. The UK, disappointingly, has not fared well in recent international comparisons and, in an overall ranking by UNICEF (2007) of 21 'rich countries' drawing on 40 separate indicators relevant to children's lives and children's rights, the UK was ranked bottom and the USA next. UNICEF reminds us why such assessments of the lives and well-being of children and adolescents are important, in its introduction to *Report Card 7* (UNICEF 2007, p.1):

> The true measure of a nation's standing is how well it attends to its children – their health and safety, their material security, their education and socialization, and their sense of being loved, valued, and included in the families and societies into which they are born.

What distinguishes the nations of the UK from others under scrutiny by UNICEF is the inequality of distribution within society – not just inequality of opportunity or inequality of access but also the inequality of rewards that results in inequality of well-being. This suggests that if child well-being is to be taken seriously in policy aspirations, then public services alone cannot be expected to deliver the desired improvement in children's outcomes. Social and economic structures are more powerful drivers than public services, and this becomes the next big child well-being challenge for government.

> *'That's a great deal to make one word mean,'*
> *Alice said in a thoughtful tone.*[2]

Notes

1   *Through the Looking Glass, and What Alice Found There*, Lewis Carroll, 1872.
2   Ibid.

CHAPTER 4

How Schools Can Contribute to Pupils' Well-Being

Pamela Munn

Introduction

This chapter considers the ways in which schools can promote the well-being of the children and young people who attend them. Schools are important public institutions that provide a universal service and are one of the first places in which young people learn about personal and social relationships that extend beyond the family and local community. They, therefore, play an important role in promoting well-being and in detecting when a young person's well-being may be at risk.

The chapter is divided into four main sections. First, it considers the contribution of schools to well-being in terms of the curriculum on offer. The curriculum is much more than the lessons on the timetable, of course. Many writers distinguish between the formal curriculum of lessons on the timetable, the informal curriculum of clubs and activities that are organised as part of school life but are voluntary for staff and pupils, and the 'hidden curriculum', of values, routines, relationships and practices that encompass the taken-for-granted part of school life. The hidden curriculum sends important messages about who and what are valued in the school. All three parts of the curriculum are interwoven but they provide a useful way of thinking about the ways in which the curriculum contributes to well-being.

Second, the chapter distinguishes whole-school approaches to well-being, designed for the whole school community, from targeted provision aimed at young people in particular need. Such provision might include nurture groups or anger-management classes, or changes to the fabric of buildings to ease access for those with physical disabilities, for example.

Third, the chapter reviews the role of adults in schools both in terms of promoting well-being through helping young people in various ways to learn, and in spotting signs that all might not be well in the life of a young person.

The chapter concludes by considering whether young people's well-being is a key priority for schools given current accountability and quality-assurance systems. It draws examples mainly from England and Scotland but the main section headings should also provide a checklist for Wales and Northern Ireland and may be a useful starting point elsewhere for those interested in reviewing schools' contribution to young people's well-being.

Before beginning, however, it is necessary to be clear about the meaning of the term 'well-being'. As discussed earlier in this book there are many different definitions. For the purposes of this chapter, it is important to stress that the term relates to both physical and mental well-being and to personal and social relations. It is important to remind ourselves, too, that young people grow and develop at different ages and stages. They do not come to school as 'empty vessels' waiting to be filled with knowledge and skills and values. Rather they arrive with their own views of the world in which schools may play an important or trivial part.

A comprehensive definition of well-being was provided by the Scottish Government in a seminar in 2007:

> a positive physical, social and mental state; it is not just the absence of pain, discomfort and incapacity. It requires that basic needs are met, that individuals have a sense of purpose, that they feel able to achieve important personal goals and participate in society. It is enhanced by conditions that include supportive personal relationships, strong and inclusive communities, good health, financial and personal security, rewarding employment, and a healthy and attractive environment. (Scottish Government 2007)

Other definitions relating more specifically to schooling can be found, for example, on the website of the Department for Children, Schools and Families (DCSF) in 2009:

> The purpose of the Department for Children, Schools and Families is to make this the best place in the world for children and young people to grow up. We want to:
>
> • make children and young people happy and healthy
>
> • keep them safe and sound

- give them a top class education
- help them stay on track.

(DCSF 2009d)

More generally, the definition of well-being for the DCSF's work is based on a legal concept (set out in the Children Act 2004 [section 10]) of well-being. This equates children and young people's well-being with the five *Every Child Matters* outcomes: being healthy, safe, enjoying and achieving, making a positive contribution, and experiencing economic well-being.

In Scotland, schooling's contribution to young people's well-being can be inferred from the single-outcome agreements between central and local government on education, which specify that both parties are accountable for the following:

- We are better educated, more skilled and more successful, renowned for our research and innovation.

- Our young people are successful learners, confident individuals, effective contributors and responsible citizens.

- Our children have the best start in life and are ready to succeed.

- We have improved the life chances for children, young people and families at risk.

(Scottish Government and COSLA 2007)

The most recent major curriculum development in Scotland, *Curriculum for Excellence*, which sets out the main purposes of the curriculum for 3–18-year-olds and provides principles of curriculum design, highlights for the first time health and well-being as a distinctive curriculum domain – albeit one that is the responsibility of all teachers, not only of subject specialists. The preamble to guidance on learning experience and outcomes on health and well-being sets out the purposes of this area of the curriculum and states the following:

Learning through health and wellbeing enables children and young people to:

- make informed decisions in order to improve their mental, social and physical wellbeing
- experience challenge and enjoyment

- experience positive aspects of healthy living and activity for themselves

- apply their mental, emotional, social and physical skills to pursue a healthy lifestyle

- make a successful move to the next stage of education or work

- establish a pattern of health and wellbeing which will be sustained into adult life, and which will help to promote the health and wellbeing of the next generation of Scottish children.

(Scottish Government 2009, p.2)

This ambitious and highly general series of purposes is followed by statements about what children and young people should know, be able to do and have experienced from early stages until they leave school. For example, under 'Social wellbeing':

As I explore the rights to which I and others are entitled, I am able to exercise these rights appropriately and accept the responsibilities that go with them. I show respect for the rights of others. (Scottish Government 2009)

Under 'Physical wellbeing':

I am developing my understanding of the human body and can use this knowledge to maintain and improve my wellbeing and health. (Scottish Government 2009)

Teachers are expected to plan a coherent set of learning experiences that will meet these outcomes. It is interesting that many of these experiences and outcomes are undifferentiated in terms of the age and stage of pupils, unlike those that are specified for more traditional curriculum areas such as mathematics and sciences. As we shall see, this raises questions about how serious the policy to promote well-being actually is.

The different degrees of specificity in the meaning of well-being relate to attempts to measure it and the progress that the UK is making in comparison to other countries. Thus two recent reports, one by UNICEF (2007), *Child Poverty in Perspective: An Overview of Child Well-Being in Rich Countries*, and one by Barnardos Scotland (2007), *The Index of Wellbeing for Children in Scotland*, use slightly different measures, but come to similar conclusions – that the UK is near the bottom of rich, or of OECD, countries in averaging out these measures. The specification of learning experiences and outcomes in curriculum guidance can be seen as the basis for school inspection schedules in Scotland but, as we shall see below, specifying valid and reliable evidence indicating a school's contribution to well-being is not straightforward.

This chapter starts with a broad definition of well-being and, using the four sections outlined above, asks how schools can promote the well-being of the young people who attend them. However, as soon as broad definitions are used, there arise legitimate questions about how schools can chart their progress and contribution in this area. A range of national statistical collections, such as those on the numbers of pupils excluded from school and attendance statistics, can provide important information about aspects of well-being and enable us to identify trends over time. Such collections are based on information collected from a wide range of schools and it is also important that individual schools analyse their own statistical information both to provide information about their current situation and to identify trends. Schools are very well accustomed to analysing the attainment results of their pupils – in itself a possible indicator of well-being, as we shall see below – but they perhaps pay less detailed attention to other aspects of school life about which they do in fact have reasonably robust information. In addition, many schools have systems for collecting pupils' views on aspects of school life: these include school and class councils, pupil fora of various kinds and regular surveys of pupils. All these sources can be put together to provide a general overview of the ways in which schools are contributing to pupils' well-being. Indeed, this is an approach that is being piloted in England and which is called the 'School Report Card' (DCSF 2009e).

The curriculum

Clearly, providing opportunities to learn about various aspects of well-being and to experience well-being are key components of schooling. But how can schools do this? The first and most obvious way is by having lessons about well-being on the timetable.

The formal curriculum

All publicly funded schools in the UK are obliged to follow national curriculum guidelines and although these differ in details in each of the four countries of the UK there are strong common features that bear directly on well-being. There is, for example, an obligation to provide formal opportunities for physical education, involving games, gymnastics and dance. This provision is supplemented by extracurricular sports activities in many schools, as we shall see below. Given current concerns about childhood obesity, having the opportunity to experience different kinds of physical activity, free of charge, is an important contribution to physical health. So, too, are programmes concerning healthy eating and cooking, drug and alcohol abuse, and sexual health. The details of these programmes vary according to the age and stage of pupils, as well as the specifics of curriculum guidance, but they do provide an important knowledge base for well-being. However, the way in which these programmes are taught is almost as important as the knowledge they are intended to convey. Active involvement of young people in discussion, and ensuring the relevance and authenticity of the learning about physical health to their own lives and enjoyment, are all associated with successful learning. Therefore a direct transmission of information from teacher to pupils is unlikely to make an impact if this is the only method used; nor is an approach that focuses on what young people should *not* do.

There are two important points to make about those aspects of the formal curriculum that are clearly directed at well-being:

1. Until relatively recently they were not badged as being directly concerned with the well-being of individual pupils and could thus be seen by both teachers and pupils as being a somewhat disparate series of lessons lacking a coherent framework. As mentioned above, it was not until 2009, for example, that the term 'well-being' was used to describe a key curriculum area in Scotland, carrying with it information about planned progression of learning experiences and learning outcomes. However, specificity in terms of ages and stages is frequently lacking.

2. The status of many of these personal and social-education, home economics/food technology and physical education programmes is relatively low. Subjects acquire status largely by their value in securing entry to higher education, the perceived complexity of their assessment and the extent to which they embody abstract reasoning. Personal and social-education programmes are not subject to national assessment, they have very little time on the timetable compared to, say, English or mathematics or sciences, and so can be regarded by both teachers and pupils (especially in secondary schools) as

being much less important than traditional subject disciplines. This is gradually changing but will need sustained effort combining imaginative teaching with raising awareness of the importance of these particular areas if well-being is to be taken seriously as an important part of the formal curriculum.

While some subjects on the timetable can contribute knowledge and understanding that directly relates to well-being, in fact *all* subjects have a part to play by providing opportunities for pupils to experience a sense of achievement in their learning. This can be done through formative assessment, which indicates what has already been learned and what the next steps are, recognising the progress that pupils have made and engendering mutual respect between teachers and pupils. Being made to feel worthless and stupid are clearly not conducive to any individual's sense of well-being.

The informal curriculum

Recognising achievement and progress is not, however, confined to the formal curriculum. Schools can provide a wide range of opportunities for pupils to develop and demonstrate their skills and talents through a variety of informal activities. Many schools have outdoor-education activities, such as climbing, orienteering, kayaking and caving, that aim to develop physical prowess and skills of team-working, problem-solving and self-sufficiency. There are also sports clubs that have similar aims. Beyond these more obvious physical activities, other clubs, such as dance, drama, music, debating, chess and opportunities for local community involvement, allow pupils to engage in wider aspects of becoming an educated person. Through the informal curriculum of clubs and societies, in other words, schools can open up to young people a wide range of opportunities to participate in and to enjoy, thereby promoting a sense of well-being through a sense of belonging and community of interest that goes beyond their class or year group.

The hidden curriculum

The hidden curriculum is a shorthand term used by academics and teachers to describe the ethos of the school and of individual classrooms, the 'taken for granted' about how things operate, and the character of the relationships that exist between teachers and pupils and among pupils themselves. One aspect of the hidden curriculum is that all schools will have an aspiration to have a positive ethos through shared values that are enacted in the daily practices of teachers and pupils.

A major challenge for schools is to ensure congruence and consistency across these three different types of curriculum. For example, if schools are teaching about the importance of a healthy and balanced diet in the formal curriculum, is this reflected in the school meals on offer (i.e. in the hidden curriculum)? Many schools have chosen to cook meals on site, rather than buy in pre-prepared food. This enables them to source local produce and to involve pupils in decision-making about menus. Thus the formal and hidden curriculum about healthy eating reinforce each other. Moreover, by consulting pupils about menus, these schools are sending a signal that pupils' views are being taken seriously when they take their preferences into account.

Similarly, are geography and science lessons that raise issues about climate change and environmental sustainability congruent with the ways in which the school uses energy and disposes of its waste? These are just two of many areas that schools could examine in order to reflect on the consistency of message between the formal and hidden curriculum.

There are also more subtle ways in which the hidden curriculum of the school can send messages about what counts as really important. These include the time allocated to various subjects on the timetable, the status and reputation of the teachers assigned to particular classes, whether classes are set or streamed and whether prizes, rewards and other forms of public recognition are given to all areas of activity or just confined to academic and sporting achievement.

Probably the most significant aspect of the hidden curriculum for pupils is the ways in which pupil-to-pupil relationships are handled. We know from a range of studies that peer relations and transitions from one stage of schooling to another are of key importance to pupils (Anderson *et al.* 2000; Boyd 2005; Lucey and Reay 2000). Thus the systems schools have in place for promoting positive relationships among pupils and tackling bullying send very important signals about whether or not well-being is really a serious concern. Many schools will involve pupils in developing, or refreshing, an anti-bullying policy. Many also have buddy systems or peer counselling in place to help pupils deal with bullying and try to ensure they feel safe and secure. Recent research on behaviour in schools has revealed that a majority of teachers, headteachers and school support staff see pupil-to-pupil verbal abuse, physical aggression and physical violence at least once a week (Munn *et al.* 2009) and this suggests that for some pupils schools can be a turbulent environment. Recent research on pupil and school effects on children's well-being (Gutman and Feinstein 2008, p.i) suggest that it is the daily experiences of pupils in school rather than the kind of school attended that are most important in understanding well-being. Gutman and Feinstein conclude:

> It is children's individual experiences such as bullying, victimisation and friendships, and their beliefs about themselves and their environment, which mainly affect their well-being, rather than school-level factors such as type of school. This highlights the importance of whole-school approaches. (Gutman and Feinstein 2008, p.i)

To sum up this first section, schools can contribute to pupils' well-being in a variety of ways:

- through formal provision of subjects on the timetable designed to increase understanding of physical health

- through approaches to teaching that value each pupil equally and aim to make lessons participative, meaningful to life outside school and enjoyable; this can contribute to *emotional* well-being

- through the informal curriculum of clubs and societies that provide opportunities for pupils to experience a range of activities and extend and develop knowledge and skills beyond the lessons on the timetable

- through the hidden curriculum of rules, routines and practices that send powerful signals about the sincerity of the school's espoused commitments to the well-being of all pupils.

Targeted intervention

All school systems are challenged by the particular difficulties and needs of their individual pupils. The commitment in the UK to inclusion of all pupils in mainstream schools that is evident in a raft of education policy (see, e.g. Allan 2008; Dyson 2005) has posed problems and challenges for schools that have a bearing upon concerns with well-being. Amongst these problems and challenges are: different, and sometimes competing, notions of the meaning of 'inclusion', a juxtaposition of the general welfare needs of all pupils in school against the needs of individual pupils, the lack of knowledge, skills and abilities of teaching staff to meet diverse needs and a lack of resources adequately to provide for pupils with different kinds of needs. Ainscow, Booth and Dyson (2006, p.13) have developed a typology of six ways of thinking about inclusion, which range from a concern only with pupils with special educational needs to education for all and a principled approach to education and society. It is within this context that targeted interventions relevant to pupils' well-being need to be understood. Underlying the practice of interventions are beliefs about the cause of a particular need, the purpose of the intervention and, fundamentally, the purpose of schooling.

Focusing only on pupils with special educational needs (and putting to one side the broader interpretations of inclusion), there are three general points that can be made about how schools can contribute to the well-being of these pupils:

1. Recognise and then tackle the attitudinal barriers towards disabilities of all kinds. This is easy to say, of course, but it is in fact a long-term and difficult undertaking. Allan reports that it is these barriers that disabled people see as most significant. 'They may include bullying or excessive admiration or pity' (Allan 2008, p.702). Underlying such attitudes, Allan argues, is a medical model of disability that sees *individual* deficits from the norm and ignores how societies define and categorise difference. The medical model is deep in our consciousness and difficult to discard. The social model of disability, in contrast, focuses attention on barriers that 'exclude or limit participation' (Allan 2008, p.702).

2. Be alert to physical features of the school and classroom environment that may impede access to locations or resources that the majority take for granted.

3. Help all pupils recognise and understand individual differences. Teachers can discuss with them why there is the need for support bases and individual help. This needs to be done sensitively and with imagination. Pupils who feel themselves to be different from the majority can also feel inferior and less worthy.

Before looking at targeted interventions for vulnerable pupils in mainstream schools it is necessary to say a few words about the existence of separate specialist schools for pupils with special educational needs or additional support needs that cannot be met in the mainstream. The desirability of separate provision remains deeply contested. Some commentators argue that pupils' well-being is more likely to be nurtured in such schools, which usually have relatively small numbers of young people and high staff–

student ratios. This point of view has been supported by Mary Warnock, the architect of policies that included pupils with special educational needs in the mainstream. She now argues that the move towards inclusion was ill-advised and claims that there is a body of evidence which suggests that the experience of disabled children in mainstream schools is generally 'traumatic' (Warnock 2005, p.43). Ainscow *et al.* (2006, pp.14–15), however, point out from a 'rights' perspective that disabled pupils or pupils otherwise categorised as having special educational needs have a right to a local mainstream education. Compulsory segregation (in a special school) is seen as contributing to the oppression of disabled people, just as other practices marginalise groups on the basis of race, gender or sexual orientation. Most commentators on either side of the argument would agree, however, that well-informed choice of provision by parents and pupils is the ideal.

Mainstream schools deploy a number of interventions targeted at vulnerable pupils, pupils who may be vulnerable in different ways. For example, they may have learning or behavioural difficulties. They may come from dysfunctional families where drug and substance abuse feature and thus have difficulties attending school regularly. They may have sensory and/or physical impairments. They may be experiencing bereavement or separation from a parent. The key point is that pupils have *different* vulnerabilities and so there is no universal targeted intervention that will meet their diverse needs. Table 4.1 provides an illustration of some of the interventions that schools can use to nurture the health and well-being of pupils with specific needs. They range from the provision of specialist staff to the creation of special teaching groups or techniques.

Table 4.1 gives only a brief indication of the range of targeted approaches schools can use to help promote well-being of individual pupils with particular needs. These approaches take time, money and particular expertise and are significant developments in schools. They are part of the general strategy to include a wider range of pupils than before in mainstream schools and policy developments such as *Every Child Matters* and *Getting It Right for Every Child*, which aim to focus on the holistic development of pupils rather than on just their academic attainments. This new policy focus makes demands on the expertise of adults working in the schools discussed below. These demands go beyond technical expertise to an awareness of the messages of 'separateness' being sent via the hidden curriculum to the valuing of the worth of pupils who are in some sense different from their mainstream peers.

Table 4.1 Examples of targeted interventions to promote well-being

Name of intervention	Purpose
Pupil support base	Location of specialist teaching related to identified needs
Specialist teachers	To provide support and assistance to mainstream teachers, and to teach individuals or small groups
Support staff/teaching assistants	To support individual pupils in mainstream classes or in support bases
Break/lunchtime supervisors	To promote positive behaviour at breaks and lunchtimes
Home–school link workers	To liaise between home and school where there are particular needs and help devise solutions to problems
Multi-agency teams	To share information about pupils in need and to co-ordinate support. Typically these involve social work and health professionals as well as teachers
Nurture groups	Small groups designed to help pupils, usually from disadvantaged backgrounds, to access the mainstream curriculum
Solution-oriented approaches	A therapeutic approach focusing on finding solutions to problems rather than a deep exploration of the problem itself. Can also be used as a whole-school approach
Targeted small-group work	Designed to develop particular strategies, e.g. anger management
Counsellors/guidance staff	To provide pastoral care and general welfare to specific pupils and year groups

These policies also stress the importance of inter-professional working so that a complete picture is built up of pupils' individual circumstances, and so that this picture is shared amongst teachers and others working with young people. We know a great deal about the challenges of effective inter-professional work, such as distinctive training provision, career development and traditions and habits of working amongst, for example, social workers, teachers and health professionals. The pragmatics of time for sharing information and budgetary and administrative arrangements are further challenges to be overcome and are likely to be intensified in a period of substantial public spending constraints. The re-organisation of departments at local and national level to bring together education and social work and new management arrangements take time before they make a real impact on front-line services. In some cases, for example in the City of Glasgow, the amalgamation of education and social work departments lasted less than three years and the departments have now reverted to separate entities. The public rationale for separation was that the new department was too large and unwieldy. In other areas of the UK departments of children's services are well established. Child-abuse and child-death cases resulting in serious-case reviews identify the continuing challenges of inter-professional working despite the best intentions of all concerned (see Vincent 2009 for an overview).

School staff and the promotion of well-being

Pupils encounter a wide variety of staff in their daily lives at school. These include headteachers, teachers, student teachers and support staff of various kinds – including finance and administrative staff, learning assistants, janitors, dinner ladies and playground assistants – as well as parent volunteers. It is clearly important that all staff are sensitive to signs that children may be neglected or abused and can take appropriate action. As a minimum, they should be aware of the school's child-protection guidelines that build on local and national guidance.

As well as staff with general responsibilities for pupils' well-being, schools have designated staff with specific responsibilities for child protection and welfare. All schools should, for example, have a designated child-protection co-ordinator whose job it is to develop policy and arrange training on child-protection matters. In addition, there will be designated staff with responsibilities for pupils' pastoral care and specialist staff with responsibilities for pupils with learning and behavioural needs.

A significant feature of current schools is the rapid increase in the numbers of support staff employed to support teachers in classrooms (usually called 'teaching' or 'learning' assistants) and the increase in staff who undertake routine administrative duties in order to free teachers to spend more time teaching. In England, figures from the Training and Development Agency in 2006 show that there has been a 97 per cent increase in the number of full-time equivalent support staff employed between 1997 and 2005, from 136,500 to 268,600 (as cited in Woods, Hammersley-Fletcher and Cole 2009).

These changes in the range and variety of staffing pose clear management challenges for headteachers. The 'development of shared values and a sense of purpose' is clearly more complex in large schools. Consistency in the 'application of shared values' in daily classroom practices present further challenges. The hidden curriculum of schools in terms of its contribution to pupils' well-being requires sustained leadership in this new staffing context. A telling example of this context was given at a recent annual conference of the British Educational Research Association. A primary headteacher reported that when she had first become a headteacher in the 1990s she had 12 staff. At the time of the conference she was managing 49 staff in the same school, with roughly the same number of pupils on roll.

Similarly, classroom teachers require training in the efficient and effective use of the range of adults now likely to be present in classrooms. Research by Blatchford *et al.* (2009, p.6) reveals that teachers are positive about the presence of support staff in their classrooms. For example, just over half the teachers in their sample reported that support staff had led to a decrease in their workload because the 'transfer of routine activities allowed more time for teaching and attending to pupils'. However, teachers found they had little time to plan and prepare lessons and activities with teaching assistants (TAs) – the staff most likely to be working directly in small groups or on an individual basis with pupils with learning or behavioural needs. This and other studies (e.g. Gunter 2007; MacBeath *et al.* undated) suggest that the increase in support staff working in classrooms as teaching assistants can in fact distance teachers from pupils with particular needs, as teachers focus attention on the class as a whole. Moreover, Blatchford *et al.* (2009, p.6) report that:

> Interactions between [teaching assistants] and pupils could be informal and personalised, aiding engagement, but they could also be reactive and unplanned on the part of the TA and encourage pupil dependency and separations from their teachers, the curriculum and their peers.

If imaginative pedagogy is a feature that promotes pupils' well-being, contributing to positive engagement with learning, then changes in the school workforce raise important questions about the continuous professional development and training of all concerned. Research by Munn *et al.* (2009) and Blatchford *et al.* (2009) suggests that teaching assistants in secondary schools tend to have fewer training opportunities than teachers and to be less satisfied with the training they receive. This is important because a systematic review by Albors *et al.* in 2009 (as cited in Blatchford *et al.* 2009) shows that when teaching assistants have been prepared and trained for specific curricular interventions, with support and guidance from the teacher and the school about practice, they tend to have positive effects on pupil progress. The wide definition of pupil well-being with which we began this chapter – one that includes a sense of achievement

– suggests that the training and development of teaching assistants is an urgent priority.

Well-being and school accountability

Schools are rightly accountable for their practices, and a number of quality assurance and accountability mechanisms are currently in place which monitor schools and provide information to parents and the general public about standards. These mechanisms include schools' self-evaluation practices, local-authority monitoring of various kinds and national monitoring through inspection systems. The most prominent indicator of school performance is undoubtedly pupil attainment as measured in national tests and in public examinations such as GCSE and A Levels.

This focus on pupil attainment reflects a core purpose of schooling – pupils' learning – and is given added emphasis by the value of qualifications for entry to higher education and the job market. In short, the possession of qualifications is a 'positional good', which confers advantages to those who possess them and disadvantages to those who do not. Furthermore, pupils' attainments are reasonably straightforward to measure and for parents and the general public to understand.[1] However, it is increasingly accepted that such a particular focus on attainment has had the perverse incentive of focusing attention only on this aspect of school life and underplaying the many other activities that take place in schools. If schools are expected to make a contribution to pupils' well-being, then it seems logical that they should evaluate the success with which they do so. This is not an easy task given the multiplicity of ways in which schools can promote a sense of well-being, many of them not amenable to robust measurement. In a review of the approaches taken to measuring well-being in high-performing education systems, Husbands, Shreeve and Jones (2008) found that health and well-being indicators were less common than pupil-attainment measures, and that these varied in different countries. It should be no surprise therefore that there are different approaches to tackling this matter in England and Scotland.

Developments are now taking place in England to pilot a new accountability mechanism mentioned briefly earlier – the 'School Report Card'. This is intended to give 'a clear coherent rounded account of school performance to be used by all stakeholders, e.g. schools, parents, Governments and Ofsted' (DCSF 2009e). Use of the report card will be piloted during the period 2009–2011 and will include measures of pupil well-being. It is clear from the proposals on measurement that, first, it is not easy to measure a school's contribution to well-being, since many other factors influence the well-being of individual pupils, and, second, that a combination of measures or indicators will be required since well-being encompasses physical and mental health, safety, enjoyment and many other aspects discussed above. The DCSF sets out the indicators to be used in the first instance and these are reproduced in Table 4.2. It also makes clear that it 'will consider how all available wellbeing indicators can be used to derive a category score for Pupil Wellbeing and test their use' (DCSF 2009e). The Department also intends to include on the report card the most recent Ofsted judgement on the behaviour of learners, a recommendation of the Steer Report (Steer 2009).

The advantage of this approach is that it brings together a range of data to produce, however imperfectly, an indicator of the school's contribution to well-being. It signals to schools the kinds of quantitative evidence that Ofsted will be using in school inspections, although the prospectus makes clear that no single indicator can be the determinant of judgement about a school's contribution to well-being and that Ofsted's experience will inform decision-making about how robust the quantitative indicators are. As far as the qualitative indicators are concerned, survey data could provide a useful source of evidence. However, there are no nationally comparable sets of survey data and Ofsted will be trialling the use of parent and pupil surveys from autumn 2009.

In Scotland the approach to evaluating the school's contribution to pupil well-being continues to be based on school self-evaluation indicators, which are also used by Her Majesty's Inspectors of Education (HMIe) (2009) in school inspections. There is no intention as yet to develop a numerical score. As can be seen from Table 4.3, the quality indicators used cover a number of aspects of school life, all of which could potentially contribute to a sense of 'well-being'. It is interesting that there is no group of indicators labelled well-being, despite there being a new 'health and well-being' curriculum area in the Curriculum for Excellence, the major curriculum reform currently being taken forward. Indicator 5.7 on care, welfare and development perhaps comes closest. Under this indicator there are three themes:

- arrangements for ensuring care, welfare and child protection

- approaches to and provision for meeting the emotional, physical and social needs of children and young people

- curricular and vocational guidance.

(HMIe 2009, p.34)

Table 4.2 Pilot quantitative and qualitative well-being indicators

Quantitative Wellbeing Indicators	Qualitative Well-being Indicators	
School measures of:	The extent to which a school:	The extent to which pupils:
• attendance and persistent absence • permanent exclusions • post-16 progression • pupils provided with at least two hours per week of high-quality PE and sport • the uptake of school lunches	• promotes healthy eating • promotes exercise and a healthy lifestyle and (for younger children) play • discourages smoking, consumption of alcohol and use of illegal drugs and other harmful substances • gives good guidance on relationships and sexual health • helps pupils to manage their feelings and be resilient • promotes equality and counteracts discrimination • provides a good range of additional activities • gives pupils good opportunities to contribute to the local community • supports pupils to make choices that will help them progress towards a chosen career/further study	• feel safe • experience bullying • know whom to approach if they have a concern • enjoy school • are making good progress • feel listened to • are able to influence decisions in the school

Key features of the indicator are given, which mention health, and highlight the particular importance of these arrangements as times of transition between nursery, primary and secondary school. As with other indicators, illustrations of an excellent and satisfactory performance in this area are provided.

**Table 4.3 Quality indicators used in inspections
in Scotland from January 2008**

	How good is our school? (version 3)		
1.1	Improvements in performance	5.5	Expectations and promoting achievement
2.1	Learners' experiences	5.6	Equality and fairness
2.2	The school's success in involving parents, carers and families	5.7	Care, welfare and development
3.1	The engagement of staff in the life and work of the school	5.9	Improvement through self-evaluation
5.1	The curriculum	8.3	Management and use of resources and space for learning
5.2	Teaching for effective learning	9.3	Developing people and partner-ships
5.3	Meeting learning needs	9.4	Leadership of improvement and change

Source: HMIe 2009

In general, across almost all the HMIe indicators there is an emphasis on a positive ethos, developing a shared sense of values and recognising a wide range of achievement. Nonetheless, the challenge for both countries is to signal that pupil well-being, *however* it is measured, is as important as pupil-attainment measures. We know from a range of research that schools will focus on those aspects of their activities for which they are seen to be directly accountable. As mentioned above, the range of ways in which a school can contribute to pupils' well-being makes it difficult to develop a robust and easily understood well-being score. The prominence given in future inspection reports to well-being will be one way of signalling its importance, as will its prominence in the new School Report Card. Time will tell.

Conclusion

We have seen in this chapter that schools can contribute to pupils' well-being in a number of different ways. These include through the formal curriculum, in which knowledge and skills are developed in relation to health and personal, social and emotional well-being. Fundamentally, of course, the formal curriculum of more traditional subjects on the timetable enables pupils to explore knowledge and ideas and to obtain national qualifications, which are important for entry to further and higher education and for entry to the job market and future *economic well-being*.

The informal curriculum of clubs and societies and out-of-school activities provides further opportunities for pupils to explore their interests and discover talents, contributing to a sense of self-esteem. The hidden curriculum of roles and relationships and what is really valued in schools also plays a key role.

The chapter has illustrated possible interconnections between these three kinds of curricula and suggested that schools need to be aware of such interconnections and any possible inconsistencies in the messages they are sending to pupils about the importance ascribed to their well-being.

The chapter has also looked at the major change in the school workforce in the recent past, with the consequent significant increase in teaching assistants and support staff of various kinds. It has drawn attention to the need for developing a shared understanding of school values and purposes across this diverse workforce and raised questions about training and the continuous professional development of support staff.

Finally, the chapter has drawn attention to the need for accountability systems to develop in ways that are supportive to the diverse ways in which schools contribute to well-being, and to avoid a reductive approach of relying on a small number of indicators that may have the unintended consequence of diverting attention from the harder-to-measure aspects of schools' contributions.

Throughout, this chapter has concentrated both on the generality of pupils in schools and highlighted a range of targeted interventions for those in need of additional support. We know from a range of studies and statistics that there are vulnerable children and young people for whom school may be especially important as a safe place where there are adults who can be trusted. We also know that young people in foster care, residential provision or otherwise being looked after by the State tend to have poorer outcomes in terms of attainment and other aspects of well-being. This makes joined-up working across education, health, social and police services all the more vital. Schools can, and do, make a significant contribution to pupils' well-being but, of course, they are not the only influence. Even greater prominence being given to the concept of well-being and encouragement at national, local and school level to develop efficient and low-cost ways of gathering together evidence about well-being would encourage greater reflection on practice and more strategic planning. Thinking about pupil well-being as a coherent curriculum area, where contributions are made by the formal, informal and hidden curriculum, should aid planning as should sensitive accountability procedures and criteria. Much has already been achieved but much also remains to be done.

Note

1   There is, of course, a widespread academic debate about how and whether schools contribute to pupils' attainment beyond what might be expected.

CHAPTER 5

Youth Civic Engagement and Support: Promoting Well-Being with the Assistance of a UNESCO Agenda

PAT DOLAN

Introduction

The prospect of promoting better well-being for young people in need is generally uncontested as the 'way to proceed' for both policy and practice in child welfare. However, the exact process or 'usable road map' required in order to achieve this outcome is less clear. For those who design, manage or deliver children services the reality of putting even well-proven or positive programmes into place can be tumultuous (Brady and Dolan 2007a, 2007b; Whittaker 2009). From the viewpoint of the academic community, while there is growing interest in promoting research that attests to improved physical and social well-being in youth and their families, this is counterbalanced by increasing awareness of a need to engage with policy and practice in a way that these parties perceive as being of value (Canavan *et al.* 2009). This backdrop of high intent but low delivery of proven methods in establishing what enables well-being can be even more contentious when dealing in research or practice with youth who present as being very difficult to engage with.

Following a brief overview of issues in relation to how well-being is conceptualised, measured and valued within an international agenda, this chapter will focus on youth from a series of perspectives:

1. The central value of social support in terms of sources, types and qualities of sustenance in youth and its connection to well-being is established.

2. The role and benefit of social-civic engagement of young people, and in particular in relation to those in adversity, is described.

3. A case example of a youth peer-mentoring programme is used to illustrate the connectivity between civic engagement, social support, coping and well-being.

4. A new conceptual model is proposed by the author that relates well-being, social support and civic engagement for young people.

How well-being is conceptualised, measured and valued within an international agenda

In recent years the focus on child well-being has been emphasised by a growing global agenda, both in UNESCO (2010) and, more particularly, within UNICEF (2007). Notably, the Innocenti Research Centre as an agent of UNICEF have focused on indicators of well-being through their 'Report Card' mechanisms, which rely centrally on a set of six core aspects measured as improvement in:

- material well-being

- health and safety

- educational well-being

- family and peer relationships

- behaviours and risks

- subjective well-being.

These components of well-being will be revisited later in the light of social-support theory and their influence by, or on, civic-engagement activities for young people. However, at this point, while the UNICEF list is an obvious portal for defining child well-being, it is worth noting that variations on this list apply in differing States. For example, within England the *Every Child Matters* policy agenda defines well-being in terms of being healthy, staying safe, enjoying and achieving, making a positive contribution and achieving economic well-being.

Additionally, the issue of the relationship between differing aspects of well-being in young people and how we measure them has been highlighted as an important issue (Axford 2009). Furthermore, it could be argued that childhood and adolescence are a process of growth and transition that, by their non-static nature and variability, require flexibility in all aspects of measurement including well-being outcomes. For example, if one divides adolescence into early, middle or late, spanning a very wide range of years and cultures (as is the case within the UNESCO global network), how one would measure well-being would necessitate some variance. If one were to simply measure 'enjoying and achieving' among youth in second- or third-level education, results would be very different for a 13-year-old compared to someone at 20 years of age.

Similar issues arise in relation to nuances such as gender, religiosity and cultural competence (Husain 2006), which by implication would require variability in describing how a young person makes a contribution to their community. More generally, extensive research on lifestyle and well-being among children and young adolescents across Great Britain and Ireland has found notable variability in results between respondents. For example, while Irish young people reported better levels of well-being, Irish girls were more likely than Irish boys to see themselves as having poorer health (Brooks *et al.* 2009).

On the positive side, there is an increasing tendency to see aspects of well-being as strengths rather than deficits in young people (Ungar 2008). Peter Benson's '40 Developmental Assets' focuses strongly on enabling positive and practical competencies in the lives of young people generally and more particularly for those at risk (Lerner and Benson 2002). Examples of these assets include a young person having at least one extended family member who remembers his or her birthday and actively cares 'for' as well as cares 'about' him or her. Similarly in a school setting, it includes at least one teacher who demonstrates knowledge of, and interest in, a young person, or at community level a young person feels fully safe when going to a local shop alone. Similarly in some States working towards better well-being in youth this is framed as activities. In the Republic of Ireland, *The Agenda for Children's Services: A Policy Handbook* (covering children and youth up to 18 years) highlights proven models of 'active' interventions coupled with a strong emphasis on youth participation and use of reflective practice among those at all levels of service provision (Office of the Minister for Children and Youth Affairs 2007). Similarly, in England the *Every Child Matters* policy highlights proactive measures for working with youth in order to enable better outcomes (Department for Children, Schools and Families 2007). These include:

- tackling social exclusion

- the problems of youth crime and anti-social behaviour

- the problems of the 'risk-taking' generation

- how to encourage citizenship, social participation and civic action.

Importantly, from the perspective of seeing the improvement of well-being through achieving better outcomes for children and youth in need (McAuley, Pecora and Rose 2006), the prospect of strength-based working with and for children and families is deemed to be 'key' (Whittaker 2009). This is further reinforced by the UNICEF message that when one does comparative analysis between rich and/or poor countries through the use of 'Report Cards' the most important indicator is not which country is doing better than others. The aim that all young people in all countries are doing better is more pertinent in terms of any global agenda, but, more importantly, within the context of the human-rights agenda contained within the UN Convention on the Rights of the Child (UNCRC).

The role of social support for youth

Since the pioneering work of Cassel in the 1970s, the central importance of social support to human existence as a process whereby acts of assistance can be exchanged between people is well established (Cassel 1976). A proven buffer to stress, both in terms of accessing help when in times of stress and as central to ongoing need, social support is core to coping in life. By far one of the more proven concepts in the applied social sciences, it is typically described across four domains: sources, types and amounts, contexts and qualities (Cutrona 2000). Importantly, one's belief in terms of support availability may be equally if not more important than the actual help on offer at any given point. Thus, for any of us, young or old, what is perceived is as good received. It can also be measured in terms of accessibility through direct one-to-one relationships, family and community and within societal contexts. Mary Levitt even suggests that, where one's social network (set of supporters) is weak, through that person's other relationships a reliable alliance can open up new relationships for accessing help. Despite known limitations to social support this positivistic approach as a strengths-building model for practice has been echoed by others (McGrath et al. 2009).

For youth, regardless of culture or class, natural sources of help including parents, peers, extended family and friendships are preferable (Pinkerton and Dolan 2007). This is applicable on the basis that the exchange of help from family and friends is non-stigmatising, more readily available and usually automatic. Informal support from others can also be reciprocated or 'paid back' and is by far the most economical form of help. This is not to say that for young people in need there are contexts in which support from professionals is not needed.

Importantly, apart from who it is that provides the support, the amount and types of support on offer to a young person within a network are crucial. Optimally, the type of support (whether practical, emotional or advisory) should match the kind of help needed at any given time. Arguably, in working with youth and their families who experience poverty, the over-supply of advice from professionals (no matter how well intentioned) will not really suffice when what is needed is something more tangible such as a supply of food or assistance to find a new school placement following expulsion. Although most people see themselves as having plentiful support on offer from others, the issue may be more around having capacity to ask for and access this help. Issues such as poor self-esteem and/or self-efficacy alone may disable a person from accessing help (Cutrona 2000). Finally, apart from ensuring that types of help (both emotional and instrumental) are present for any young person, ensuring that support does not wane over time may be a key issue – particularly in the context of over-burdened professionals who may be skills-rich but time-poor.

The quality of support that is available can in many ways be crucial to a young person's well-being. Where there is a sense of closeness to others despite adversity or problematic relationships, coupled with some degree of dependability or capacity to know help is there, positive support will be most accessible. Importantly, the presence of criticism that is constructive and never demeaning and the retention of a potential to reciprocate help is equally crucial for any young person. First, this enables youth to change behaviours towards coping better, and, second, it ensures that they do not completely use up their bank of goodwill from family and friends without giving something in return.

Finally, the context in which support is provided is often not considered. If a young person experiences multiple stressors simultaneously his or her capacity to either access or accept help may be impaired. For some youth dealing with too many problems at the same time can be so difficult that they reject help and/or move into a mode of despair and turn away from all supporters. Similarly, issues of timing of support can be crucial. For example, in a case of bereavement, while, initially, support can be plentiful if not, indeed, over-supplied, very often this help wanes and may not be available six weeks later when really needed by a young person in mourning.

Social support and the specific challenge of adolescence

While all these principles, practices and underpinnings for social-network support have resonance for all youth, for those in need there are other specific nuances that have particular 'currency'. Adolescence has been described as a developmental journey between childhood and adulthood (Feldman and Elliot 1993). It is typically described as 'stage-like' in terms of early, middle and late phases, starting post-latency at about 12 years and seen, in some of the UNICEF and UNESCO literature, as finishing in the late twenties. In itself, this process, which brings such physical, sexual, emotional and intellectual change in a young person, is accompanied by a strong need for all types of social support – particularly from parents and other familial relationships (Pinkerton and Dolan 2007). Whether in the context of normative or non-normative adolescent development, the need for practical support (including financial assistance) as well as emotional support in dealing with the tumultuous times of the teenage years is well established (Kroger 2004).

Youth may be selective among parents and friends when seeking advice support, particularly in relation to issues that may be taboo in families, but their need for *esteem* support is filled by a wide range of sources within the family. Longitudinal research in Ireland and comparative research on Ireland and the USA (McGrath *et al.* 2009) suggest that many young people can identify casual friendships they can use to work through issues during adolescence, although a significant number cannot identify close friends. For young people who have difficulties, this need for support may be even more apparent and the need to enable success in and support from non-school leisure and hobby activities has been highlighted (Gilligan 2009).

Thankfully, however, youth are not by their very nature problematic, and the evidence is that most do fine in life: the perception and portrayal of adolescence as the 'terrible teens' may be mythical. In addition, young people are not 'empty vessels' during their maturation. In addition to the support they receive, they also have much to offer to others, which may go untapped in many contexts (UNICEF 2007). We will now explore this positive capacity in youth within a civic-engagement agenda.

Civic engagement by youth as support within and beyond family

While one might be inclined to think of civic engagement in youth as only occurring in formal settings such as community youth-leadership programmes or school activities, there are many other situations in which they provide social support. For instance, youth who act as main carers for their disabled parents in the home should be deemed to be 'informally civic active' (Office of the Minister for Children and Youth Affairs 2007). In such cases not only can their acts of altruism be invisible, these are also rarely given acknowledgement as evidence of civic engagement on the part of the young person. Similarly, in countries in development where youth take on the role of caring for siblings as a result of parents dying prematurely – for example, with the HIV/AIDS epidemic (UNICEF 2007) – their role as premature family carers can also be overlooked. To a much lesser extent, many youth offer support to elders as well as other family and community members, sometimes as a side-product of a hobby or school activities and relationships (Liebenberg and Ungar 2009).

Although it might be assumed that agreeing a definition for civic engagement in itself should be simple, it may be more assumed than actually known. While Carpini's definition of 'individual and collective actions designed to identify and address issues of public concern' helps, nevertheless there is the limitation that, while there are plentiful definitions and they are all good, they are not the same or used as common currency (Carpini 2006). More specifically in respect of defining civic engagement for adolescent populations, James Youniss *et al.* (2002) have advocated starting with the concept of civic competence before moving to a more expansive definition in order to establish a better fit for the real-world circumstances in which youth function.

The extent to which civic engagement and social-support enlistment are directly connected is unknown, but certainly in addition to informal caring contexts there are obvious connections that can be highlighted. At a very basic level, when thinking about civic engagement, the benefits to youth in terms of better social support, enlistment from others and a greater capacity to be resilient to stress or risk are likely to be associated, although causal links have yet to be formally established. So although we do not know for sure whether a youth who is civicly active has a resultant better social network and great coping capacity, listed below are four associated benefits that can accrue:

1. *Deepening existing relationships and accessing new ones:* by being involved with existing relationships, including friends, in civic activity one can deepen positive ties, or gain introduction to new possible friends.

2. *Reciprocity of support:* through acting with, or on behalf of, others, the donation of support is more likely to lead to conditions where a young person can get 'pay back'. This may occur from individuals, groups or organisations or via other associated sets of relationships.

3. *Increase in self and external sources of esteem:* as a result of civic engagement and a desire to be involved with others in a positive way, feelings of enthusiasm and achievement will bring an associated sense of improved self-esteem and self-efficacy.

4. *Respite from focusing on one's own difficulties:* working with others can enable youth to realise that they are not alone in having needs. By focusing on others, a young person can gain respite from his or her personal, family, school or community-located worries.

An illustrative case example of peer youth-mentoring

Peer youth-mentoring is an interesting illustration of the connection between civic engagement, social support and well-being for youth and a community-based service where the evidence of the four benefits listed above may be located. Since the well-cited randomised control trial study by Tierney and colleagues in Public Private Ventures (Tierney, Grossman and Resch 1995) and a more recent school study, the interest in youth mentoring, including peer mentoring, has become centre stage in working with young people in adversity (Rhodes 2005). While there is some debate over whether in fact mentor-rich environments and communities are required more than individualised programmes (and particularly so in relation to resilience building) (Philip 2003), the aspects of peer mentoring associated with civic engagement as part of developing altruism in young people is uncontested.

Youth peer-mentoring friendship programmes usually take place within school sites and involve older youth providing regular support to younger students over time. Most programmes are constructed as one-to-one matches of mentor and mentees spending set time together in social activities in order to establish friendship. In addition to activities, mentors are also available for advice and support if crisis occurs and, in many cases, offer assistance informally in the school and/or community setting. In such cases of obvious civic activity, it is very easy to see how social-network principles of sources, types, amounts and good quality of support are enabled for both the mentor and mentee. In the context of non-normative adolescent development – for example, in youth gangs – the prospect of utilising their capacity to be positively civically engaged through mentorship is noteworthy (Frank 2005).

Whether through one-to-one peer-mentoring programmes like the 'Big Brothers Big Sisters Program', which has now moved from a century-old USA-based service to an internationally transported model (Brady and Dolan 2007a), or through more innovative and naturally constructed relationship programmes, their connection as both a social-support enabler and assistance toward enhancing well-being is worthy of further development. Finally, intergenerational mentoring, which focuses on older people passing wisdom to youth and they reciprocally providing practical and protective support to elders, is gaining interest among philanthropic communities as well as researchers (Flanagan 2001).

A global agenda on youth, well-being and civic engagement

Since the turn of this century, the role and contribution of young people as active global actors in civil society has been well documented by many UN organisations. The acknowledgement by the World Bank (which has invested substantially in programmes for youth) highlights the value of non-educational projects across a range of spheres, including the private sector, rural and urban development, social policies such as protection of citizens, education and environmental protection.

Furthermore, the World Bank in collaboration with Innovations in Civic Participation, through the advice of an expert group and utilisation of high-quality research methods, have identified the impact of youth volunteer-service programmes that promote civic engagement. They highlight potential benefits, including cost efficacy, that can accrue as a result of youth civic engagement through established formal programmes. For example, in relation to the IRS Survey of Arci Servizio Civile ASC, benefits identified for youth ranged from better relations with others to enhanced vocational skills and practical aptitudes, including better time-management. This echoes similar benefits identified by Constance Flanagan and colleagues – for example, hopefulness, self-efficacy and better familial and school-based relationships (Flanagan and Nakesha 2001).

For over a decade UNESCO has held a bi-annual World Youth Forum whereby young people from the six UN Regions have their voice and give advice on issues that they see as key to society. For example, in the forum held in October 2009, youth considered the global economic crisis and best methods to address poverty. Concurrent to this forum and on the advice of youth, UNESCO (in press) have developed a Global Strategy for Youth with three core objectives, namely: knowledge building/management, youth participation, and programme development. All of these are framed within a context of aiming for better outcomes for young people. Established in 2008, the UNESCO Chair in Children, Youth and Civic Engagement is also focused on contributing strongly to this UNESCO global strategy.

Since its foundation, just over 60 years ago, as a human rights and advocacy international movement, the United Nations has at a broad level forwarded the rights of children and youth. Most famously, this position has been well branded through the establishment of the United Nations Convention on the Rights of the Child (UNCRC), that has now been in existence over 20 years and adopted internationally by almost all countries. Of particular interest to us here, under Article 12 of the convention, is young people's right to participation, which declares that:

> State Parties shall assure to the child who is capable of forming his or her own views the right to express those views freely in all matters affecting the child, the views of the child being given due weight in accordance with the age and maturity of the child. For this purpose, the child shall in particular be provided the opportunity to be heard in any judicial and administrative proceedings affecting the child, either directly, or through a representative or an appropriate body, in a manner consistent with the procedural rules of national law. (United Nations 1989)

On the basis that young people's right to participation is not a new concept (Dolan 2010), has been well aired and is uncontested within the field of children's welfare, for the purpose of this chapter and brevity, the UNCRC is assumed as ever-present and taken as a given. This then underpins a conceptual model provided in the next section that connects social-civic engagement of young people to social support and resilience-building as vehicles for enabling better well-being in youth.

Towards a conceptual model connecting civic engagement, social support, resilience and well-being in youth

The connection between supporting youth, resilience and well-being has been well established and given much expression in recent years. In the main, this has been based on a focus on supportive actions aimed directly at individual youth (things they can do for themselves) rather than at their family and friends, semi-formal helpers such as mentors, or professionals (including youth workers). However, of late, there has been a shift towards seeing social support and resilience as occurring at a wider 'outside of the young person' ecological level (Ungar 2008). The support and capacity for resilience at family (both nuclear and extended), school and community levels through increasing protective factors and decreasing aspects of risk is gaining some attention (Dolan 2008). Although success in hobbies and leisure activities such as sports and music has been well identified (Gilligan 2009), the prospect of civic engagement as a means of enabling better social-support enlistment, increasing resiliency and better well-being has not as such received much attention.

With youth rights assumed, building on the prospects of their social-civic engagement activation, conditions can be created to enable two benefits for young people:

1. Civic engagement can enable better enlistment of more support, including new social relationships and/or enhancement of a young person's existing social-support landscape.

2. A focus on acts for others at informal and formal levels of family, school and community levels, a focus on respite from self and self problems, and recognition of others and their predicaments can help build the capacity to be resilient.

The culmination of this double positive effect can lead to the creation of improved well-being for youth, as illustrated in Figure 5.1.

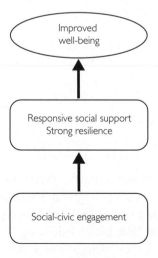

Figure 5.1 Conceptual model connecting social-civic engagement, social support, resilience and well-being in youth

This is not to suggest that civic-engagement activation is the only source of support enlistment and/or improvement in well-being. Moreover, this connection is posited here as one of a range of associated components for improved well-being for youth. In order to further clarify this conceptualisation, these connections are explored in Table 5.1, which summarises how UNICEF's six facets of well-being presented earlier get played out as components in social-support theory and as activities of civic engagement. Each component of well-being is first matched to a feature of social-support theory, and an accompanying example of youth social-civic engagement activity is identified.

Table 5.1 UNICEF indicators of well-being matched to aspects of social support and civic-engagement activities

UNICEF indicator of well-being	Social-support factor	Civic-engagement activity
Material well-being	Concrete support	Environmental community clean-up schemes
Health and safety	Concrete and advice support	Youth participation in personal/community safety projects
Educational well-being	Advice/esteem support from durable relations	Communal in-school educational and social assignments
Family and peer relationships	Closeness and reciprocity of support	Intergenerational projects
Behaviours and risks	Mitigated by a positive social network membership	Peer-mentoring projects
Subjective well-being	Perceived social support	Activities where youth fundraise for others in need

Note: a concrete support applies to practical and tangible help, for example loaning money to or providing a lift in a car for someone else.

In terms of ordering and activating the overall factors contained in each column of Table 5.1, it is suggested that activation of civic engagement of youth will lead to their having better social-support capacity, which, in turn, will enable them to have better well-being. For service planning and intervention purposes, service managers or practitioners in collaboration with youth should identify which element of well-being is being targeted and the related civic activity should be activated with a view to creating better social support.

Applying social-civic engagement across contexts for youth

In order to ground this hypothesis and to marry it to the incoming UNESCO agenda, this framework is considered across two specific youth populations and issues within differing international contexts – those in conflict with the law, and youth who live in fragile post-conflict States and/or countries in development.

Civically engaging young people in conflict with the law

Although young people who are seen as being disruptive, and even a danger to communities, may seem most unlikely candidates for positive civic engagement, this idea is in fact not that far-fetched. There is some evidence that this idea dates back to the 1960s in projects such as the Winthrop Community Youth Program, which pioneered altruism in youth in conflict with the law by getting them to complete positive acts towards others locally. More recently, there have been other projects and programmes that work on the same principle of youth-work practice (Frank 2005). Thus, the notion of youth leadership as a 'nice' activity only for youth of 'good character' may be ill-founded and therefore the prospect of it applying to a more diverse population can be easily overlooked.

Importantly, the benefits to these young people themselves in terms of their well-being can easily be forgotten. Seeing youth civic leadership in social as well as political contexts amongst those in conflict with the law becomes even more important when one considers its possible connection with self-compassion (Neff, Rude and Kirkpatrick 2007). Positive attributes in youth – including happiness, optimism, wisdom, positive affect, personal initiative, curiosity and exploration, extroversion and conscientiousness – have been associated with self-compassion. Neff and colleagues also found that giving attention to the pursuit of innovative challenges can also have benefits. Young people who are leaders of social actions for the good of others therefore gain as individuals as well as benefiting society.

The creation of ripe conditions for such social-leadership development in this population can also be influenced by issues of cultural competence (Husain 2006). Ideas about the ways in which youth (particularly detached youth in poor urban communities) can demonstrate their leadership must not just be culturally sensitive but also need to guard against over-importation from other state models by adults who plan services projects or programmes. For example, in certain countries issues of religiosity may be a strong force for youth leadership where in others entrepreneurship (which is social or non-social) may be a determining factor. So 'self-compassion' as an underpinning strength (coupled with culturally sensitive targeting of the youth leadership required) can be a key influence in designing programmes of civic engagement for those who are known to be or at risk of being in conflict with the law.

One obvious forum in which such youth leadership can be developed is that of inter-generational activities. Where youth can be enabled to work positively with, and for, older people in the community not only will there be positive benefits for young people in terms of their accessing wisdom from elders but there will also be a benefit to older people in terms of protection (as opposed to risk of harm) and practical support from youth. In fact, it could be argued that rather than youth being perceived as a threat by such older populations the value of younger people as protectors who look out for familial and non-familial elderly in the community could be enhanced.

Young people living in fragile States and countries in development

Although the need for strong social-support landscapes for young people who live in fragile and/or post-conflict States is obvious, knowledge of how to build conditions whereby these young people can both access and activate such help in relationships beyond the family is lacking. Nonetheless, UNICEF has highlighted the benefits of programmes that involve civic engagement in such contexts by stating that 'youth service programmes have the potential to address needs by providing a participatory cross-sectoral framework for engaging youth in post-conflict recovery' (2007, p.2).

It could be argued that dealing with issues such as loss of family members and the personal threat resulting from war, coupled with the fear of such events, is likely to leave youth immobilised. However, there are instances where young people have shown organic strength, not only in overcoming the odds and bouncing back, but also by being civicly engaged ahead of adults. For example, there is some evidence that in crises young people are the first to offer assistance, often ahead of adults. This was found to be the case in three world disasters in recent times – the attack on the World

Trade Center (9/11), the Tsunami and Hurricane Katrina. In all cases, it was youth who acted quickly to try and assist victims.

Nevertheless, we should not need world disasters to become aware of the civic-engagement potential of youth and particularly so in relation to working in fragile States. Apart from the fact that positive engagement of youth in such situations can enable better support networks and resilience, it can also provide them with respite from the ongoing stress of witnessing dangers and/or experiencing harm. Furthermore, this attests to the value of young people 'in the present' and not just as potential adults who if endowed with strong civic responsibility will provide payback to the community at a later point. More negatively, an obvious fear within the UN system relates to child soldiering as part of civic-engagement activity – a phenomenon that sees young people's civic engagement as becoming not only political rather than social, but also involving them in violence to others at a very premature stage of their lives.

A less controversial area is the context in which well-being can be promoted within countries in development and transition. Supporting countries to develop on the continent of Africa is a major focus for UN agencies – for example, in both education and human rights (UNICEF 2009). In some African countries where the life expectancy is relatively short with fewer elders and many parents dying young, the role of youth as carers is of notable concern. In such cases young people are forced to adopt a parental-like role in which civic engagement is a necessity. Perhaps there is a need to both highlight and value this capacity more, as well as seeking greater prevention strategies to avoid youth having to take familial responsibilities in advance of their maturation.

Conclusion

This chapter has focused on exploring the potential relationship between social support (and, to a lesser extent, resilience) and civic engagement of youth with a view towards the betterment of their well-being. Utilising a United Nations and UNESCO agenda, it has been suggested that social-civic engagement in youth has untapped potential, particularly for those who experience adversity. Although the examples of youth in conflict with the law, living in post-conflict communities or living in countries in development have been highlighted, one can easily see how this potential can have resonance for other groups – for example, young people with a learning difficulty.

From an international perspective, while the form and agenda for social-civic engagement may differ globally across the six United Nations regions, the need for social support and a capacity to be resilient will remain for all young people. At a very basic 'common denominator level', over the past decade through the UNESCO Global Youth Forum we know that young people are not that different and have generally very similar needs. For instance, recent research by McGrath and colleagues (McGrath *et al.* 2009) has shown that youth in Ireland and the United States have similar support needs in relation to their well-being.

Just as the causal relationship between support and well-being is unknown (UNICEF 2009), whether a young person's capacity to be civically engaged comes from nature or nurture is also unclear. However, the key question may not be one of chromosome or culture, but rather what are the conditions that society needs to create in order to enable youth civic participation with a view to their full involvement in society, and thus enabling their well-being.

From the perspective of the agenda of the UNESCO Chair presented earlier, the current hypothesis that civic engagement in youth can accrue as much benefit for them as for others is untested but holds promise. And even though over time the work of the UNESCO agenda may lead to more questions than answers, the journey of 'finding out' in itself will be worthwhile. However, whether youth in need are seen as myopic or even labelled negatively as mad, sad or bad, the need to better their well-being remains for us all. More specifically, at international, national and local levels, these questions will also be of importance to service planners and practitioners who work with, and for, youth, as well as for the interested academic community. Ultimately, if as a result of exploring this connection between youth civic engagement and well-being more is known about how best to support those who experience adversity, then the journey will be well worthwhile.

PART 2

Child Well-Being:
International Policy and
Research Developments

CHAPTER 6

Developing Indicators for Child Well-Being in a Changing Context

ASHER BEN-ARIEH

Introduction

As so many of the previous chapters have shown, the concept of children well-being is changing. Scholars have termed this shift as one of moving from 'child-saving' to child development (Kahn 2010) or from child welfare to child well-being (Kamerman, Phipps and Ben-Arieh 2010). This changing context, which in many ways is still developing and which still has a long way to go (Ben-Arieh 2008), is complicating efforts to develop appropriate indicators and outcome measures of children's quality of life and status.

Further complicating things, the relationship between efforts to define the concept of children's well-being and efforts to measure and monitor it are not a 'one-way-only' sequence. On the contrary, the field of child indicators is changing in a way best described as interacting with the changing understanding of child well-being. Thus, new technologies and sources of information shed more light on children's lives, and in doing so influence how we understand and conceptualize children's well-being. This interaction, in turn, calls for new indicators, just as new theories and norms reshape the concept of children's well-being (Ben-Arieh 2010).

This chapter presents the child indicators perspective on these changes and shifts. It does so by focusing on changes influenced by new theories and norms as well as changes in the more 'technical' aspects of measures and measurement. It starts with a brief history of the child indicators movement (and its parent movement of social indicators). Then the chapter discusses the recent changes and shifts in the field as well as its current status. The third section attempts to explain what led to the rapid development and shifts in the child indicators movement by focusing on three major catalysts for change:

1. changes in the demand for indicators

2. methodological and measurement changes

3. normative and theoretical changes.

The chapter ends with a short discussion on where the field is likely heading in the future.

The development of the child indicators movement

The use of statistical data and indicators specifically to study the well-being of children is not new. Pioneering 'State of the Child' reports were published as early as the 1940s (Ben-Arieh 2006; Ben-Arieh and Goerge 2001). Nevertheless, most scholars would agree that the current field of child well-being indicators has its substantive origins in the 'social indicators movement' of the 1960s. This movement arose in a climate of rapid social change and as a result of a sense among social scientists and public officials that accurately measured and consistently collected social indicators could provide a way to monitor the condition of groups in society, including the conditions of children and families (Aborn 1985; Land 2000).

Although there is a long history of studies of social trends using statistical indicators, it was the publication of Bauer's (1966) book *Social Indicators* that prompted the widespread use of the term 'social indicators'. A key objective of the early social indicators efforts was to assess the extent to which government programs or policies were achieving their stated objectives. To evaluate or monitor changes taking place in society, policy makers and others emphasized the utility of social indicators within social-system models (Land 1975).

Indeed, the child indicators movement was based on these earlier efforts, and really sprung into life at the end of the last two decades of the twentieth century. UNICEF published its first *State of the World's Children* report in 1979. This annual review of basic indicators of children's survival and development has helped create a global awareness of the need to monitor how children fare. There have been various initiatives, such as the 'European Childhood Project', that were specific and accurate in describing the situation of children using quantitative data. And certainly there have been many local initiatives to obtain better and more reliable information on the situation of children. Scholars, public agencies and nongovernmental organizations have initiated these efforts within their spheres of interest or operation (Miljeteig 1997).

By identifying key indicators and their relationships to specific outcomes or social well-being measures, these modeling efforts emphasized not only the descriptive function of child indicators, but their analytic function as well. By and large, these functions provide a better understanding of the impact on child well-being of changes in policies and socio-demographic trends (Zill, Sigal and Brim 1982).

Social indicators could thus be strategically used to shape how we think about important issues in our personal lives and the life of a nation; the use of indicators falls well within the long-established 'public enlightenment' function of social indicators (Frones 2007). Child advocacy groups, policy makers, scholars, the media and service providers all use indicators of children's well-being for several reasons (for example, to describe the condition of children, to monitor or track child outcomes, or to set goals). Although there are notable gaps and inadequacies in existing child and family well-being indicators (Ben-Arieh 2000), there also are literally dozens of data series and indicators from which to form opinions and draw conclusions (Bradshaw, Hoelscher and Richardson 2007).

The rapidly growing interest in child indicators stems, in part, from a movement toward accountability-based public policy. This policy demands more accurate measures of the conditions children face and the outcomes of various programs designed to address those conditions. At the same time, the rapid changes in family life have increased demand from child-development professionals, social scientists and the general public for a better picture of children's well-being (Ben-Arieh and Wintersberger 1997; Casas 2000). Beyond these general explanations, I would argue that the development of the child indicators movement can be attributed to 'new' demands and, with regard to the policy utility of the indicators, to new methodological advancements and to 'new' normative and conceptual theories.

Recent changes in the child indicators movement

The child indicators movement has seen a number of changes and shifts during recent decades. Its current status can be best understood in regard to nine major shifts:

1. Early indicators tended to focus on child survival, whereas recent indicators look beyond survival to child well-being.

2. Early indicators primarily focused on negative outcomes in life, while recent indicators look also at positive outcomes.

3. Current indicators incorporate a children's rights perspective but look beyond it as well.

4. Early indicators emphasized children's 'well-becoming', that is, their subsequent achievement or well-being; recent indicators focus also on children's current well-being.

5. Early indicators were derived from 'traditional' domains of child well-being, primarily those determined by professions, while recent indicators are emerging from new domains that cut across professions.

6. Early indicators focused on the adult's perspective, whereas new indicators consider the child's perspective as well.

7. Early indicators were usually looking at national geographic units, while recent indicators are measured at a variety of geographical units.

8. Recent years have seen efforts to develop various composite indices of children's well-being.

9. Recent efforts are guided by their policy relevance.

This evolution has occurred virtually everywhere, although at varying paces (Ben-Arieh 2002, 2006). These changes are detailed below.

1. From survival and basic needs to development and well-being
Children's physical survival and basic needs have long been a focus of child indicators research, particularly threats to children's survival. The use of such indicators has spurred programs to save children's lives (Ben-Arieh 2000; Bradshaw *et al.* 2007). Infant and child mortality, school enrollment and dropout, immunizations and childhood disease are all examples of indicators of basic needs. However, a fundamental shift occurred when the focus moved from survival to well-being. Scholars argued in the late 1990s for indicators that moved beyond basic needs and beyond the phenomenon of deviance to those that promote child development (Aber 1997; Pittman and Irby 1997). Indeed, the field moved from efforts to determine minimums, as in saving a life, to those that focus on quality of life. This move was supported by efforts to understand what constitutes 'quality of life' and its implications for children (Casas 2000; Huebner 1997, 2004).

2. From negative to positive

The absence of problems or failures does not necessarily indicate proper growth and success (Ben-Arieh 2005; Moore, Lippman and Brown 2004). Measures of risk factors or negative behaviors are not the same as measures of protective factors or positive behaviors (Aber and Jones 1997). Thus, the challenge became developing indicators that hold societies accountable for more than the safe warehousing of children and youth (Pittman and Irby 1997). As Resnick (1995, p.3) states: 'Children's well-being indicators are on the move from concentrating only on trends of dying, distress, disability and discomfort, to tackling the issue of indicators of sparkle, satisfaction, and well-being.'

3. Incorporating children's rights and beyond

Although inspired and to some extent guided by the children's rights movement, the child indicators movement looks beyond simply monitoring rights. Perhaps the most crucial difference is the standard used to measure children's status. Children's well-being is normally focused on what is desired, but rights monitoring addresses legally established minimums. Another significant distinction between monitoring rights and monitoring well-being came into play as the field developed indicators for policy makers.

Monitoring rights and establishing when they have (or have not) been met requires clear, concrete and observable phenomena. Indicators that are abstract and suggestive and even, perhaps, persuasive about children's well-being are less powerful for monitoring rights. On the other hand, indicators of children's rights and indicators of their well-being share common features. The United Nation's Convention on the Rights of the Child (CRC) is, at its most fundamental, based on recognizing and enhancing the dignity of the child. The child indicators movement was inspired by and conscious of the need to be, at a minimum, consistent with a concept of dignity for the child. Monitoring rights and well-being also share a focus on indicators that can be measured at the level of the child (i.e. child-centered). Such indicators draw attention to the actual situation of children and allow for nuanced and culturally anchored treatment of children on the basis of race, class, gender, special needs, religion or minority status.

4. From well-becoming to well-being

In contrast to the immediacy of well-*being*, well-*becoming* focuses on the future (i.e. preparing children to be productive and happy adults). Qvortrup (1999) laid the foundation for considering children's well-being, rather than just their well-becoming, by arguing that the conventional preoccupation with the next generation is a preoccupation of adults. Although not a necessarily harmful view, anyone interested in children and childhood should *also* be interested in both the present and the future. In other words, in the former view children were instrumentalized in the sense that their 'good life' was postponed until adulthood. As such, perspectives of well-becoming focus on opportunities rather than provisions (De Lone 1979). Accepting the arguments of Qvortrup (1999) and others on the need to concentrate on the well-being of children does not deny the relevance of a child's development toward adulthood. However, focusing on preparing children to become citizens suggests that they are not citizens during childhood, a concept that is hard to reconcile with a belief in children's rights. It is not uncommon to find in the literature reference to the importance of rearing children who will be creative, ethical and moral adult members of community.

It is harder to find reference to children's well-being in their childhood. Even indicators of poverty or health, which on the surface are indicators of current well-being, are discussed in a context that is forward-looking: the results of child poverty are diminished future prospects. Indeed, each of the two perspectives is legitimate and necessary, both for social science and public policy. However, the emergence of the child-centered perspective, and its focus on children's well-being, introduced new ideas and energy to the child indicators movement.

5. From traditional to new domains

The previous three shifts are interrelated and are both the reason for and the outcome of one another (Ben-Arieh 2006). Until recently, when measuring the state of children, scholars concerned themselves with traditional domains, those defined either by profession or by a social service (i.e. education, health, foster care). Looking at children's well-being rather than just at their well-becoming naturally brings into focus new domains of children's well-being, including children's life-skills, their civic involvement and participation, and children's culture (Ben-Arieh 2000).

6. From an adult to a child's perspective

The above changes forced the field to ask at least some of the following questions: What are children doing? What do children need? What do children have? What do children think and feel? To whom or what are children connected and related? What do children contribute? Answering such questions demanded a better picture of children as human beings in their present life, including the positive aspects of their life.

However, most of the existing data do not help much in seeking answers to these questions. A good example would be the remarkable work by Land, Lamb and Mustillo (2001), who studied children's well-being in the United States during the last quarter of the twentieth century. Their reliance on existing databases led them to use traditional indicators of children's well-being, and thus their work has limited potential in answering such questions as outlined above.

In order to better answer these questions, the field began to focus on children's daily lives, which is something that children know the most about. Studies have found, for example, that parents do not really know how children spend their time (Funk, Hagan and Schimming 1999) or what they are worried about (Gottlieb and Bronstein 1996). Hence, to answer such questions, children had to be involved in such studies, at least as the primary source of information.

7. The changing geographical focus

Interest in communities and neighborhoods as the context of children's well-being is growing, as is the need to focus policies and programs in these areas. With this comes added interest in the level at which data are collected (e.g. at the level of the child or community), and in the necessity of incorporating such data in planning, policy making, and evaluation (Coulton, Korbin and McDonell 2009). Thus, it has become increasingly clear that collecting and analyzing data cannot be considered an exclusively national or governmental responsibility. Around the world, we have seen a shift in the responsibility for our children's well-being from federal or national agencies to regional, district, municipal or community-level agencies. In virtually all countries, this has led to efforts to produce indicators and data on children's well-being at these 'new' levels. Local and regional reports on children's well-being are multiplying, and this trend seems here to stay (Coulton et al. 2009).

8. Becoming policy oriented

There is an evident shift toward policy-oriented efforts (Granger 2006; Klein 2006; O'Hare 2008). A major advantage of indicators is the ability to mobilize activities and resources across agency and organizational boundaries (Hogan 2006). Indeed, the field moved from a conceptual discussion of potential uses, to the implementation of real efforts in practice (Bradshaw 2006; Little 2006; Phipps 2006). With considerable agreement on the uses of indicators, and in some cases examples of actual use, the child indicators movement was ready to address the question of what difference indicators make in advancing child well-being.

9. Toward a composite index of child well-being

Although expanding data on children provide policy makers and the media with important information (Brown and Moore 2003), this increasing supply of information has also led to calls for a single summary number to capture the circumstances of children. Such a composite would, it is argued, facilitate easier assessment of progress or decline. Moreover, it might be easier to hold policy makers accountable if a single number were used. In addition, it would be simpler to compare trends across demographic groups and different localities and regions (UNICEF 2007). Scholars have since attempted to develop summary indices (Land *et al.* 2001; Moore *et al.* 2007).

Why did the focus shift?

So what contributed to the emergence and development of the child indicators movement? I would argue that this rapid development is a consequence of three major sources: a 'new' demand for policy-oriented indicators; changes in the technical and methodological ability to produce indicators; and 'new' normative and theoretical advancements.

The 'new' demand for policy-oriented indicators

In recent years, the call for research and indicators with a bigger impact on policy has grown louder (Aber *et al.* 2010). This demand for policy-oriented indicators contributed to the development and advancement of the child indicators movement (Ben-Arieh and Goerge 2006). In this regard, some indicators and measurements have clearly led to new policies and programs for children and some have not (Ben-Arieh and Goerge 2006). One clear example is the child poverty indicator in the UK, which for many years had no real impact but then (following a Beveridge Memorial talk by then Prime Minister Tony Blair) became a dominant indicator influencing social policy (Bradshaw 2006). It is also evident that the same indicator, when used in certain contexts, has led to desired outcomes, while in others it has not. Here a good example would be the UNICEF child well-being index and the way it was accepted and treated in different countries (Richardson 2010). The effort to develop better policy-oriented indicators led to a thorough examination of existing indicators and to better data collection, including across new domains of life (Teitler and Ben-Arieh 2006).

New methodological and technical developments

Just as the new demand for policy-oriented indicators created the context in which the child indicators movement flourished, three methodological perspectives contributed to its rapid evolution. These methodological perspectives were:

1. the call for using the child as the unit of observation

2. the emerging importance of subjective perspectives

3. the expanded use of administrative data, and the growing variety of data sources.

CHILDREN AS THE UNIT OF OBSERVATION

If children have basic rights and their childhood is worthy of study by itself, then making the child the unit of observation seems obvious (Jensen and Saporiti 1992). The child indicators movement thus began incorporating child-centered indicators, ones that begin from the child and move outward, separating, at least for measurement purposes, the child from his or her family. Sen (1997) has argued for measures that reflect the life a person is actually living rather than the resources or means a person may have available. Sen's approach takes into account personal choices, constraints, circumstances and abilities to achieve a preferred living standard. Applying Sen's approach to a child's living conditions highlights the need to focus on the child, rather than the household or community, as the unit of analysis (Ben-Arieh *et al.* 2001).

An informative example can be drawn from Sauli's (1997) work on families in Finland. If scholars use the family as the unit of analysis, one-half of the families with children are one-child families. However, using the child as the unit of analysis reveals that only one-fourth of them live without siblings. If the field is to gain an accurate picture of children and their experience, it must develop indicators that focus on the child as the unit of observation. This also means disaggregating information in traditional databases to more reliably assess their well-being.

THE EMERGENCE OF THE SUBJECTIVE PERSPECTIVE

Prout (1997, p.96) argued that 'large-scale social phenomena and small-scale inter subjective action implicate each other such that the complexity of the social world cannot be expressed through a simple asymmetry of objective social structure and subjective actors'. Yet, much research on children's lives has, until recently, focused on objective descriptions, treating children as passive objects who are acted on by the adult world. As the child indicators movement accepted and built on the theoretical foundations outlined above, it became clear that a new role for children had emerged – a role that coupled the search for objective measures with a subjective view of childhood (Casas *et al.* 2004; Mareš 2006). This has proved particularly important given that studies have shown, particularly during adolescence, that parents do not always accurately convey their child's feelings (Shek 1998; Sweeting 2001). Further, studies have shown that including the perspectives of children is important not only because they differ from those of the adults, but because doing so respects children as persons, better informs policy makers, provides a foundation for child advocacy, and enhances legal and political socialization of children (Melton and Limber 1992).

The child indicators movement, which traditionally was based on aggregate statistics, bloomed as new indicators sought to capture children's own account of their lives and living conditions. The field quickly realized that although there are areas in which indirect information may be superior – such as on the household economy as reported by parents, or grades from school records – in most instances, and particularly for crucial indicators, such as mental well-being and social relations, children's own reports are necessary (Lohan and Murphy 2001; O'Hannessian *et al.* 1995; Shek 1998).

Indeed, recent years have brought a surge in interest in trying to capture the subjective well-being of children and how to measure it (see McAuley, Morgan and Rose, Chapter 2, this volume, and Bradshaw *et al.*, Chapter 9, this volume). One approach was to conduct surveys with children asking them about their well-being while using an array of scales (Andresen and Fegter in press; Burton and Phipps 2010; Huebner 2004). The second approach was to work with the children to conceptualize child well-being and to build together measures (Fattore, Mason and Watson 2009).

THE EMERGENCE OF ADMINISTRATIVE DATA AND THE
VARIABILITY OF DATA SOURCES
The richness of children's lives and their domains of well-being mean that any single source of information will be incomplete. Therefore, the field sought three different sources of information: administrative data, census and surveys, and social research (longitudinal and *ad hoc*). Although scholars had used the latter two regularly in the past, administrative data emerged in the 'era of information' during the second half of the twentieth century and contributed to the evolution of the child indicators movement.

Administrative data, even though collected primarily for purposes other than research, are a powerful resource for research (Goerge 1997). The data, maintained by organizations that serve children and families daily, are an important source of information on the condition of children. Until recently, administrative data were confined to paper files. However, as governments and others computerized information systems, administrative data emerged as a rich, accessible source of information for developing indicators of children's well-being. For example, administrative data, by definition, cover the population of individuals or families with a particular status or receiving a particular service. In addition to recording service receipt, the files often contain information on these people's addresses or neighborhoods, thus contributing to the development of indicators at the regional or local level and the consequent 'small region monitoring' (Bannister 1994).

Further, administrative data may be the best option for quickly developing more timely or new community and local indicators of children's well-being. Given the expense of new or continuing social surveys, and given that much administrative data already exist, this source is ideal for the short-term development of indicators that can be used to inform the public and policy makers.

'New' normative and theoretical approaches
Theories and normative approaches to children welfare abound. Many have contributed to this effort and many more continue to carry out work in this field. Three such approaches are singled out in this chapter. They have not only influenced the child welfare field at large, but have had a

particular contribution to the emergence and rapid development of the child indicators movement. These include:

1. ecological theories of child development

2. the normative concept of children's rights

3. the 'new' sociology of childhood as a stage in and of itself.

THE ECOLOGY OF CHILD DEVELOPMENT

Today, children's capabilities are understood in the context of their development and well-being (see Aldgate, Chapter 1, this volume, for a more detailed description). These are dynamic processes, influenced by a multitude of factors. Children interact with their environment and thus play an active role in creating their well-being by balancing the different factors, developing and making use of resources, and responding to stress. Bronfenbrenner's ecological model of human development (Bronfenbrenner and Morris 1998) conceptualizes child development on the basis of four concentric circles of environmental influence, with time as an underlying factor, recognizing both individual changes over time and historic time.

The child, with all his or her personal characteristics, interacts first and foremost with the family, but also a range of other people and systems: friends, neighbors, health care, child care, school, and so forth. These direct interactions compose the child's *microsystem*, and this is the level with the most direct influence on children. Connections between the different structures within the microsystem, for example between parents and school, occur in the *mesosystem*. One level up, the *exosystem* represents the societal context in which families live, including parents' social networks, the conditions in the local community, access to and quality of services, parents' workplace, and the media. The exosystem affects the child mainly indirectly by influencing the different structures within the microsystem. The *macrosystem*, finally, points to the wider societal context of cultural norms and values, policies, economic conditions and global developments. The different systems are dynamic and interdependent, influencing one another and changing over time (Lippman 2004; Olk 2004; Stevens *et al.* 2005).

In interacting with the different systems and subsystems, children and their families encounter both barriers and facilitators. These barriers and facilitators can, in many respects, be considered as indicators of child well-being. Together with the various outcomes at the different levels, this ecological perspective had immense impact on the child indicators movement and its development (Bradshaw *et al.* 2007).

CHILDREN'S RIGHTS AS HUMAN RIGHT

The UN Convention on the Rights of the Child (CRC) offers a normative framework for understanding children's well-being. Its four general principles fit closely with conceptualizations of child well-being. The first of these is nondiscrimination. Article 2 of the CRC argues for recognizing the life situations and well-being of excluded groups of children, such as those with disabilities, children in institutions, or refugee children, and to disaggregate available data by age, gender, ethnicity, geography, and economic background. The second principle, the best interest of the child (article 3), itself implies a child focus and strengthens children's role as citizens in their own right. From this principle comes the imperative to use the child as a unit of analysis. The complexity of children's lives is reflected in the third principle, that of survival and development (article 6). The CRC promotes a holistic view of child development and well-being, giving equal weight to children's civic, political, social, economic and cultural rights, and stressing that these rights are interrelated, universal and indivisible. Concepts of child well-being must, accordingly, be multidimensional and ecological. The fourth principle calls for respecting the view of the child (article 12), acknowledging children's rights to be heard and to have their view taken into account in matters that affect them (Santos-Pais 1999).

These views of children's rights contributed to the child indicators movement in several important ways. First, they have placed children on the agenda, thus calling for more data on their life and well-being. Second, they call for indicators to monitor the implementation of the CRC and the fulfillment of children's rights. Third, by the breadth of topics and issues covered, these views demand indicators in subdomains and areas of interest that were not measured or monitored before.

THE 'NEW' SOCIOLOGY OF CHILDHOOD

One of the most important concepts that has shaped the child indicators movement is that of childhood as a stage in and of itself. The discourse on child well-being is thus also one of well-being and well-becoming (Frones 2007). The more traditional perspective was one that looked on child well-being in terms of children's future, focusing on their education and future employability. The 'new' perspective on child well-being focuses on children's current (during childhood) life situation.

One can argue that it is reasonable to develop indicators of child well-being that focus on children as 'future adults' or members of the next generation. Such approaches, however, often fail to consider the life-stage of childhood, a stage that has its own sociological characteristics

(Alanen 2001; Olk 2004; Qvortrup 1999). The CRC, for example, makes clear that children's immediate well-being is important in its own right. Children's present life and development and future life-chances thus must be reconciled in conceptualizations of well-being by looking both into the conditions under which children are doing well and child outcomes across a range of domains (Ben-Arieh *et al.* 2001).

Future perspectives

The child indicators movement is clearly growing and on the move. The number of 'State of the Child' reports alone has more than doubled since the 1980s, with one example being discussed in Chapter 7 in this volume by Brooks, Hanafin and Langford (and in Ben-Arieh 2006). Although the field has indeed changed dramatically, we are still in the midst of the process. None of the above shifts has reached its final destination. However, all have definitely left the station. Therefore, the first reasonable conclusion is that the field will continue to move in these directions. Further, as some have claimed, the continuation of these trends will eventually lead to the creation of a new role for children in measuring and monitoring their own well-being. In a field that looks beyond survival and to the full range of child well-being, including children and their own perspectives would be a natural evolution. Indeed, incorporating children's subjective perceptions is both a prerequisite and a consequence of the changing field of measuring and monitoring child well-being. This, in turn, will lead to making children active actors in the effort to measure and monitor their own well-being as a natural progression (Ben-Arieh 2005).

Finally, the field is maturing and getting more organized. What started with several international and national projects (see, e.g. Ben-Arieh *et al.* 2001; http://multinational-indicators.chapinhall.org; Hauser, Brown and Prosser 1997; Qvortrup 199) had developed by 2006 into the International Society for Child Indicators (ISCI) (www.childindicators.org) and the launch of the *Child Indicators Research* journal. These accomplishments and advances will no doubt continue apace.

CHAPTER 7

National Reporting on Child Well-Being: The *State of the Nation's Children* Reports in the Republic of Ireland

ANNE-MARIE BROOKS, SINÉAD HANAFIN
AND SYLDA LANGFORD

Introduction

In the absence of good information about children, partial and inexact understandings of their lives (based on anecdotal and subjective experience) abound. These understandings may or may not reflect the reality of their lives. It is a disservice to children and their parents to base important decisions that can have an impact on children's lives on such an approach. The development, implementation, monitoring and evaluation of policy needs good information. In its absence it is not possible to make appropriate judgements. In recent times, there has been a significant increase in the demand for better information, and an improvement in the availability and accessibility of good-quality statistical data is now an integral part of the policy design and evaluation process in Ireland (National Statistics Board 2009) and elsewhere (Trewin 2006). One way in which this demand is met is through the publication of *State of the Nation's Children* reports.

The *State of the Nation's Children* reports in Ireland are compiled by the Office of the Minister for Children and Youth Affairs in association with the Central Statistics Office and the National University of Ireland, Galway. These reports are compiled to fulfil a commitment given in the National Children's Strategy (Department of Health and Children 2000) that a regularly updated statement of key indicators of children's well-being would be made available. This commitment reflects a more global effort to measure child well-being (Ben-Arieh *et al.* 2001) and State of the Child reports such as these are a feature in a number of other countries including the United States (Federal Interagency Program on Child and Family Statistics 2009) and the United Kingdom (Bradshaw 2002). Since 1979, UNICEF has published *The State of the World's Children,* a publication that is specifically focused on a review of basic indicators of children's survival and development across a number of different countries (e.g. UNICEF 2008). The *State of the Nation's Children* reports in Ireland are based on the National Set of Child Well-Being Indicators, which were developed in 2005.

This chapter sets out an overview of the National Set of Child Well-Being Indicators, including the methodology applied to develop the indicators. Within this, particular attention is paid to the role played by children themselves in the development process. Since the National Set of Child Well-Being Indicators was first developed in 2005, some revisions have taken place to take account of improved data and changing demography, and a summary of these revisions is also presented. An overview of the *State of the Nation's Children* reports published since 2005 and the challenges faced in compiling these reports are presented. The chapter concludes with an outline of future developments for reporting on child well-being in Ireland.

Development of the National Set of Child Well-Being Indicators: An overview

Nationally, prior to the development of the National Set of Child Well-Being Indicators, there was no overall policy focus on measuring child well-being in Ireland (Fitzgerald 2004). However, considerable progress had been made in some areas (Hanafin and Brooks 2005a) and it was possible to build on this. Further, a background search of the national and international literature identified three broad approaches to developing the National Set of Child Well-Being Indicators. These were:

- *data-driven development,* where indicators are selected on the basis of the availability of data and where existing data sets are exploited to best characterise the state of the subject area under investigation

- *policy-driven development,* where indicators are developed for those phenomena that are currently on the political agenda and for which data are requested by policy makers

- *theory-driven development*, which focuses on selecting the best possible indicators from a theoretical point of view. It has been noted, however, that the availability of data often restricts the outcome of this approach (Kohler and Rigby 2003; Niemeijer 2002; Rigby and Kohler 2002).

Bauer *et al.* (2003) have suggested that all three approaches be combined in order to 'arrive at measurable, meaningful indicators that are considered in the policy making process' (Bauer *et al.* 2003, p.107). Indeed, for the development of the National Set of Child Well-Being Indicators, all three approaches were combined and the theoretical understanding was conceptually guided by a holistic understanding of children's lives. Andrews *et al.*'s definition of child well-being, as follows, provided this conceptual guidance:

> healthy and successful individual functioning (involving physiological, psychological and behavioural levels of organisation), positive social relationships (with family members, peers, adult caregivers and community and societal institutions, for instance, school and faith and civic organisations), and a social ecology that provides safety (e.g. freedom from interpersonal violence, war and crime), human and civil rights, social justice and participation in civil society. (Andrews *et al.* 2002, p.103)

This definition was used because it facilitated the inclusion of many different dimensions of children's lives, as well as highlighting the importance of children's relationships and formal and informal supports. This understanding of children's lives is in keeping with the conceptualisation of the child as described in the 'Whole Child Perspective' of the National Children's Strategy (Department of Health and Children 2000).

In addition to this, account was also taken of Ben-Arieh *et al.*'s (2001) conclusions that 'the field of child well-being indicators is undergoing four major shifts, from survival to well-being, from negative to positive, from well-becoming to well-being and from traditional to new domains' (Ben-Arieh *et al.* 2001, p.47). Further, widely accepted selection criteria identified by Moore (1997) and reviewed for their applicability in the Irish context (Carroll 2002), along with guidance in the literature relating to the number of indicators, was also considered.

According to the New Policy Institute (2002), when building indicator sets, one major challenge is 'to select a manageable number of indicators which adequately cover the wide range of issues associated with [the topic under investigation] such that they collectively provide a reasonably comprehensive picture of [the topic] and how it is changing' (New Policy

Institute 2002, p.9). Hogan also stresses the importance of selecting a manageable number of indicators and limiting their number to avoid confusion and attention being diverted from the priorities of purpose of the work (Reidy and Winje 2002). According to the National Economic and Social Council (2002), a small number of indicators are important for three reasons:

1. A small number of indicators keeps the project manageable and focused.

2. A small number of indicators have a greater chance of acceptance in the policy arena and among a potential audience of policy makers and politicians.

3. A small number of indicators, which are readily understood, are more likely to become part of a generalised understanding (of child well-being) than a more exhaustive list.

They suggest that the number of indicators within an indicator set should range between 15 and 20, while the New Policy Institute (2002) suggested that the total number of indicators should range between 50 and 100, with 100 indicators reaching the absolute limits of manageability.

Development of the National Set of Child Well-Being Indicators: Methodology

The methodology applied to develop the National Set of Child Well-Being Indicators incorporated four main components. These were:

1. a background review of indicator sets in use elsewhere and the compilation of an inventory of key indicator, domains and selection criteria

2. a feasibility study of the availability of national statistics to construct the indicator identified in the previous step

3. a study on 'children's understandings of well-being'

4. a consensus process referred to as a 'Delphi technique' (described later), whereby participants on 'a panel of expertise' agreed indicators for use in the Irish context.

Background review of indicator sets and compilation of an inventory
A review of 76 international, national and regional indicator sets was undertaken. Each of these were reviewed for content, domain, sub-domain, number of indicators used and country of origin. The criteria for selecting the indicators were also examined. The final inventory (Brooks and Hanafin 2005) included:

- several thousand child well-being indicators, which were drawn from six international collaborations including *The State of the World's Children* (UNICEF 2005) and the *Child Health Indicators of Life and Development* (Rigby and Kohler 2002)

- 39 national indicator sets, including *America's Children* (Federal Interagency Program on Child and Family Statistics 2002), *Australia's Children: Their Health and Well-Being* (Al-Yaman, Bryant and Sargeant 2002) and *The Well-Being of Canada's Young Children* (Government of Canada 2002)

- 28 regional indicator sets drawn largely on material from Canada, the United States and Australia.

A feasibility study of the availability of national statistics to construct the indicators identified in the inventory
The inventory was followed by a feasibility study in which the aim was to identify indicators that could be readily compiled from data currently available in Ireland and to pinpoint areas where further development of data systems was necessary. This involved the examination of the inventory of child well-being indicators on an indicator-by-indicator basis to assess the extent to which Ireland was able to provide data to construct the indicators and at what frequency (Fitzgerald 2004).

A study on children's understanding of well-being
In Ireland, there is a strong policy commitment to giving children a voice in matters that affect them (Department of Health and Children 2000). Consequently, a study was undertaken on children's own views of well-being. The study ran in parallel to the process of the Delphi technique (described later) and used photography as the main method. A total of 33 groups of children were involved in the overall study, which commenced with 266 children taking a total of 4,073 photographs of things, people

and/or places that 'make them well' or 'keep them well'. When developed, the photographs were returned to the children who had taken them and they were asked to annotate them. The second stage of the study involved other groups of children looking at the developed photographs and dividing them into sets of mutually exclusive categories, while the third stage comprised further groups of children in developing schematic representations of well-being, using photographic examples of the categories. Schema were first developed by single gender groups, then by mixed gender groups, and a final integration was undertaken by a group of older youth, which aimed to provide a comprehensive representation of well-being relevant to Irish children.

There was considerable overlap between the areas considered important by children and adult stakeholders. However, three areas – those of 'pets and animals', 'things to do' and 'places to go' – had not been identified by adult stakeholders. These three areas were incorporated into the Delphi Study and subsequently into the National Set of Child Well-Being Indicators (Nic Gabhainn and Sixsmith 2005).

The Delphi Study

The Delphi technique has been defined as a research approach used to gain consensus through a series of rounds of questionnaire surveys, usually two or three, where information and results are fed back to panel members between each round (Linstone and Turoff 1975). The main purpose of adopting a Delphi technique to decision-making is to provide a structured approach to collecting data in situations where the only available alternative may be an anecdotal or an entirely subjective approach. A systematic review of empirical studies ($n = 25$) comparing the Delphi technique with standard interacting groups concluded, with some caution, that Delphi groups outperform groups in decision-making and forecasting (Rowe and Wright 1999).

For this study, 'a panel of expertise' comprising 69 policy makers, service providers, non-governmental organisations and parents was formed and a three-round Delphi study carried out, with feedback on the individual and group responses provided at each round. Response rates varied between 72 per cent and 84 per cent and this methodology facilitated an integrated, systematic and transparent approach to the development of an agreed National Set of Child Well-Being Indicators (Hanafin and Brooks 2005a, 2005b; Hanafin et al. 2007).

Development of the National Set of Child Well-Being Indicators: Results

The agreed National Set of Child Well-Being Indicators comprised 42 child well-being indicators and seven socio-demographic indicators, which would be used to contextualise children's lives in Ireland (Hanafin and Brooks 2005a, 2005b; Hanafin et al. 2007). Of these indicators, four required new data (on pets and animals, values and respect, quality of early childhood care, and education and nutritional outcomes).

Overall, over 90 per cent of the 'panel of expertise' reported they were very satisfied with the National Set of Child Well-Being Indicators and, when asked to consider the indicator set in light of the selection criteria (Carroll 2002; Moore 1997), the results were equally positive. Some concerns did emerge, however, that related to the 'children of all ages' selection criterion, with some reporting that the National Set of Child Well-Being Indicators did not adequately address the middle childhood period (Hanafin and Brooks 2005a).

Since the development of the National Set of Child Well-Being Indicators, some revisions have been made. Most notably, in an attempt to close critical data-gaps around the middle childhood period, the Office of the Minister for Children and Youth Affairs provided additional funding to the Health Promotion Research Centre, who conducts the Health Behaviour in School-Aged Children (HBSC) survey in Ireland. This additional funding allowed for the age threshold for this survey to be extended. Instead of collecting data on children from the age of 11, this survey now collects data on children from as early as nine years (Nic Gabhainn, Molcho and Kelly 2009). Therefore, the indicators, which use data drawn from this survey, have been improved.

Further data-gaps have been closed by developing data for the indicators on pets and animals, which is now collected on a quadrennial basis through the HBSC Survey (Nic Gabhainn, Kelly and Molcho 2007), and the quality of early childhood care and education, which is now collected on a triennial basis through the Quarterly National Household Survey (Central Statistics Office 2009a). More recently, a data source for the indicator on nutritional outcomes has also been identified. These data are now being collected through the government-funded, World Health Organization-led project known as the Surveillance of Obesity in Irish School Children.

Finally, indicators reporting on attainment in reading, mathematics and science, which were included as a special feature of the original indicator set, are now incorporated as regular indicators and, to take account of the recent demographic changes in Ireland (Central Statistics Office 2007), a new indicator on ethnicity has also been added. The National Set of Child Well-Being Indicators, which include all of these revisions, can be found in Hanafin and Brooks (2009).

Reporting on child well-being through the *State of the Nation's Children* reports: An overview

The development of the National Set of Child Well-Being Indicators was a crucial milestone in evaluating child well-being as it provided a comprehensive framework for understanding children's well-being in Ireland. As mentioned earlier, two reports on children's well-being, titled the *State of the Nation's Children* (Office of the Minister for Children and Youth Affairs 2006, 2008), have been compiled since the completion of the work on the National Set of Child Well-Being Indicators and there is an on-going commitment to a biennial report (Department of Health and Children 2000).

The *State of the Nation's Children* reports draw on some 22 data sources. These sources range from international surveys (e.g. the Health Behaviour in School-Aged Children Survey and the Programme for International Student Assessment Survey) to administrative data sources (e.g. Post-Primary Pupil Database and the National Psychiatric In-Patient Reporting System) to other official sources of data from the Central Statistics Office (e.g. Census of Population and Vital Statistics).

The conceptual framework for these reports, like the development of the National Set of Child Well-Being Indicators, is underpinned by the 'Whole Child Perspective', which was, in turn, based on the seminal work of Urie Bronfenbrenner (Bronfenbrenner 1979; Bronfenbrenner and Morris 1998). Specifically, the domains used in the *State of the Nation's Children* reports are:

- children's outcomes, specifically:

  ○ children's health outcomes

  ○ children's educational outcomes

  ○ children's socio-emotional–behavioural outcomes

- children's relationships

- children's formal and informal supports.

An additional domain (socio-demographics), which provides contextual data through the use of socio-demographic indicators, is also included. This domain essentially describes the characteristics of the child population as well as children's family settings and living arrangements. This conceptual framework, and specifically the domains used, is broadly similar to ones adopted in State of the Child reports published in other countries (Ben-Arieh *et al.* 2001; Brooks and Hanafin 2005).

Reporting on child well-being through the *State of the Nation's Children* reports: The practice

The *State of the Nation's Children* reports provide the most up-to-date aggregated data on all indicators in the National Set of Child Well-Being Indicators. Along with this, data for each indicator is disaggregated across sub-groups of children, across regions and across time. In addition, comparisons across countries are also drawn (where possible and where appropriate). Drawing on some examples for the most recent *State of the Nation's Children* report (Office of the Minister for Children and Youth Affairs 2008), the rationale for – and, indeed, the strength of – adopting this approach is now demonstrated.

Across sub-groups

It is crucial to have the capacity to disaggregate data across sub-groups as otherwise important variations amenable to policy intervention in child well-being can be hidden (Ben-Arieh *et al.* 2001). The most recent *State of the Nation's Children* report (Office of the Minister for Children and Youth Affairs 2008), for example, noted the following:

- The percentage of children aged 9–17 who reported being physically active for at least 60 minutes per day on more than 4 days per week was 54.8 per cent. However, these data showed significant variations across gender (45.9% girls versus 63.4% boys) and also age groups.

- The percentage of children aged 9–17 who reported being bullied at school was 24.5 per cent. Again, however, further disaggregation of the data showed significant variations across age groups (38.3% aged 8–9, 29.3% aged 10–11, 26.2% aged 12–14 and 20.8% aged 15–17).

- The percentage of babies born at low birth-weight to all mothers was 5.3 per cent. However, further disaggregation of the data showed substantial variations across social class. For example, the percentage of babies born at low birth-weight to unemployed mothers was 8.1 per cent.

Currently, in the *State of the Nation's Children* reports, indicators are disaggregated across gender, age and social class where such data is available. Future data developments will take account of the need to disaggregate data beyond demographic variables in order to identify differences across ethnicity and disability, amongst others.

Across regions

Many services are initiated, developed and delivered at local level and the availability of local information is therefore critical to identifying where improvements can be made. Without local-level data, variations in service delivery, and in child well-being, may be missed. In the most recent *State of the Nation's Children* report, for example, the rate of immunisations for Measles, Mumps and Rubella (MMR) at 24 months of age was 86 per cent. However, further disaggregation of the data showed significant variations across former health-board regions, with the Eastern Regional Health Authority reporting a rate of 82 per cent compared with the Midland Health Board, who reported a rate of 94 per cent (Office of the Minister for Children and Youth Affairs 2008). By highlighting these variations in the *State of the Nation's Children* reports, attention can be focused on why these variations exist and how they might be equalised.

Across time

The impact of interventions on children's lives may only become apparent over time (McAuley, Pecora and Rose 2006) and it is essential to measure progress over time as well as reporting on the current status. Without such data, improvements (or disimprovements) cannot be measured. Again, drawing from the most recent *State of the Nation's Children* report, we found that breastfeeding initiation rates (exclusive or combined) were 47.5 per cent in 2006. While this remains low compared with international trends, a year-on-year increase in these rates has been observed since 2001, when breastfeeding initiation rates stood at just 41.3 per cent. Likewise, in 2006, infant mortality rates were 3.9 per 1,000 live births. Again, by examining these data over time, we have observed a year-on-year decrease in these rates since 2002, when the infant mortality rate was 5.6 per 1,000 live births (Office of the Minister for Children and Youth Affairs 2008). While these are promising results, on their own they do not necessarily tell us that breastfeeding rates or infant mortality rates are at an acceptable level. For this, examining data across countries is helpful.

Across countries

While it can be difficult to identify good (or poor) performance in any absolute sense (Phipps 2006), a significantly better or worse performance compared with similarly affluent countries can help to benchmark the position (Fitzgerald 2004).

Again, using the infant mortality rate as an example, we see that if we rely solely on data over time alone, which has shown an impressive year-on-year decrease since 2001 to a rate of 3.9 per 1,000 live births, this record would be considered satisfactory. By comparing this data across similarly affluent countries, however, it is clear that improvements can still be made. In 2006, infant mortality rates in Ireland were 3.9 per 1,000 live births. This compares with Luxembourg, who reported infant mortality rates of 2.5 per 1,000 live births and both Sweden and Finland who reported rates of 2.8 per 1,000 live births (Office of the Minister for Children and Youth Affairs 2008). International comparisons can offer guidance on what is achievable.

In practice, disaggregating data across sub-groups of children, across regions and across time, and drawing comparisons across countries, has presented some of the many challenges that arose in compiling the *State of the Nation's Children* reports. Some of these challenges are discussed in the next section.

Reporting on child well-being through the *State of the Nation's Children* reports: The challenges

A number of challenges arose in compiling the *State of the Nation's Children* reports (Hanafin and Brooks 2009). These are now outlined.

Data availability

One of the greatest challenges in compiling the *State of the Nation's Children* reports is data availability. Indeed, for the first report, because of limited data, four indicators could not be reported on at all, while for other indicators only a partial picture could be presented. This included the indicator on 'public expenditure on children's lives', which only presented data on 'public expenditure on education', and 'breastfeeding', which only presented data on 'breastfeeding initiation' (i.e. at discharge from hospital). Further, because of limited data, the period of middle childhood could not be subjected to the same level of scrutiny as, for example, the period of infancy or adolescence. Despite investments and improvements in data, some of these challenges persist.

Even when data are available, the continued availability of these data also presents a challenge. When the National Set of Child Well-Being Indicators was developed, for example, a number of indicators used data that were drawn from the Programme for International Student Assessment. This programme is an internationally standardised survey, jointly developed by participating OECD countries and administered to 15-year-old children in schools. The survey was implemented in 43 countries in the first assessment (2000), in 41 countries in the second assessment (2003) and in 58 countries in the third assessment (2006). In the fourth assessment, which took place in 2009, there were 62 countries participating. Tests are typically administered to between 4,500 and 10,000 students in each country. Among the indicators drawn from this survey were:

- the percentage of children aged 15 who report that their parents spend time just talking with them several times a week

- the percentage of children aged 15 who report that their parents discuss with them how well they are doing at school several times a week

- the percentage of children aged 15 who report that their parents eat a main meal with them around a table several times a week.

Data to construct these indicators were collected via questions included in the internationally agreed instrumentation administered in 2000; however, these questions were removed from the instrumentation for subsequent data-collection periods. As these indicators were included in the National Set of Child Well-Being Indicators, the Office of the Minister for Children and Youth Affairs had to secure a commitment from the Education Research Centre (who conduct this survey in Ireland) to ensure instrumentation administered at a national level would continue to include these questions in future waves of data collection. Fortunately, this commitment was secured. However, as these questions have now been removed from the internationally agreed instrumentation, the ability to examine data across countries for these indicators is no longer possible (Eivers, Shiel and Cunningham 2008).

Similarly, when the National Set of Child Well-Being Indicators was developed, one indicator used data that were drawn from KIDSCREEN. For example:

- the percentage of children aged 8–17 who report feeling happy with the way they are.

Following this, however, funding for KIDSCREEN was discontinued. As this indicator was included in the National Set of Child Well-Being Indicators, the Office of the Minister for Children and Youth Affairs had to secure agreement from the Health Promotion Research Centre (who conduct the Health Behaviour in School-Aged Children in Ireland) to include this question on instrumentation administered at a national level, thus enabling us to continue reporting on this indicator.

Data disaggregation

As mentioned earlier, in compiling the *State of the Nation's Children* reports, indicators are disaggregated across several basic socio-demographic markers (i.e. across gender, age, social class and region at a minimum). In practice, however, this is not always possible. In some data sources, only specific age-groups are included (e.g. the European Schools Project on Alcohol and Drugs Survey is administered to 15-year-old children only). In other data sources, the number of cases may be too small to allow data to be disaggregated in this way (e.g. the number of births to girls aged 10–17 collected through Vital Statistics).[1] For others, which collect data on rare issues, disaggregated data could potentially compromise anonymity (e.g. the number of suicides among children aged 10–17 collected through Vital Statistics). This is particularly relevant to a small country such as Ireland, which has a child population of approximately one million.

Finally, for other data sources, some of these basic socio-demographic markers are simply not collected at all at this time (e.g. Child Care Interim Data Set).

Comparisons across countries

Drawing comparisons across countries is another challenge, and the removal of questions from international surveys (such as in the case described earlier) is one factor that has contributed to this; however, there are also others. To facilitate international comparisons, the definitions of indicators should be identical (Lack *et al.* 2003). This is not always straightforward. This is the case for the indicator on 'ante-natal care in first trimester of pregnancy', for example. In Ireland, the National Perinatal Reporting System defines the first trimester of pregnancy as up to 12 weeks, whereas the World Health Organization defines the first trimester of pregnancy as up to 14 weeks. Because of this, drawing comparisons across countries for this indicator has not been possible. Drawing comparison across countries has also not been possible in cases where indicators refer to a local service or policy that is specific only to Ireland. This is the case for the indicators on 'the number of children referred to the Garda Juvenile Liaison Programme' or 'the percentage of mothers of newborn children visited by a Public Health Nurse (PHN) within 48 hours of discharge from hospital'.

Data timeliness

As mentioned earlier, there is a commitment to publish the *State of the Nation's Children* report on a biennial basis. While many of the data sources collect and update data on an annual basis to facilitate this, others do not. Indeed, there is considerable variation in the frequency of data collection for each data source. Some data sources collect data on an annual basis (e.g. Vital Statistics) while others collect data on a triennial (European Schools Project on Alcohol and Drugs and the Programme for International Student Assessment), quadrennial (Health Behaviour in School-Aged Children Survey) or even on a quinquennial (Census of the Population) basis. Even when data is collected on an annual or biennial basis, often there is a time-lag of three years or more before that data is available. Therefore, a biennial update of each indicator is simply not possible and often, due to time-lags, we are forced to rely on data that is out of date. The biennial reporting of this data is under review at present and it may be that a change in the reporting period will occur in future.

Data quality

As mentioned above, some 22 data sources were used in the compilation of the *State of the Nation's Children* reports. Some of these data sources are of higher quality than others. Data sources, such as the Census of Population, adopt a survey methodology and data are collated, analysed and disseminated according to a very high standard as required by legislation in Ireland. Not all data sources, however, collect, analyse and disseminate data in this way and under these conditions. Many administrative data sources have evolved over time, sometimes in an *ad hoc* way, and their purpose is to support daily routine activities rather than to provide statistical data, while others do not have full coverage. An example of this is the disability databases – the National Intellectual Disability Database and the National Physical and Sensory Disability Database – which currently boast 95 per cent and 65 per cent coverage respectively. Consequently, the quality of some data is of a lower quality than others, and this can lead to some difficulties in using the data to report on children's well-being.

Reporting on child well-being through the *State of the Nation's Children* reports: Going forward

A recent consultation was undertaken to review the National Set of Child Well-Being Indicators. For this, respondents were asked to consider the National Set of Child Well-Being Indicators (including the revisions made since 2005) in light of the original selection criteria, to signal their overall level of satisfaction with the indicator set and also to suggest improvements to the indicator set through either the removal of existing indicators and/or addition of new indicators. This consultation also sought respondents' views on the *State of the Nation's Children* reports published heretofore, alongside suggestions for future reports.

A total of 32 submissions were received from various stakeholders, including government departments (e.g. the Department of Health and Children and the Department of Education and Science), agencies (e.g. the Health Research Board and the National Disability Authority) and non-governmental organisations (e.g. Barnardos and the Children's Rights Alliance). Some original members from the 'panel of expertise' from the Delphi Study were also included.

National Set of Child Well-Being Indicators

The results of this consultation found that the revised National Set of Child Well-Being Indicators continues broadly to meet the original selection criteria, and overall satisfaction with the indicator set remains high. Despite this, some concerns have been raised, and suggestions for further revision have been recommended.

Most notably, concerns were raised over the 'striking' data gaps in the middle childhood period that continue to persist despite improvements made to the Health Behaviour in School-Aged Children Survey data. As one respondent noted, 'the indicators do not adequately reflect primary school-aged children, specifically 4–11-year-olds'. While this is a concern that besets indicator sets in many other countries (Brooks and Hanafin 2005), efforts to address this will continue. Other concerns related to the current inability to disaggregate data across various sub-groups of children such as Traveller children and children with disabilities. Recently, the European Schools Project on Alcohol and Drugs and Health Behaviour in School-Aged Children Surveys have included Traveller and Disability markers in their instrumentation and this will go some way to address these concerns. Again, further efforts will continue.

A number of specific suggestions for improvement were also made and *Growing Up in Ireland: The National Longitudinal Study of Children* (www. growingup.ie) was promoted as a possible data source in this context. Among these were recommendations to expand, or make existing indicators more comprehensive. For example:

- recommendations to measure breastfeeding rates beyond initiation

- recommendations to measure public expenditure on children beyond education

- recommendations to measure participation in decision-making beyond participation in decision-making in schools to other contexts

- recommendations to measure the incidence of chronic health and mental health beyond those that require hospitalisation.

Other suggestions included a need to replace existing indicators, which are considered unsatisfactory, for more appropriate indicators. Among these was the indicator on sexual health and behaviour, which currently measures births to girls aged 10–17. Instead, it was suggested measuring sexual activity, condom-use or incidence of sexually transmitted diseases. Another example here is the indicator on nutritional behaviour, with some suggesting the Body Mass Index (BMI) to be a more appropriate measure. (As mentioned earlier, BMI data will be available through the Surveillance of Obesity in Irish School Children Study.) Finally, a number of new indicators were also suggested, including indicators on arts and culture; access to, and use of, computers and the Internet; civic participation and social capital, among others.

All of these suggestions will be considered as the National Set of Child Well-Being Indicators evolves, and, more generally, through the development of the National Data Strategy on Children's Lives, which will be described later. In considering these suggestions, however, we need to be cognisant of the need to limit the number of indicators included in the indicator set and also some of the data quality and availability issues mentioned earlier.

State of the Nation's Children reports

The results of this consultation also demonstrated high overall satisfaction with these reports, with the majority of respondents reporting that they found these reports useful. Further, a large majority rated these reports as 'excellent' or 'good' in meeting the aims of:

1. describing the lives of children

2. tracking changes over time

3. benchmarking progress in Ireland relative to other countries.

Overall, respondents identified the following benefits of these reports:

1. provides a broad-based description of children's lives, which draws attention to the many different areas of children's lives

2. gives a one-stop snapshot of children's lives

3. provides a concise evaluation of children's lives

4. supplements other data that are available

5. gives a good understanding of children in Ireland compared with those in other countries

6. provides a focus on issues of concern

7. reinforces the importance of individual indicator areas

8. useful tool for teaching, research and making submissions.

In general, most respondents believed that this report should continue to be compiled on a biennial basis. In some cases some respondents suggest the report should only include indicators that have updated data. In other cases, respondents suggested that the report should include all indicators, irrespective of whether updated data for each indicator is available or not.

In this context biennial web-based reports, and less frequent printed reports in cases where new data for all/most indicators is available, were suggested. Further, the introduction of special reports on various sub-groups of children (e.g. Traveller children, children with a disability, international children and early school-leavers) would also be considered a welcomed addition.

Overall, these reports appear to be making a contribution to improving our understanding of child well-being. Indeed, there is some evidence to suggest that they have stimulated an interest in measuring and monitoring child well-being nationally. Since the first report was published in 2006, a number of national reports on child well-being have been published by other government departments and non-governmental organisations (e.g. Barnardos Ireland 2008; Central Statistics Office 2009b; Children's Rights Alliance 2009; Department of Social and Family Affairs 2007; National Economic and Social Council 2009) and this all helps to build a generalised understanding of children's lives.

Conclusion

The *State of the Nation's Children* report has been an effective vehicle to improve and maximise data on child well-being. As mentioned earlier, already considerable improvements (within a very short time period) have been made to existing data sources. Data on the middle childhood period has been strengthened, and data to construct three indicators from the National Set of Child Well-Being Indicators for which there was no data originally available has now been developed. Steps to improve the data, particularly from administrative data sources, are continuing across a number of government departments through the development of Departmental Data Strategies, and a National Data Strategy on Children's Lives is currently in development. This strategy will set out a short-, medium- and long-term approach to ensuring that information about children's lives is available, of good quality and utilised in a way that improves understandings about children in Irish society.

Note

1   Vital Statistics are prepared by the Central Statistics Office for the Minister for Health and Children in accordance with the provisions of Section 2 of the Vital Statistics and Births, Deaths and Marriages Registration Act 1952 and Section 73 of the Civil Registration Act 2004.

CHAPTER 8

The Challenge of Improving Children's Well-Being and Measuring Outcomes: An American Perspective

PETER J. PECORA
AND MARKELL HARRISON-JACKSON

Introduction

This chapter describes how child well-being is measured in the United States, including some of the methodological challenges inherent in this work. There is a special focus on the advances and challenges in measuring child well-being in the field of child and family services. Data about the well-being indicators of children placed in foster care and young adults who have exited out of home care are also presented.

National indicators of general child well-being: Measuring child well-being in the United States[1]

As other authors in this volume discuss, there is a long and important history relating to how to measure child indicators of functioning and other areas of well-being (Ben-Arieh 2006; Ben-Arieh and Goerge 2001; Hauser, Brown and Prosser 1997). In the United States, as in other countries, there is an ongoing need for high-quality data.

How the United States tracks general child well-being

A variety of local, county, State and federal government agencies track child and adult health, income, housing, demographic, social and other indicators. Some of these indicators were originally developed from public health and economic perspectives, while others have been added as the United States needed a more comprehensive set of general population census data. States often differed from each other and the US Federal Government has struggled to try to achieve more uniformity across all communities. As discussed later, while some measurement challenges exist, significant progress has been made. For example, Table 8.1 includes a sample of the most important child well-being indicators that are gathered regularly every year from every State so they can be aggregated nationally.

One of the advantages of this approach is that vulnerable sub-groups can be identified in relation to certain indicators. For example, we consistently find huge high-school dropout and disproportionally high unemployment rates among African-American, Native American and Latino youth, with data about Native American youth sparse. (For high-school dropout rates see http://nces.ed.gov/fastfacts/display.asp?id=16 and for employment www.bls.gov/news.release/youth.t01.htm.)

Table 8.1 Key indicators of the Annie E. Casey Foundation's KIDS COUNT

Key indicators	Percentage
Percent low-birthweight babies 2006	6
Infant mortality rate (deaths per 1,000 live births) 2006	4.7
Child death rate (deaths per 100,000 children, ages 1–14) 2006	9
Teen death rate (deaths per 100,000 teens, ages 15–19) 2006	34
Teen birth rate (births per 1,000 females, ages 15–19) 2006	19
Percent of teens who are high-school dropouts (ages 16–19) 2007	2
Percent of teens not attending school and not working (ages 16–19) 2007	4
Percent of children living in families where no parent has full-time, year-round employment 2007	24
Percent of children in poverty (income below $21,027 for a family of two adults and two children in 2007)	9
Percent of children in single-parent families 2007	18

Source: The Annie E. Casey Foundation 2009, p.37

There are two publications that the child indicators field in the United States relies on for summarizing the most essential data on the well-being of children in the United States: the *KIDS COUNT Data Book* and *America's Children: Key National Indicators of Well-Being*.

The first, the *KIDS COUNT Data Book*, a publication of the Annie E. Casey Foundation (AECF), celebrated its 20th anniversary with the 2009 edition. A State-by-State look at the ten key indicators of well-being, the Data Book tracks progress over time and assigns ranks to States, in both overall well-being and by indicator. The KIDS COUNT Data Center website has incorporated a number of impressive features. Each indicator can be portrayed on maps and line-graphs, and in rankings by State. Customized State-level profiles can also be created online. For all States, county-level data are also provided, and for many States, community-level data are available. Besides the ten KIDS COUNT key indicators, the site includes many additional indicators grouped by category.[2]

The second publication is sponsored by the national government. The US Federal Interagency Forum on Child and Family Statistics publishes *America's Children: Key National Indicators of Well-Being*, the 12th annual edition of which was released early in 2009. The report includes 40 indicators in seven sections: family and social environment, economic circumstances, health care, physical environment and safety, behavior, education, and health. Each section also highlights one or more indicators to draw attention to current data-gaps regarding the country's assessment of child well-being. In alternate years the report also has a special focus: in 2009 it was children with special health-care needs. Charts or tables show trend data over time (typically, 10–20 years), and are supplemented by an appendix with detailed tables.[3]

While these are two vital resources, readers should note that there is a huge amount of work under way in this area in the United States and elsewhere (e.g. Ben-Arieh and Frones 2009; Hauser *et al.* 1997).[4] For example, a State-focused initiative was launched in 2004 by the Packard Foundation. Called *KidsData*, this provides many different types of data on children, being a comprehensive website that tracks hundreds of indicators on the health and well-being of children in California – on topics ranging from alcohol use to immigration, to weight. Data are continually updated, and, depending on the source, available for cities, school districts and counties, along with State-wide comparisons. Data can be customized by year, locale, ethnicity, age and more (again, depending on the source). The results can be viewed as tables and maps or bar, trend and pie graphs. The site offers descriptions of why each issue matters and what the data mean, as well as links to related news and research.[5]

Challenges in measuring general child well-being

One of the shortcomings in measurement that we face is how poverty, child poverty and other forms of deprivation are defined in the United States. For example, poverty is measured using outdated criteria and the 'poverty line' is too low because the factors that are used to calculate it have not been updated and revised for many years (see www.irp.wisc.edu/faqs/faq1. htm). The under-count of certain ethnic groups and many immigrants in the US decennial census make it difficult to measure accurately the diversity of our citizens and trends over time – including gaps in our knowledge of particular sub-groups of children. How data has been gathered regarding Latino and Native American groups has been controversial (e.g. Lieberson and Waters 1989; US Census Bureau 2008).

In addition, there is a need to strengthen the collection and use of data within a number of federal and State administrative systems (Nelson 2009). Organizations like the US Census Bureau, Child Trends and the Annie E. Casey Foundation have made strong endorsements of the value of child well-being indicators and the potential for their improvement:

> The Casey Foundation has made these investments based on our conviction that data-driven decision-making offers a powerful – and sorely underutilized – tool to improve results for children. Results matter, and achieving positive results requires us to keep our eyes on the prize: carefully measuring the well-being of children; setting meaningful goals for their care and development; identifying those who are suffering or being left behind; strategically publicizing the performance of public programs; and maintaining society's focus on the evolving, objectively measured needs of the next generation. (Nelson 2009, p.6)

Measuring child-welfare outcomes in the United States: Mission and goals of child-welfare services

The mission of child welfare has long been to respond specifically to the needs of children reported to public child-protection agencies as abused or neglected, at risk of child maltreatment, or who are a risk to themselves or others because of emotional or behavioral problems. This mission, involving the need to protect children from child abuse and neglect, affects what kinds of child well-being outcomes are measured in child welfare.[6] System goals and expected outcomes are discussed in the next section.

Key goals and outcomes for child welfare services[7]

Child-welfare services as a field is gaining more clarity and consensus about its primary mission. There is one primary goal and two secondary goals for child-welfare services:

- The primary goal is to protect children from harm.

- The second goal is to preserve existing family units, which we understand to include both birth-family and relative families as appropriate.

- The third goal is to promote children's development into adults who can live independently and contribute to their community, which may require a variety of permanency planning alternatives such as family reunification, placement with relatives, different forms of guardianship (depending upon local law), and adoption – including in rare situations *planned* long-term foster care or kinship care with some kind of legal safeguards such as guardianship (US Department of Health and Human Services 2003).

There is some debate in the field about placing child safety as a superior goal to family support – some organizations such as the Child Welfare League of America (2003) argue that, without an emphasis upon both child safety and family support simultaneously, neither will happen in an equitable manner. Yet, the effectiveness of the existing system in achieving positive child development and *well-being* has also been rightly criticized (e.g. Berrick *et al.* 1998; Maluccio and Pecora 2006). The key components of each of these major goals (also called 'outcome domains') are summarized below.

Safety

The core goal for child-welfare services (CWS), according to federal policy and most States, is keeping children safe from child abuse and neglect. This includes children living with their birth families, those returned home to their families, and children placed in out-of-home care. In terms of concrete outcomes, citizens should be looking to child-welfare services to prevent children from being maltreated and to keep families safely together that are functioning at a minimum standard of parenting. Child-welfare workers operate on the philosophical basis that all children have a right to live in a safe environment and receive protection from abuse and neglect. For example, the focus of child-welfare services should be to deliver services that are preventive and non-punitive; and that are geared toward parent rehabilitation through identification and treatment of the factors that underlie the problem.

Permanence[8]

When the State steps in to protect an abused or neglected child, it is not enough for the State to make the child safe; the State must also consider the child's needs for permanent and stable family ties. Besides protecting a child, the State should ensure that the children will be brought up by stable and legally secure permanent families, rather than in temporary foster care under the supervision of the State. This principle has been well established in federal law, first by the Adoption Assistance and Child Welfare Act of 1980, then by the Adoption and Safe Families Act of 1997, and then by the Adoption Promotion Act of 2003 (Casey Family Programs 2003; Kerman, Maluccio and Freundlich 2008).

Child well-being

Achieving child well-being in child welfare services means, foremost, that a child is safe from child abuse or neglect. This requires that a child's basic needs are met and the child has the opportunity to grow and develop in an environment that provides adequate nurture, support and stimulation. In this outcome domain we include children's education, mental health, health and social behavior (Wulczyn *et al.* 2005a, 2005b). Although child-welfare services is not singularly responsible for these, CWS should be expected to work with other parties to achieve these goals, and when children are under the guardianship of CWS should take the lead in co-ordinating efforts related to achieving these outcomes.

Family well-being

Family well-being is generally not viewed as an outcome of today's child-welfare services but might be thought of as an outcome in a reformulated child and family services program that is concerned not only about the impact of services on children but on each family member. In this usage, family well-being means that a family has the capacity to care for its children and fulfill their basic developmental, health, educational, social, cultural, spiritual and housing needs. It would imply that children's services workers have some responsibility for locating these essential services and supports for the sake of the family's well-being.

Measuring outcomes in child welfare

Each of these outcome domains is exemplified, albeit imperfectly, by new federal outcome standards as shown in Table 8.2. A US Government Accountability Office report (2004) summarized the issue this way for the original standards:

> It is against these benchmarks for statewide data indicators that a state is measured. Any state whose performance is found to fall short of substantial conformity (based upon data analysis and an on-site review of individual cases) is given an opportunity to develop and implement a plan to improve performance and avoid the withholding of federal funds. AFSA also required HHS to prepare and submit to Congress an annual report on the performance of each state on each outcome measure. (As cited in McDonald, Salyers and Shaver 2004, p.5)

For the new indicators, during a Child and Family Services Review (CFSR), the review team assesses the State's substantial conformity with the following:

1. seven outcomes in the domains of safety, permanency, and child and family well-being

2. seven systemic factors that affect outcomes for children and families.

To measure a State's substantial achievement of the outcomes, the review team assesses items (on-site review) or items and data indicators (on-site review and State-wide assessment). To measure substantial achievement of the systemic factors, the review team assesses items to determine whether the systemic factors are in place and functioning satisfactorily. The items and/or data indicators associated with the outcomes and systemic factors are listed in Table 8.2.[9]

The CFSR outcome definitions and performance measurement methods have stimulated helpful introspection and discussion in most States. But many experts advocate for their refinement, which may occur within the next two or three years because of a change in federal leaders. These refinements will likely center on broadening and improving the precision of the data indicators, as well as expanding the sample size used for case reviews and key informant interviews (e.g. US Accountability Office 2004; Wulczyn *et al.* 2005b; Wulczyn, Orlebeke and Haight 2009).

Table 8.2 National Child and Family Services Review standards for child welfare: Non-systemic standards

Standard	Description
Safety	*Safety Outcome 1:* Children are, first and foremost, protected from abuse and neglect. Timeliness of initiating investigations of reports of child maltreatment (Item 1) Repeat maltreatment (Item 2) Absence of recurrence of maltreatment (data indicator) Absence of maltreatment of children in foster care (data indicator)
	Safety Outcome 2: Children are safely maintained in their homes whenever possible and appropriate. Services to family to protect child(ren) in home and prevent removal or re-entry into foster care (Item 3) Risk assessment and safety management (Item 4)
Permanency	*Permanency Outcome 1:* Children have permanency and stability in their living situations. Foster care re-entries (Item 5) Stability of foster-care placement (Item 6) Permanency goal for child (Item 7) Reunification, guardianship, or permanent placement with relatives (Item 8) Adoption (Item 9) Other planned permanent living arrangement (Item 10) Timeliness and permanency of reunifications (Permanency Composite 1) Timeliness of adoptions (Permanency Composite 2) Achieving permanency for children in foster care (Permanency Composite 3) Placement stability (Permanency Composite 4)
	Permanency Outcome 2: The continuity of family relationships and connections is preserved for children. Proximity of foster-care placement (Item 11) Placement with siblings (Item 12) Visiting with parents and siblings in foster care (Item 13) Preserving connections (Item 14) Relative placement (Item 15) Relationship of child in care with parents (Item 16)

Child and Family Well-Being	*Child and Family Well-Being Outcome 1:* Families have enhanced capacity to provide for their children's needs.
	Needs and services of child, parents, and foster parents (Item 17)
	Child and family involvement in case planning (Item 18)
	Caseworker visits with child (Item 19)
	Caseworker visits with parent(s) (Item 20)
	Child and Family Well-Being Outcome 2: Children receive appropriate services to meet their educational needs.
	Educational needs of the child (Item 21)
	Child and Family Well-Being Outcome 3: Children receive adequate services to meet their physical and mental health needs.
	Physical health of the child (Item 22)
	Mental/behavioral health of the child (Item 23)

Note that the CFSR also measures a number of systemic areas: (1) Statewide Information System; (2) Case Review System; (3) Quality Assurance System; (4) Staff and Provider Training; (5) Service Array and Resource Development; (6) Agency Responsiveness to the Community; and (7) Foster and Adoptive Parent Licensing, Recruitment, and Retention.

Source: US Department of Health and Human Services 2006

The movement to measure more child well-being outcomes in child welfare

Measuring the well-being of children in foster care is evolving in the United States, aided by studies that underscore the importance of paying attention to child development, child functioning, and placement stability (Berrick *et al.* 1998; Pecora *et al.* 2010; Shonkoff and Phillips 2000).[10] One example of an attempt to improve measurement of child indicators in the child-abuse prevention and family-support field is presented in Table 8.3.

Another example of where progress is slowly being made is in the studies of youth in foster care that measure their mental-health functioning and educational achievement (e.g. Courtney and Dworsky 2005; White *et al.* 2007). The Chapin Hall Midwest Study and the Casey Family Programs Adolescent Mental-Health Study both used standardized surveys and some survey items that were used in general population surveys of children.

Another area of innovative work has been the measurement of how alumni of foster care are functioning after return home or emancipation from foster care (see Tables 8.4–8.6). The Chapin Hall Midwest Study team interviewed youth who were emancipating from foster care as adults at the ages of 19, 21 and 23. The Northwest Alumni Study compared the

Table 8.3 Selected characteristics of child well-being indicators with special attention to placement prevention programs

Child well-being indicators

Health

   Children with vaccinations up to date

   Caregivers who rate overall child health rating as very good or excellent

   Children with emergency room visits for injuries

   Children with stable medical provider (person or place)

   Children receiving yearly dental care

   Children with dental caries

   Children with health insurance

Education and cognitive well-being

   Children attending an accredited nursery school, pre-K or Head Start program

   Children whose families read to them or tell them stories regularly

   Children evaluated for developmental delays and learning disabilities

   Eligible children in early intervention programs

Socio-emotional well-being

   Children who are screened for socio-emotional well-being

   Children with negative screens for socio-emotional well-being who receive appropriate services from licensed providers

Home and community risk and protective factors

Social connectedness

   Emergency support available

   Group membership

   Service access

Home safety

Child maltreatment

Parenting capacity

Substance use

Economic hardship

   Poverty status

   Income

Family conflict

Source: Adapted from Ross and Vandivere 2009

functioning of foster care alumni aged 20–33 who were served by private versus public agencies in Washington and Oregon. All of these studies examined the needs and functioning of children in the child-welfare system in relation to their peers in the general population, and each study used different sections that measured a slightly different number of disorders or a different generation of the same instrument: the Composite International Diagnostic Interview (CIDI).

Table 8.4 Mental-health functioning: Rates for lifetime symptoms, symptoms in the past 12 months and lifetime recovery of the northwest foster care alumni[a]

Mental health outcomes	Northwest Alumni			NCS-R (general population)		
	Northwest Alumni Study: % who had symptoms – Lifetime	Northwest Alumni Study: % who had symptoms in past 12 months	Northwest Alumni Study: % recovered	Gen. pop. (NCS-R) for ages 20–33: % who had symptoms – Lifetime	Gen. pop. (NCS-R) for ages 20–33: % who had symptoms in past 12 months	Gen. pop. (NCS-R): % recovered[b]
CIDI diagnosis[c]	–	54.4 (2.7)	–	–	22.1 (1.0)*[d]	–
3 or more CIDI diagnoses[c]	–	19.9 (2.3)	–	–	2.9 (0.5)*[d]	–
Major depression episode	41.1 (2.8)	20.1 (2.3)	51.0 (4.5)	21.0 (1.4)*	11.1 (0.8)*	48.3 (2.2)
Panic syndrome	21.1 (2.2)	14.8 (1.9)	30.1 (5.4)	4.8 (0.5)*	3.5 (0.4)*	30.4 (4.7)
Modified social phobia	23.3 (2.5)	17.1 (2.3)	26.6 (5.2)	15.9 (1.6)*	9.4 (1.0)*	36.7 (3.1)*
Generalized anxiety disorder	19.1 (2.4)	11.5 (2.0)	39.6 (7.3)	7.0 (0.8)*	4.0 (0.6)*	39.8 (3.8)

continued

Table 8.4 Mental-health functioning: Rates for lifetime
symptoms, symptoms in the past 12 months and lifetime
recovery of the northwest foster care alumni[a] *cont.*

Mental health outcomes	Northwest Alumni			NCS-R (general population)		
	Northwest Alumni Study: % who had symptoms – Lifetime	Northwest Alumni Study: % who had symptoms in past 12 months	Northwest Alumni Study: % recovered	Gen. pop. (NCS-R) for ages 20–33: % who had symptoms – Lifetime	Gen. pop. (NCS-R) for ages 20–33: % who had symptoms in past 12 months	Gen. pop. (NCS-R): % recovered[b]
PTSD[c]	30.0 (2.5)	25.2 (2.5)	15.7 (2.4)	7.6 (0.7)*	4.6 (0.5)*	41.9 (4.1)*
Alcohol problem	Not measured	11.9 (1.6)	–	Not measured	Not measured	–
Alcohol dependence	11.3 (1.2)	3.6 (0.6)	67.9 (4.5)	7.1 (0.1)*	2.3 (0.6)	63.4 (5.4)
Drug problem	Not measured	12.3 (2.2)	–	Not measured	Not measured	–
Drug dependence	21.0 (2.3)	8.0 (1.8)	61.8 (6.6)	4.5 (0.7)*	0.7 (0.2)*	80.4 (4.8)*
Anorexia[f]	1.2 (0.3)	0.0	100.0	0.3 (0.1)*	0.0	–
Bulimia	4.9 (1.4)	3.6 (1.3)	25.8 (1.1)	0.8 (0.2)*	0.5 (0.2)*	48.3 (13.6)*
SF-12* mental health score of 50 or above	–	50.6 (2.8)	–	–	–	–
Sample size	479			1601		

* Indicates a significant difference between the Northwest Alumni Study and the
National Co-Morbidity Study – Replication (NCS-R), p<.05, two-tailed.

a This analysis takes the NCS-R data matched to ages 20–33 and post-stratifies the NCS-R data to match the northwest distribution of race, sex and age. The NCS-R prevalence estimates were then run on this post-stratified data set. These numbers are slightly different from the NCS-R mental health comparison statistics published previously in the Northwest Alumni Study report (Pecora *et al.* 2005) because those original numbers did not take into account the post-stratification.

b Alumni were considered to have recovered if the lifetime occurrence of a mental-health symptom was not present in the past 12 months.

c Because alcohol and drug problems were not assessed during the lifetime, the CIDI diagnosis and three or more CIDI diagnoses could not be computed for the lifetime; consequently, no recovery rate could be computed for either item.

d Not adjusted by race or gender.

e The NCS-R PTSD section included some additional specific trauma items, but the Northwest Alumni Study version of the CIDI PTSD items included some general questions that were designed to identify potentially traumatic events. The purpose was to help the respondent identify at least one event, so the focus was on measuring whether the reactions to any of these events constituted PTSD rather than measuring the number or type of items *per se*. The measures, therefore, should be comparable.

f Anorexia is extremely rare in the general population.

Source: Pecora *et al.* 2010, pp.110–111. Reprinted with permission of Oxford University Press, Inc.

Table 8.5 Physical health functioning of the northwest foster care alumni ages 20–33

Physical health	Northwest alumni % (SE)
No chronic physical disorder[a]	72.5 (2.4)
SF-12° physical health score of 50 or above	68.8 (2.5)
Does not smoke currently	57.2 (2.6)
Smokes fewer than 10 cigarettes per day	75.3 (2.0)
Does not drink currently	53.1 (2.8)
Drinks fewer than 150 drinks per year	75.9 (2.2)
Sample size	479

a Chronic physical disorder includes heart disease, high blood pressure, chronic lung disease, ulcers and HIV. It does not include diabetes or asthma.

Source: Pecora *et al.* 2010, p.115

**Table 8.6 Educational outcomes for northwest
alumni and comparison groups[a]**

Educational outcomes	Total % (SE)	Census Bureau data %	Other alumni studies	
			%	Study
Completed high school – high school diploma or GED	84.8 (1.9)	Between 70 and 87, depending upon the age range and study	71% at 36.7 years old	Buehler *et al.* 2000
			77% at 22 years old	Blome 1997 national study of alumni
			90% at 22.8 years old	Casey Family Services 1999 with long-term extended alumni from foster care
			44% at 22.8 years old	Casey Family Services 1999 with non-extended alumni from foster care[b]
			63% at about 20 years old	Courtney *et al.* 2001 Wisconsin study of high school completion 12 to 18 months after discharge
			54% at 21 years	Westat national study of alumni (Cook, Fleishman and Grimes 1989)
Completed high school – high school diploma only	56.3 (2.7)	About 75	28.6%	Mech 2003 (Very few alumni studies have delineated completion of diplomas vs. GEDs.)
Completed high school – with a GED	28.5 (2.5)		11%	Mech and Fung 1999

Any education past high school (any type of post-secondary education)	42.7 (2.7)	About 52 – some college (ages 25 and older)	27% at 22 years old	Alexander and Huberty 1993 alumni with some college or vocational training
			45% at 22 years old	Blome 1997 national study of alumni
			73% at 22.8 years old	Casey Family Services 1999 with long-term extended alumni from care[b]
			18% at 22.8 years old	Casey Family Services 1999 with non-extended alumni from foster care[b]
			33%	Westat national study of alumni (Cook et al. 1989)
Completed any degree/certificate beyond high school (vocational, BA, etc.)	20.6 (1.8)		N/A	N/A
Completed college or more (has BA or more)	1.8 (0.4)	24 (ages 25 and older)	8%	Casey Family Services 1999 with non-extended alumni from foster care[b]
			2% at 21 years	Westat national study of alumni (Cook et al. 1989)
			1.6%	Zimmerman 1982
Sample size	479			

a These comparative data from earlier studies must be viewed with special caution as only the Blome (ages 22 and older) and Westat studies (up to age 24) included older alumni.

b In the Casey Family Services Study, two main groups were differentiated: (1) those who were placed with the agency for a long period of time; and (2) those alumni who had left the program early.

Source: Adapted from Pecora et al. 2010, pp.122–123

From measuring child safety and permanence to child well-being in child welfare

As agencies have improved their management-information systems and, more importantly, their thinking about performance measurement in child welfare, it has advanced our thinking about what and how to measure child well-being. The child indicators measurement movement has been of support because experts in that field have tackled variable definition, research methods and data analyses challenges.

What has helped to propel this work are research findings that indicate that, for example, many youth in foster care are coping with mental-health disorders or have left foster care with poor skills for independent living; and that about 25 percent experience homelessness within one year of leaving care. The child well-being and other outcome data also provide an urgent call to improve services; and show that children and parents deserve evidence-based interventions to improve success rates.

Implementing those services has proven challenging (Fixsen *et al.* 2005), but must be done:

> Evidence-based policy and practice has been the subject of considerable debate in the UK, US and Europe. Increasingly in the UK and US, there is a move towards evidence-based policy, leading to a recognition within most helping professions of the need to develop an evidence base to justify policy and practice developments. Increased scrutiny of public expenditure, coupled with concern that limited resources should be targeted where there is most likelihood of tangible benefits, has fuelled a preoccupation with determining outcomes of interventions. (McAuley, Pecora and Rose 2006, p.322)

Another child well-being research challenge is the choice of study methods. Many studies involve user views but lack objective/standardized outcome measures (McAuley *et al.* 2006). Herein lies an important tension in how best to bring together the views of children and parents with data from other sources. Bradshaw and colleagues address the important area of subjective well-being in Chapter 9 of this volume, looking at the promising new directions they are pursuing to measure and incorporate subjective well-being in future indices.

Further tensions are highlighted by Whittaker (2009, p.167) who indicates that there are many 'fault lines' that exist in the child and family services field:

- the continuing tensions between 'front-end', preventive services and 'deep-end' highly intensive treatment services and the unhelpful dichotomies these tend to create and perpetuate

- the tensions between a widely shared desire to adopt more evidence-based practices and the genuinely felt resistances to these, particularly when they are employed in a lock-step or cookie-cutter fashion requiring strict adherence to established protocols with little opportunity for experimentation, customization or practitioner discretion

- the tension as manifest in North America and elsewhere between evidence-based and culturally competent practices reflecting, among other things, antagonism towards certain practice strategies based on perceptions of the under-representation of ethnic minorities in the study samples on which certain models have been validated.

Whittaker cautions us that since model programs proliferate and are increasingly removed from the particular political and cultural niches within which they were developed, we should heed the cautions offered by Munro, Stein and Ward (2005) – i.e. that researchers, planners and youth and family practitioners are at a 'moment in time' when cross-national perspectives are critical in helping identify new ways of framing problems, gathering data and shaping service-solutions:

> Cross-national dialogue can help in identifying different formats for collecting, analyzing and utilizing routinely gathered client information, analyzing subtle local adaptations of internationally recognized evidence-based services and examining the effects of differing policy contexts on service outcomes. (Whittaker 2009, p.167)

Comparing outcomes of child-welfare interventions is complex because studies use a variety of outcome measures and different ways of describing processes, and include data on diverse groups of children with differing needs in different types of placement. Agency administrative data needs to include more child well-being outcome indicators, and worker completion rates often need to be increased to improve data completeness. Agency administrative data should be enriched with more child well-being outcome indicators.

In addition, we need to identify and then systematically address barriers to conducting follow-up studies in order to measure intermediate and more distal program outcomes. What might help us be more successful is the involvement of more youths in care, alumni and caregivers in study design and data interpretation. In addition, we should more routinely measure and think about *iatrogenic* effects of our services, i.e. which types of people get *worse?* Finally, confidentiality myths and other barriers sometimes prevent more frequent use of cross-agency administrative databases to measure key child well-being and other program outcomes. One blocking strategy that bureaucrats often use to prevent collaboration is the 'need to protect client confidentiality'.[11]

Conclusion

The United States is at an important crossroads: many groups want to improve child well-being of *all* children because they believe that the outcomes for the more vulnerable children will improve as well, especially if the more intensive services are carefully targeted (National Research Council and the Institute of Medicine 2009; Pew Foundation 2008; Prinz *et al.* 2009). Studies summarized in this chapter illustrate some of those areas for youth in foster care and foster care alumni. But federal, State and county governments are struggling with how to afford this approach.

Nevertheless, measurement of a key set of child indicators will continue because refining how we conceptualize and measure child well-being is improving the situation of children in the United States, as more firm research data are amassed about how youth are doing, how that has changed over time, and the effects of interventions to improve child well-being outcomes. Practical breakthroughs occur when policy makers and service managers work together with researchers and other scholars to advance measurement methods in order to assess the impact of new services in terms of outcomes at the micro and macro levels (Ben-Arieh and Frones 2009).

Focusing on a few key child and adolescent outcomes within a context of cross-program efforts to support children and their families is a promising approach. As Nelson (2009) emphasized, these are some of the most important functions of government, business and community partners: carefully measuring the well-being of children; setting meaningful goals for their care and development; identifying those who are being left behind; strategically publicizing the performance of service delivery programs; and maintaining a focus on the objectively measured needs of our children – the next generation.

Notes

1   See also www.childtrend.org/Files//Child_Trends-2009_01_05_FR_ChildIndicatorGuide.pdf.
2   For more on the *KIDS COUNT 2009 Data Book* and Data Center, see http://datacenter. kidscount.org.
3   For more on the *America's Children* report, see www.childstats.gov.
4   See, for example, www.financeproject.org/Publications/indicatorsofchildwellbeingresource. htm.
5   See www.kidsdata.org.
6   During the Federal fiscal year 2007, an estimated 3.2 million US children were reported as abused and neglected, with 794,000 confirmed victims (US Department of Health and Human Services 2009, p.xii). The Child Abuse Prevention and Treatment Act of 1974 was the federal government's landmark legislation to reduce child maltreatment nationwide.
7   Adapted from Pecora *et al.* (2009), Chapter 1.
8   Adapted from Hardin (1992) pp.11–12.
9   The numerical performance standards can be found in Appendix H of the federal CFSR manual: www.acf.hhs.gov/programs/cb/cwmonitoring/tools_guide/procedures/appendixh.htm.
10 The United States Federal Government estimated that 496,000 children were placed in foster care in family and non-family settings as of 30 September 2007 with about 783,000 children served during the 2007 federal fiscal year. While about 18 percent may be placed because of some emotional or behavioral disorder, most are placed to protect them from child maltreatment.
11 See a recent American Bar Association report for how to break through these barriers at www.abanet.org/child/education.

CHAPTER 9

The Subjective Well-Being of Children

JONATHAN BRADSHAW, GWYTHER REES,
ANTONIA KEUNG AND HARIDHAN GOSWAMI

Background

For most dimensions of child well-being there are now some pretty good indicators that can be used to monitor progress over time. In the UK we have been monitoring the child-poverty strategy since 1999 using the set of indicators in *Opportunity for All* (Department for Work and Pensions 2009), which as well as material well-being indicators also cover health, education, housing and looked-after children. The five domains of the *Every Child Matters* (ECM) Outcomes Framework for England (be healthy; stay safe; enjoy and achieve; make a positive contribution; achieve economic well-being) have National Public Service Agreement (PSA) targets and a host of national quality-of-life and quality-of-service indicators associated with them – though they do not (all) seem to have been populated with data. When we produced the books (Bradshaw 2002; Bradshaw and Mayhew 2005) on the well-being of children in the UK there was no shortage of material out there to monitor change – we could say that some things had got better for children and some had got worse. Even international comparisons of child well-being (Bradshaw and Richardson 2009; Bradshaw, Hoelscher and Richardson 2007; OECD 2009; Richardson, Hoelscher and Bradshaw 2008; UNICEF 2007) have been able to draw on a rich variety of comparable indicators from sample surveys and international series, and Richardson (2010) has been able to use some of these indicators to trace change over time. The European Union has been investing heavily in developing the so-called 'Laeken' indicators, set to include indicators of well-being that go beyond the conventional child-income poverty measures

(European Commission 2008; European Union 2010), and the EU Statistics on Income and Living Conditions has included a special module on child well-being in the 2009 survey.

One important exception to this picture of plenty is subjective well-being – by which we mean (to avoid a lengthy discussion) the expressed views of children about their personal well-being and their relationships. There is no indicator of subjective well-being in *Opportunity for All* (Department for Work and Pensions 2009) and there is only one indicator in the ECM outcomes framework – under 'Be healthy', young people's perception of their emotional health and well-being (see NI50/PSA 12/DSO1, DCSF 2009c).[1] It is operationalised by a very simple question in the 'Tellus' survey launched by Ofsted as an online survey in 2007, which 'gathers the views of children and young people in Years 6, 8 and 10, on their life, their school and their local area' (Tellus4 2009). The findings from this are intended to inform policy making and to measure progress and performance across the five ECM outcomes at both local and national (England) levels. The survey ran again in 2008 (Tellus3) and the Department for Children, Schools and Families (DCSF) is responsible for Tellus4 as well as having commissioned the National Foundation for Educational Research (NFER) to further develop and deliver the survey in autumn 2009 (Tellus4 2009). The Tellus survey has five simple questions covering happiness and relationships with friends and family. Among them 69 per cent of respondents say that it is true that they 'feel happy about life at the moment'.

At present there are really only two other national sources of data in the UK on children's subjective well-being over time. The first is the British Household Panel youth questionnaire that has asked 11–15-year-olds about their happiness, feeling troubled and self-esteem since 1994. Each of these three dimensions of subjective well-being is assessed by a number of questions where a score is given to each response (see Table 9.1). A scale is created for each dimension by summing up the scores to each set of corresponding questions. The happiness scale ranges from 0 to 30; the troubled-feeling scale ranges from 0 to 6; and the self-esteem scale ranges from 0 to 15. Thus, the higher the score, the better is the subjective well-being on all three scales. (The internal reliability of each scale is deemed reasonable with Cronbach's Alpha[2] ranges between 0.6 and 0.7.)

Table 9.1 Questions set from the British Household Panel Survey measuring subjective well-being

SWB	Questions	Scoring	α coefficient
Happiness	How you feel about your a) school work b) appearance c) family d) friends e) life as a whole	Scale of 0–6 per question, where: 0 = not happy at all; 6 = very happy Total scale: 0–30	0.70
Feeling (less) troubled	In the past month, how many days have you felt unhappy or depressed? (Feeling sad) 0) 11+ 1) 4–10 2) 1–3 3) None In the past week how many nights have you lost sleep worrying about things? (Feeling worried) 0) 6–7 1) 3–5 2) 1–2 3) None	Scale of 0–3 per question, where: 0 = a lot of trouble; 3 = no trouble at all Total scale: 0–6	0.60
Self-esteem	Please say whether you strongly agree, agree, disagree or strongly disagree that the following statements apply to yourself. a) no good qualities b) I certainly feel useless at times c) not a likeable person d) all in all, I am inclined to feel I am a failure e) at times I feel I am no good at all	Scale of 0–3 per question, where: 0 = strongly agree; 3 = strongly disagree Total scale: 0–15	0.71

Source: Keung 2007, p.81

Figure 9.1 presents results based on our own analysis of successive waves and shows that there is little evidence of change in subjective well-being over this period (Keung 2007).

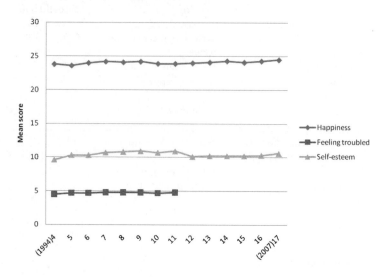

Figure 9.1 Subjective well-being of 11–15-year-old young people from the 1994/5–2007/8 British Household Panel Survey

Source: Keung 2007, p.90.

The other main source is an international survey, the *Health Behaviour of School-Aged Children* (HBSC), which is based on a school-based sample of 11, 13 and 15-year-olds undertaken every four years – the most recent being in 2005–6 (Currie *et al.* 2008). There are a number of questions covering subjective well-being in this survey.

We (Bradshaw and Richardson 2009) have used the following in our domains of subjective well-being and children's relationships:

Subjective well-being

- Personal well-being
    - % who report high life satisfaction using Cantril's Ladder (Cantril 1965)
- Well-being at school
    - % who feel pressured by school work
    - % liking school a lot

- Self-defined health
  - ∘ % who rate their health as fair or poor

Children's relationships

- Quality of family relations
  - ∘ % who find it easy to talk to mothers
  - ∘ % who find it easy to talk to fathers
- Peer relationships
  - ∘ % who find their classmates kind and helpful.

It is possible to use these questions to trace change over time (Richardson 2010). Figure 9.2 shows the distribution of the percentage with high life satisfaction in 2001–2 and 2005–6. The level of life satisfaction has remained quite stable in Great Britain but improved in Estonia and deteriorated in Hungary.

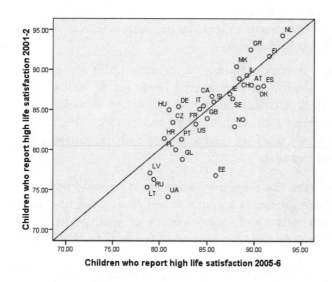

Figure 9.2 Children who report high life satisfaction in 2001–2 and 2005–6 (HBSC)

There is currently a debate in progress about whether we need to be worried about subjective well-being. In their index of child well-being that followed our earlier work very closely, the OECD (2009) left out the subjective well-being domain (except well-being at school) and any indicator on relationships – on the grounds that their member governments did not consider these were policy-amenable: 'It is unclear how governments concerned with family and peer relationships and subjective well-being would go about designing policies to improve outcomes in these dimensions' (OECD 2009, p.29). In the Third OECD World Forum on 'Statistics, Knowledge and Policy' in 2009, there was also discussion about whether the development of the initiative *Measuring of Australia's Progress* (MAP) should include 'some subjective indicators, most notably a measure of happiness' (Pink 2009, p.6).

The EU report (Tarki/Applica 2010) on child poverty and child well-being has also excluded subjective well-being but (at the time of writing) suggests that relationship indicators might be included, because social capital – 'bonding' and 'bridging' social links – has been shown to be important in long-term career success as well as to the cohesiveness of society. (This is, incidentally, a lovely example of well-becoming having precedence over well-being.)

Another argument that one hears is that subjective well-being is subjective – soft – in contrast to some harder, more objective indicators. Thus Pink (2009, p.6) argues that:

> although the Australian Bureau of Statistics (ABS) has given primacy to objective over subjective measures of wellbeing, apparently there is continuing community interest in measuring subjective concepts such as quality of life and happiness. The users have continuously raised the need to include both these subjective and objective measures.

We would argue here that subjective well-being is measured using well-established scales in surveys, and so it is no less hard or soft or objective or subjective than measures of income poverty or reading literacy. The argument is confusing the ideas of subjective/self expressed with subjective/qualitative.

Another argument given for ignoring subjective well-being in international comparisons is that it is a function of national cultural differences. So, for example, the argument goes, Hungarian children have lower subjective well-being because they are 'naturally' morose, and, in contrast, Dutch children are somehow 'naturally' happier – even controlling for all the influences on happiness. Therefore international differences in happiness are not real, but just cultural artefacts. We have seen no evidence to support this view. There is a small literature on self-perceived health that tends to suggest that a very small proportion of variation can be explained by type of welfare regime (see, e.g. Eikemo *et al.* 2008). Torsheim *et al.* (2006) found that adolescents' self-perceived health varied with the degree of inequality within a country, but that is not an indicator of national cultural difference.

Of course, there may be different linguistic understandings of happiness (or more specifically in the case of Cantril's ladder (see pp.188–9) 'the best possible life'), and this may influence responses, but, again, this is not necessarily a cultural factor. In fact, this view is supported by research evidence that demonstrates that unobserved variables (such as diverse cultural differences, expectations and norms) that cause the problem of systematic reporting can be mitigated by the use of 'anchoring vignettes' (Rice, Robone and Smith 2010). This technique has been used in recent comparative research of health-system performance in 17 EU countries, based on the World Health Survey data, conducted by Rice *et al.* (2010) to reduce the problem systematic reporting of behaviours. Rice and his research team show that, once the data is adjusted for differential reporting behaviour, it is possible to 'partition observed differences in self-reported responses into differences due to reporting behaviour and genuine differences in the underlying latent construct under scrutiny' (Rice *et al.* 2010, p.85). This technique can potentially be applied to international child well-being research, though the technique itself is still being developed.

There is also, admittedly, a good deal of uncertainty about how subjective well-being should be measured, which may also be deterring analysts from including it. At the International Society for Child Indicators Conference in 2009 the Australian Institute of Health and Welfare used this argument as objection to incorporating subjective indicators in their battery of child well-being indicators.

In contrast there are those that see subjective well-being as the *essence* of well-being. Health is health, education is education, but well-being is what children feel and express. There is some support for this view in the United Nations Convention on the Rights of the Child: 'the primary consideration in all actions concerning children must be in their best interest and their views must be taken into account' (Articles 3 and 12, UNICEF 2009). One way in which we can take their views into account is by asking children what they think and feel in surveys.

Children's Society surveys

This is the view that has been taken by the Children's Society in England. In the absence of good data on subjective well-being in 2005 they launched a school-based survey, one of the main objectives of which was to estimate the prevalence of runaways (Rees and Lee 2005). But the survey also contained a lot of questions relating to subjective well-being and we subsequently explored this data (Bradshaw *et al.* 2009). In 2008 the Children's Society repeated the survey but this time its *main* purpose was to investigate subjective well-being. The survey was a random sample of mainstream primary and secondary schools in England, covering Years 6, 8 and 10 (10–15-year-olds). One class was randomly selected in each school. The total sample was just under 7,000 – over 2,000 in each of the three age groups. Respondents completed a self-completion questionnaire in a classroom setting. The questions covered a great variety of approaches to subjective well-being, drawing on questions, scales and measures that had been used in previous research. One of the objectives was to establish a reliable and valid set of measures of subjective well-being that could be used in subsequent surveys. A report on the survey was then published (Rees *et al.* 2010).

In the rest of this chapter we are focusing on three issues. In the next section we compare and contrast three scales of subjective well-being. Then we analyse variations in subjective well-being. Finally, we develop an explanatory framework for subjective well-being. In general, our objective is to shift thinking forward on the subject and leave those who come after us with a battery of measures to draw on.

Measures of subjective well-being

The Children's Society survey used three existing measures of subjective well-being. The first of these is Cantril's ladder (Cantril 1965). Young people are shown a picture of a vertical ladder with 11 rungs and asked to place themselves on the ladder, with 10 being the best possible life for you and 0 being the worst possible life for you. The second approach was developed by Cummins and Lau (2006) for use with adults and later developed by Casas *et al.* (2007) for children. It is an 11-point Likert Scale on 'Happiness with life as a whole'. The third approach was adapted from Huebner's life-satisfaction scale (1994). Huebner's original scale had five-point Likert Scales in response to seven items:

1. 'My life is going well.'

2. 'My life is just right.'

3. 'I would like to change things in my life.'*

4. 'I wish I had a different kind of life.'

5. 'I have a good life.'

6. 'I have what I want in life.'

7. 'My life is better than most young people.'*[3]

On testing the scalability of these items we found that we could drop the two items marked with asterisks without any loss of explanatory power.

The original intention was to use all three scales separately as we thought that there was a distinction to be made between life satisfaction and happiness. However, it became apparent that there was such a degree of overlap between these scales that we were merely repeating ourselves in a tedious manner. So, which scale to choose? As the answer did not seem to be obvious we decided to combine all three scales into a composite scale by taking the average of the standardised (z) scores. Table 9.2 shows the correlation between each of the scales and shows they are all closely related to the composite scale.

Table 9.2 Correlation matrix of subjective well-being scales

	Cantril's ladder	Happiness with life as a whole	Huebner's life satisfaction	Composite
Cantril's ladder	1	.57**	.70**	.87**
Happiness with life as a whole		1	.66**	.86**
Huebner's life satisfaction			1	.90**
Composite				1

**p<0.01

The overall distribution of subjective well-being is generally positive (they are happy) with a tail of those with lower than average well-being.

Variations in subjective well-being

We then sought to explore how subjective well-being varied. This task was approached by first exploring the individual characteristics of the child and then the family characteristics.

The individual characteristics were:

- age**

- gender**

- disability**

- religious affiliation*

- ethnicity*

- country of birth.

As indicated by the asterisks, there were some statistically significant variation by each of these factors except country of birth. Age was the most important factor, with older children having lower subjective well-being than younger ones. Girls had lower subjective well-being than boys. However, the most striking finding was that very little of the variation in subjective well-being (3–4%) could be explained by these individual characteristics.

We then looked at family factors. These were:

- poverty**

- family structure*

- number of siblings.

Poverty and family structure (being in a lone-parent family) were associated with lower subjective well-being. But again, the contribution was only marginal – between them explaining only between 1 and 2.5 per cent of variation in subjective well-being.

We then put these variables together in a regression and the results are presented in Table 9.3. It can be seen that age, gender, disability, learning difficulties, single parents and adults in work make a contribution to explaining variation in subjective well-being. Ethnicity and country of origin do not. Religion is marginal. However, all these factors together only explain 7 per cent of the variation in subjective well-being.

Table 9.3 Regression of subjective well-being against individual and family characteristics

Socio-demographic characteristics	B	SE B	ß	t	Sig.
Constant	.266	.096		2.768	.006
Year group (base 10)					
6	1.007	.097	.190	10.341	.000
8	.391	.093	.077	4.221	.000
Gender (base male)					
Female	-.269	.078	-.055	-3.452	.001
Disability (base no)					
Yes	-1.003	.354	-.046	-2.834	.005
Learning difficulty (base no)					
Yes	-1.030	.159	-.105	-6.486	.000
Ethnicity (base White)					
Black	-.338	.229	-.024	-1.472	.141
Pakistani/Bangladeshi	-.578	.310	-.049	-1.865	.062
Indian	-.045	.267	-.003	-.168	.867
Mixed	-.316	.188	-.027	-1.679	.093
Other	-.562	.257	-.037	-2.185	.029
Country of origin (base UK born)					
Non-UK born	-.156	.177	-.015	-.884	.377
Religious affiliation (base none)					
Christian	.229	.085	.046	2.696	.007
Muslim	.436	.271	.044	1.608	.108
Other	-.004	.177	.000	-.023	.982
Family structure (base both parents)					
Step-parents	-.166	.148	-.021	-1.126	.260
Single parent	-.446	.127	-.073	-3.520	.000

continued

Table 9.3 Regression of subjective well-being against
individual and family characteristcs *cont.*

Socio-demographic characteristics	B	SE B	ß	t	Sig.
Other	-.407	-.108	-.068	-2.777	.000
Living with siblings, 1st home only (base yes)					
No	-.288	.120	-.049	-2.403	.016
Adults in paid job (base two or more)					
None	-.615	.204	-.050	-3.017	.003
One	-.258	.092	-.046	-2.805	.005

R^2 = .072 (Adjusted R^2 = .067), F = 14.724, p = .000, N = 3809

In order to explore whether we could explain more of subjective well-being we undertook two further analyses. First, we tested the hypothesis that subjective well-being might be associated with recent life events. The survey asked whether the child had experienced any of the following life events in the previous 12 months:

- change in family structure**
- change in home
- change in school
- change in local area
- experiences of being bullied**
- experiences of being treated unfairly by adults.**

Experiences of changes in family structure, being bullied and being treated unfairly by adults were associated with lower subjective well-being but between them they only explained 12–13 per cent of the variation. It is interesting that children who had moved home, school and area did not have lower subjective well-being.

We then investigated whether an accumulation of life experiences might result in lower subjective well-being. In Figure 9.3 we include disability, poverty and change in family structure. Children having none of these problems had higher subjective well-being than those having all three – but the differences were not large.

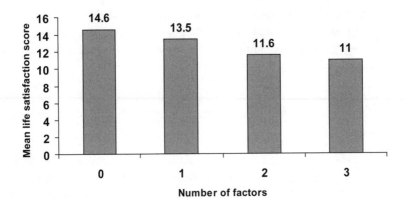

Figure 9.3 Subjective well-being by accumulation of problems

As we have reported above we found that children have generally high levels of subjective well-being, though there is a tail at the bottom of the distribution. We have explored the characteristics of those who were in the bottom 10 per cent of the distribution by using logistic regression. We found that the experience of high levels of family conflict, living in a workless household or being bullied significantly increases the odds of falling into the bottom 10 per cent of the overall well-being distribution. Being a girl or having learning difficulty also increases such odds; being a Christian is, however, associated with lower odds. These variables explained more of the overall subjective well-being (Nagelkerke $R^2 = 0.20$).[4] The 'change' variables, family types and other socio-economic variables analysed were excluded by the model.

These results are quite perplexing but they are not unexpected. We know from previous studies that subjective well-being varies with age and gender (see, e.g. Currie *et al*. 2008; Quilgars, Searle and Keung 2006). Others who have attempted to explain subjective well-being have also had limited success (see Bradshaw *et al*. 2009; Clarke, Bradshaw and Williams 2000; Keung 2006, 2007).

What are the possible explanations for these results?

- There may be problems with our dependent variable – our measures of subjective well-being. For example, are these merely picking up transient moods, rather than a substantive emotional state or core affect (Russell 2003)?

- There are certainly some problems with our independent variables – for example, it is not easy to ask children about their material well-being and in this analysis we classified as poor those children who lacked an employed adult in the household or who were in receipt of free school meals.

- It is possible that cross-sectional survey data fails to pick up the impact of important events – in, for example, early childhood or later child abuse.

- There is evidence that personality traits and genetics may be important determining factors in subjective well-being (Diener and Lucas 1998; Diener *et al.* 1999). We did not include questions on personality in our questionnaire, though we will do in future research.

- Possibly the best explanation of these results is the theory of dynamic equilibrium or homeostasis. Cummins (2009) argues that subjective well-being is an innate personal characteristic – managed by a system of psychological devices (not personality), which have evolved to ensure a Homeostatically Protected Mood (HPMood). Cummins explains:

> We experience HPMood as a combination of contentment, happiness and positive arousal thus giving us a normally positive view of ourselves. It is further proposed that when homeostasis fails, due to the overwhelming nature of a negative challenge, people lose contact with HPMood and experience the dominance of negative rather than positive affect. When this condition is chronic, people experience depression. (Cummins 2009, p.17)

So, if this is true, we do not pick up variation associated with socio-demographic differences or life events because they have been mitigated by the automatic processes of adaptation and habituation. Cummins (2009) argues that homeostasis does involve both external and internal buffers. Thus external factors like wealth or relationships can help to protect against homeostatic failure. Also internal buffers – a mixture of affect and cognition – such as a sense of control or self-esteem can assist adaptation. But basically adaptation is a genetically adaptive process.

All this could lead us to conclude that those who are sceptical about the value of taking account of subjective well-being are right. But to be so they are not *entirely* right – the fact that we have significant coefficients on socio-demographic factors demonstrates that subjective well-being is to some extent policy-amenable. But the fact that so little variation has been explained may nevertheless lead one to conclude that the outcome may not be worth the effort. However, before we reach such a conclusion we need to further explore the nature of well-being.

The construction of subjective well-being

Our understanding from previous work on the subject led us to develop a framework for understanding what contributes to subjective well-being (Rees, Francis and Robbins 2005). We hypothesised that subjective well-being would be influenced by three key domains of a child's life: social relationships, feelings about themselves, and material and physical environment. We then identified a sense of safety and freedom as two important cross-cutting themes that we also wished to explore, although there is room for debate about the latter – for example, Cummins and Lau (2006) have argued that freedom is not of the same order as the other domains.

Each of these domains could be measured using related indicators. The Children's Society survey had included a very large number of questions covering these domains, and the first task was to undertake a data-reduction exercise. This was accomplished using factor analysis. The results are summarised in Tables 9.4 to 9.8.

Table 9.4 shows that we started with 25 indicators on relationships and, using factor analysis, we found (as expected) that they can be divided into three components – relationships with families, relationships with friends and relationships with neighbours. The indicators extracted for each component are in italics. We found that five indicators maximised the variation in relationship with family, four relationships with friends and two relationships with neighbours, each with good levels of internal reliability with Cronbach's Alpha above 0.8.

Table 9.4 Factor analysis of relationship indicators

25 indicators on relationships	Factor extracted
I enjoy being at home with my family. I like spending time with my carers. *My parents or carers treat me fairly.* *My family get along well together.* *My parents or carers and I do fun things together.* *My parents listen to my views and take me seriously.* Members of my family talk nicely to one another. How happy are you with your family? My family is better than most. My parents or carers care about me. I help make decisions in my family.	Relationship with family 57.74% explained variance α = 0.87
My friends treat me well. My friends are nice to me. I wish I had different friends. My friends are mean to me. *My friends are great.* I have a bad time with my friends. *I have a lot of fun with my friends.* I have enough friends. *My friends will help me if I need it.* How happy are you with your friends?	Relationship with friends 58.70% explained variance α = 0.85
Adults in my area listen to young people's views. I like my neighbours. *Adults in my area treat young people fairly.* I wish there were different people in my area.	Relationship with neighbours 68.49% explained variance α = 0.81

(Side label: Relationships domain)

Table 9.5 covers the factor analysis of 35 items relating to self. They formed into the following components – a self-concept (or esteem) with six indicators, health with two indicators, school work with four indicators, the future (or, possibly, resilience) with five indicators, and leisure with two indicators. The indicators in these components had adequate to good levels of internal reliability.

Table 9.5 Factor analysis of self indicators

	35 indicators on 'self'	Factor extracted
Self domain	*A lot of things about me are good.* I can't do anything right [reverse coded]. *In general, I like being the way I am.* I do lots of important things. *Overall I have a lot to be proud of.* *I can do things as well as most other people.* Overall I am no good [reverse coded]. Other people think I am a good person. *I am as good as most other people.* *When I do something, I do it well.* I think I am doing pretty well. I am doing just as well as other young people my age.	Self-concept 51.55% variance explained α = 0.86
	How happy are you with your health? *Would you say your health is good or bad?* [Good–bad scale] In the last month how often did a health problem cause you to miss doing things? Emotional-health problem scale.	Health 81.09% variance explained α = 0.60
	How happy are you about your school work? How well do you feel you are doing at school? *I look forward to going to school.* *I wish I didn't have to go to school* [reverse coded]. *School is interesting.* I like being in school. *There are many things about school I don't like* [reverse coded]. I enjoy school activities.	School work 58.60% variance explained α = 0.76

continued

Table 9.5 Factor analysis of self indicators *cont.*

	35 indicators on 'self'	Factor extracted
Self domain	I learn a lot at school. I feel bad at school [reverse coded]. How important do you think it is for you to get good marks?	School work 58.60% variance explained α = 0.76
	I think the things I have done in the past will help me in the future. *I feel positive about my future.* *If I succeed in life it will be because of my efforts.* *My own efforts and actions are what will determine my future.* *What I do and how I do it will determine my successes in life.*	The future 49.33% variance explained α = 0.83
	How happy are you about how you spend your time? *How happy are you about how you enjoy yourself?* Leisure scale.	Leisure 83.25% variance explained α = 0.80

In Table 9.6 nine indicators of personal freedom could be reduced to five to form a single component. Again, the internal reliability of the indicators is reasonably good.

Table 9.6 Factor analysis of freedom indicators

	9 indicators on freedom	Factor extracted
Freedom domain	*I have enough choice about how I spend my time.* *How happy are you about the amount of choice you have in life?* *I feel like I am free to decide for myself how to live my life.* *How happy are you about the amount of freedom you have?* *I generally feel free to express my ideas and opinions.* I feel pressured in my life. In my daily life, I often have to do what I am told. I feel like I can pretty much be myself in my daily situation. I have plenty of freedom in the area I live in.	Personal freedom 55.49% variance explained α = 0.73

There were 16 indicators covering the environment domain in Table 9.7. We were unable to produce a solution that summarised the indicators of material well-being, so in order to represent that component we used two proxy indicators of family economic condition – 'adults with a paid job' and 'free school meals'. Living environment was represented by two subcomponents – residence and recreation – each of which has four and three indicators respectively, and they both have good levels of internal reliability.

Table 9.7 Factor analysis of living environment indicators

	16 indicators on environment	Factor extracted
Living environment domain	How happy are you about the things you have? On average, how much money of your own do you have to spend each week? How well off do you think your family is? *How many adults that you live with have a paid job?* *Do you receive free school meals?*	Un-factorable The italicised two indicators on the left are selected to assess family economic condition
	How happy are you about the home you live in? I have enough privacy at home. How happy are you with your local area? I have plenty of freedom in the area I live in. *I wish I lived in a different house.* *I wish I lived somewhere else.* *I like where I live.* *My home is nice.* *There are lots of fun things to do where I live.* *There are places for me to go in my area.* *There is nothing to do in my area.*	Living environment 55.42% variance explained 2 factors extracted: 1st factor: Residence α = 0.79 2nd factor: Recreation α = 0.81

There were seven indicators relating to the safety domain in Table 9.8 and we did not succeed in obtaining a factor score from them. So, instead, we used one proxy variable, which asks about how happy respondents feel about their own safety.

Table 9.8 Factor analysis of safety indicators

	7 indicators on safety	Factor extracted
Safety domain	*How happy are you about how safe you feel?*	Un-factorable
	I feel safe at home.	The italicised indicator on the left is selected to access feeling safe in general
	I feel safe with my friends.	
	In the past 12 months how often have you been bullied by other young people?	
	I feel safe at school.	
	I feel safe when I am out in my local area during the day.	
	I feel safe when I am out in my local area at night.	

After this process of data reduction we had measures (either factor scores or individual variables) representing the five domains, and within them we have identified ten separate components. How do these domains and components relate to our composite subjective well-being measure? Table 9.9 presents correlation coefficients between the domain and components and the overall child well-being. The 'self' domain has the strongest association with overall well-being, followed by 'freedom' and 'relationships'. 'Safety' is less important than these. Within 'relationships' family is much more closely associated with overall well-being than are friends and neighbours. Within 'self', leisure, health and self-concept are more important than school work and future. We are not able to correlate material well-being because it is a dichotomous variable; however, living environment appears to be fairly closely associated with overall well-being.

These are bivariate correlations. In Table 9.10 we explore the relationship between overall subjective well-being and the well-being components. The model explains 58 per cent of the variation in overall subjective well-being. Personal freedom, health, family relations and leisure explain most of the variation in subjective well-being. Personal freedom by itself explains 35 per cent of the variation. Although all the other variables make a contribution to subjective well-being, relationships with friends, safety, economic conditions and school work are only marginally important, contributing only 1.3 per cent.

Table 9.9 Correlation between overall subjective
well-being and domains and components of well-being

Domain	r with overall well-being	Component	r with overall well-being
Relationships	0.58**	Family	0.54**
		Friends	0.27**
		Neighbours	0.19**
Self	0.63**	Self-concept	0.51**
		Health	0.51**
		School work	0.32**
		Future	0.32**
		Leisure	0.54**
Freedom	0.60**	–	–
Environment	–	Material	–
		Living environment	0.48**
Safety	0.47**	–	–

** $p<0.01$

Table 9.10 Regression of the overall subjective
well-being against all the well-being components

	Unstandardised coefficients		Standardised coefficients		
	B	Std. error	Beta	t	Sig.
(Constant)	.024	.014		1.750	.080
Personal freedom	.114	.019	.132	6.120	.000
Health	.142	.015	.168	9.633	.000
Family	.182	.016	.217	11.356	.000
Leisure	.163	.017	.186	9.645	.000
Self-concept	.118	.016	.140	7.386	.000
Living environment	.109	.019	.106	5.779	.000

continurd

Table 9.10 Regression of the overall subjective well-being against all the well-being components *cont.*

	Unstandardised coefficients		Standardised coefficients		
	B	Std. error	Beta	t	Sig.
Friends	.069	.014	.081	4.898	.000
Happiness: about how safe you feel (1 = unhappy)	-.247	.048	-.081	-5.131	.000
Family economic condition (1 = poor)	-.178	.042	-.064	-4.228	.000
School work	.050	.014	.060	3.671	.000

$R^2 = 0.58$; $F (10, 1863) = 254.20$; $p<0.001$ (based on Stepwise; n = 1874)

We also explored the bottom 10 per cent of the overall well-being distribution by using logistic regression to see which well-being components might be important in reducing the odds of being in the bottom 10 per cent of the distribution. After controlling for the effect of the other well-being components, family relations, self-concept, school work, leisure, health, living environment and freedom all reduce the risk of falling into the bottom 10 per cent of the overall well-being distribution. Unhappiness about material possession and feeling safe significantly increases the risk. Relationships with friends and neighbours, the future and recreation make no difference.

Discussion and conclusion

This chapter has explored subjective well-being of children drawing on the Children's Society Survey 2008. We have explored three standard scales of subjective well-being and combined them into an overall measure. We find that many characteristics of the child and the family are associated with subjective well-being but none of them are particularly important, and, having controlled for them, the vast majority of variation in subjective well-being remains unexplained. We have discussed the possible reasons for this. In future research it would be useful to include some measures of personality in order to be able to assess its impact on well-being. But the theory of homeostasis seems to present the best explanation for these findings.

We then explored the construction of subjective well-being. This started with a data-reduction exercise that identified a subset of variables that contributed to measures of well-being domains and components. This exercise was successful for all domains except that we could not develop a factor score for material well-being and safety. We then explored the association between these elements of well-being and the overall well-being measure and found that we could explain well over half of the variation in overall well-being using these measures. Some very interesting findings emerged. Children's sense of 'freedom' (perhaps self-reliance) is very important to their overall well-being. This finding has some resonance with the Whitehall studies that found that health and well-being was more associated with self-efficacy than other factors (see, e.g. Bosma, Stansfeld and Marmot 1998; Marmot *et al.* 1997). In the relationship domain, relationship with family is much more important than relationship with friends and neighbours even for these teenage children. School work, family economic condition and feelings of safety were much less important.

If these findings are right then a number of conclusions follow. Reducing poverty or attempting to maintain traditional family structures are unlikely in themselves to have major impacts on subjective well-being – though they may have other benefits. Enabling children to feel in control of their own lives and maintaining non-conflictual family relationships (whatever the structure) are likely to have more impact. Girls need more of this than boys to maintain their well-being and, if we can discover why it happens, we need to see how to reduce the deterioration in subjective well-being by age.

There remain a number of challenges. We still believe that the level of subjective well-being matters and that it matters even though it may not be 'policy-amenable'. However, we expect that it *is* policy-amenable, and evaluation studies of areas such as anti-bullying strategies, rights-respecting schools and social and emotional education could *demonstrate* that it is – despite homeostasis. There have been some of these (see, e.g. Coleman 2007, 2009; Hallam 2009; NICE 2008; Seligman *et al.* 2009) but there is a need for more. We will be doing more work on the individual components of subjective well-being. We have yet to understand why there are such variations between countries when we are unable to explain much of the variation *within* countries. We need more studies of subjective well-being at the micro (national population) level that enable us to compare results at the macro (country) level, and there are a number of countries that have started doing studies that can help here. Work on subjective well-being is really only in its infancy but we believe it is both really interesting and potentially very important.

Notes

1   The indicator is one of the 64 indicators that are drawn from the national indicator set (NIS) and used by central government to monitor and manage performance of local authorities and their local partners in their delivery of services to children, young people and families. Thus the director and lead member of children's services are being held accountable for performance of the overall children's services.
2   Cronbach's Alpha is a measure of scalability – the nearer to 1.0 the more reliable the item in the scale.
3   The asterisks found here and throughout the chapter are conventional indicators of statistical significance: * = <0.05; ** = <0.01 and *** = 0.001.
4   The Nagelkerke R^2 indicates the proportion of variance explained by the model.

Part 3

Child Well-Being: Looking Towards the Future

CHAPTER 10

Child Well-Being: Current Issues and Future Directions

Colette McAuley and Wendy Rose

Introduction

In this concluding chapter we reflect on four sets of issues that have emerged from this volume about how the child well-being agenda is adding to our understanding of children's lives, and how the landscape of policy and practice is changing as a result. Although academics, professionals and policy makers are comfortable using child well-being as a way of capturing our aspirations for all children (contested though the definition may be), as yet there is still some way to go before it could be said that children and families are fully included in the debate. Their perspectives on well-being are therefore examined further in this chapter.

Throughout the chapters we have been struck by the opening up of debates about dimensions of well-being that do not seem to be contained in some of the frameworks, such as the five *Every Child Matters* outcomes. We look again at some of the implications about taking an ecological perspective (the fit between child well-being and the well-being of families and the community) and embracing the new thinking about happiness. The importance of families and the wider community to the well-being of children becomes even more apparent.

The third set of issues on which we reflect is the diversity with which the term child well-being is currently being used and, as a result, is providing a shared language that is reaping benefits as well as opening up more dilemmas and questions.

Finally, we turn to the thorny issues of measurement – *how* do we know how well our children are doing? Looking to future directions we pick up the importance of the child indicators movement and the growing interest in subjective well-being as another important dimension.

We conclude where we started – thinking again about how children can help to shape our understanding of their lives and how they can become even more actively involved in measuring and monitoring their own well-being.

Child well-being – The views of parents and children

One of the most interesting points arising from a recent consultation with parents, carers and young people about what constitutes a 'good' or 'content' childhood was the finding that this important topic was actually rarely publicly discussed among parents and children or in society in general (Counterpoint 2008).

> It's incredibly important. I don't think we talk about this often enough!
>
> *(A single-parent mother cited in Counterpoint 2008)*

And although parents' and carers' immediate reaction was that it was 'common sense' and that everyone was aware of the definitions and components, on discussion they reached the conclusion that it was in fact a challenging topic. Where they became uncomfortable was in identifying the components of a 'good' or 'content' childhood. Parents felt they were being judgemental when discussing other families. They also felt the weight of responsibility when discussing what made their children happy, whilst feeling relatively powerless about the influences on their children outside of the family. Nevertheless, after considerable debate, the parents and young people reached an extraordinary degree of consensus. They identified the following key factors (in the order given) as being essential for a good/content childhood:

- family
- friends
- schools
- wider community/other influences.

(Counterpoint 2008, p.36)

Family was absolutely paramount in their minds.

In contrast, key factors identified by parents and carers as *undermining* a good, content childhood were:

- no 'safe environment'
- financial pressures
- limited opportunities for 'quality' family time
- pressure to buy things for children/young people
- political correctness 'gone mad'
- 'It's our culture, we don't like children'.

(Counterpoint 2008, p.54)

In McAuley, Morgan and Rose (Chapter 2, this volume), the need to ask young people directly about their lived experiences was highlighted. In their review of children's perspectives, a number of common messages emerged. One was the importance children attached to not wanting to be seen to stand out as being different from their peers. This was, not least, because that might well lead to bullying. Another, and not unrelated message, was of feeling unsafe. In the Counterpoint consultation, many of the preoccupations of the parents and children centred around the same issues. The young people's perspectives on what could undermine a good childhood were illuminating. Feeling insecure and unsafe appeared to underpin their worries:

> They worried about having nowhere to play or 'hang out'; that it wasn't safe 'outside' (in their neighbourhood, on the roads); families arguing and falling out; not having the same 'stuff' as their friends, or being different in some way; and not having anyone around who's there for you, looking out for you. (Counterpoint 2008, p.19)

Of interest to us here also was the fact that the term 'well-being' was not one with which the parents or young people were familiar. And, further, they had difficulty relating it to their everyday lives. Given that the sample of families were drawn from a range of households from different social groups, included different family types and were drawn from across England, this is a very important finding. The researchers reached the conclusion that parents, carers and young people had become distanced from the debate about what makes for a good childhood.

There is another important underlying issue, too. If government, academics and professionals are constructing conceptualisations without including parents and children in those debates, there is a very serious danger of disenfranchisement of families. Considering the sense of engagement with the issue that emerged in this consultation, however, there is every possibility that children and their families would welcome being part of a much greater debate with policy makers and professionals about the quality of childhood they would like every child in the UK to experience. As has been demonstrated, many authors in this volume see child well-being as a social construct, serving a purpose for people in society at this point. If it is to be the dominant discourse around children, parents and children need to be given the opportunity to shape the concept. Their involvement as key stakeholders would then mean that the discourse is grounded in reality. It might also allow families to feel more involvement and investment in policy development.

Child well-being: Making sense of the theoretical background

Of all the theoretical influences on the concept of child well-being, four stand out as particularly important:

- the ecological perspective on children's development

- the concept of wellness

- the sociology of childhood

- the new science of happiness.

Since children's rights and the sociology of childhood have been addressed in earlier chapters (see Ben-Arieh, Chapter 6, this volume; McAuley, Morgan and Rose, Chapter 2, this volume), we want to concentrate here on why the ecological perspective and the current work by psychologists on wellness and happiness are so important.

Increasingly, children's development is considered from an ecological perspective, that is within the context of their social environment. In an ecological model, children are seen as actively influencing their environment through their behaviour and contacts with others:

> This considers the child within their environment surrounded by layers of successively larger and more complex social groupings, which have an influence on him or her. These include the family and extended family, friendship networks, school, neighbourhood,

and work influences, and the family's place within the community. Still wider is the influence of the culture within which the family live. (Jones and Ramchandani 1999, p.2)

Children's personalities and intrinsic capabilities influence how they interact with others in their environment. How they function socially and their cultural norms are also thought to be important factors in this interchange.

Psychologists developing the concept of child and family wellness have also adopted an ecological approach:

Child wellness is predicated on the satisfaction of material, physical, affective, and psychological needs. Wellness is an ecological concept: a child's wellness is determined by the level of parental, familial, communal and social wellness. (Prilleltensky and Nelson 2000 p.87)

Prilleltensky and Nelson define family wellness as 'the presence of supportive, affectionate and gratifying relationships that serve to promote the personal development of family members and the collective well-being of the family as a whole' (Prilleltensky and Nelson 2000, p.87). The issue is that this comes through the satisfaction of personal and family wishes at the same time. Further, they see wellness at these levels as intricately linked to the state of the wider community in which they live:

Parents who enjoy physical and psychological health, and who have access to adequate financial resources, will be in a good position to provide a wellness-enhancing environment for their children. Parental wellness, in turn, is based on the opportunities afforded them by the community in which they reside. (Prilleltensky and Nelson 2000, p.87)

These authors recognise the powerful impact of socio-economic, cultural and contextual factors in shaping the lives of children and families. Hence their framework for interventions to promote child and family wellness includes consideration of interventions/services needed at child, family, community and society levels. However, it also introduces a values dimension that locates interventions along a continuum ranging from the individualist to the collectivist model. They see balancing individualist with collectivist values as crucial as, they argue, strong communities are vital in supporting private citizens to achieve their goals.

> Collectivist values support the equalization of access to valued societal resources and foster a sense of community that is missing from today's society. (Prilleltensky and Nelson 2000, p.90)

Recent research on happiness has also been influential. Most of this research has been adult-focused and concerned with the quality of life, specifically in relation to people with disabilities. Research on the concept of happiness has its roots in 'hedonic psychology', which concerns itself with self-assessed evaluations of quality of life. The work of Daniel Kahneman and colleagues has particularly advanced our thinking on the concept and its measurement. They have examined complex issues such as how moments of pleasure relate to overall assessment of well-being and, indeed, which aspects of life contribute most significantly to levels of satisfaction (Kahneman, Diener and Schwarz 1999).

Deeply influenced by Kahneman's work, economists such as Layard (2005) have turned their attention to the 'new science of happiness' to attempt to explain the disparity between the increasing wealth in countries such as the UK and the lack of increased life satisfaction. Drawing on a range of evidence predominantly from the new science of happiness, Layard concludes that increasing wealth does not bring associated happiness. He recognises that to explain a person's level of happiness we need to consider external and internal factors. With regard to sources of happiness, he highlights two areas: humans are deeply social beings and, as social beings, we want to trust each other. His thesis is that material and financial inequity does not create trusting relationships or, indeed, a trustful society. Overall, his message is that it is relationships that are central to our happiness and that we need to take the pursuit of happiness seriously as a policy goal for the sake of everyone's well-being in our society.

Both research on happiness and Layard's reflections are based upon consideration of adults' sense of satisfaction with their lives. However, they open up a whole new set of questions in relation to children and *their* sense of satisfaction, happiness and well-being. We already have strong evidence of the importance of close family relationships in children's lives (see McAuley, Morgan and Rose, Chapter 2, this volume). In the Counterpoint consultation with parents and young people, family was seen to be by far the most important factor in achieving a good/content childhood (Counterpoint 2008). And a considerable amount of emphasis was placed by children in a range of family situations on the need to feel safe, secure and be with people you can trust (McAuley, Morgan and Rose, Chapter 2, this volume). We also know from these sources that children and their parents want to feel safe in the communities in which they live out their daily lives. Given our growing understanding of the importance of the environment, working to create strong, safe communities wherein people feel they can trust each other would appear to be one of the greatest investments we could make in improving children's well-being.

Child well-being: Facilitating positive change

Underpinning the current discourse about child well-being are some important shifts (discussed above) in our thinking about childhood, children, human well-being generally, and the respective roles of families and the State. These are long-running themes that individually can be traced back through the last century and beyond, but their current potency is in the way they have come together for debate in public arenas, crossing the boundaries of different disciplines. These shifts are changing the landscape. We have economists talking about happiness, psychologists exploring community wellness and the impact of social policy, and the Archbishop of Canterbury arguing 'for a systematic willingness to pay attention to how children and young people actually talk about themselves, and perhaps above all for a realistic and grateful appreciation of who and what our young people really are' (Layard and Dunn 2009, p.178).

Against this backcloth, the term 'child well-being' is being used widely and in very different ways. The two studies of child well-being commissioned by the Department for Children, Schools and Families (Counterpoint 2008; Ereaut and Whiting 2008) give ample evidence of uncertainty, ambiguity and instability in its definition, usage and function (let alone its spelling, be it one word, two words or hyphenated).

> Wellbeing is a cultural construct and represents a shifting set of meanings — wellbeing is no less than what a group or groups of people collectively agree makes 'a good life'. (Ereaut and Whiting 2008, p.1)

It is not a term that trips off the tongue or is part of the everyday language of the wider population, as discussed earlier. As one mother asked, 'Should we know what it means?' (Counterpoint 2008, p.1).

Furthermore, the definition and use of child well-being will continue to be subject to change. Three contributory factors to this can be identified:

1. The changing context inevitably has an impact. In addition to the influence of new thinking and new research about children, there are political events, such as elections and economic crises, which lead to reordering of priorities, commitment and resources. New

interests may emerge, such as a focus on issues of cost-effectiveness over the life trajectory, i.e. attempting to cost what might be the effects on later public expenditure of *not* addressing aspects of child well-being.

2. It all depends on the *purpose* of defining child well-being and who is defining it. This may influence the weight given to involving children in the process and how their contributions are used, and how the pendulum swings in giving emphasis to well-becoming or children's current experiences. Definitions may vary, for instance, if child-welfare agencies or service providers are defining child well-being for the group of vulnerable children in their care according to their terms of reference or mission rather than the outcomes considered desirable for all children in the population.

3. The search for indicators inevitably interacts with how child well-being is defined and 'is not a one-way relationship' (Ben-Arieh, Chapter 6, this volume). Ben-Arieh argues that:

> Thus, new technologies and sources of information shed more light on children's lives, and in doing so influence how we understand and conceptualize children's well-being. This interaction, in turn, calls for new indicators, just as new theories and norms reshape the concept of children's well-being.

Child well-being is, therefore, a term that can be, and is being, used in many different ways but the consequences of this flexibility are not necessarily negative. It can be argued that its use has contributed positively to the changing landscape of debate about children. First, it has provided a unifying framework for exchange and collaboration between the many different disciplines with an interest in children – between sociologists, economists, psychologists, social-policy analysts, criminologists, public-health epidemiologists, educationalists, social workers and many others. This has allowed debates about what is happening to children and what is important in order for them to be able to flourish and be opened up across the public, private and voluntary sectors, between parliamentarians, academics, professionals and the public, and involving children and young people. It has extended into far-reaching international exchange about how well children are doing, about why some children do better than others (within nation states and in comparison with other countries), and about the evidence of the effectiveness of strategies and interventions to bring about desired improvements.

Second, child well-being has provided an all-embracing vision for children's social policy. This vision can assist in the co-ordination of policy aims across disparate areas of government responsibility, and permit analysis of the impact of government departments' activities on the overall policy ambitions of improving children's well-being. Ereaut and Whiting (2008) refer to this as an inspiring ambition but observe that there are some risks involved for policy development by the lead government department, then the Department for Children, Schools and Families (DCSF), now the Department for Education, following the 2010 general election:

> If DCSF aspires to holism, a question arises as to how the Department can possibly measure the kind of 'wellbeing' that is high-level, visionary, ambitious, holistic. (p.17)

Further risks arise by appearing to have captured 'the huge and abstract ideal' of well-being within the five outcomes of *Every Child Matters* (Ereaut and Whiting 2008, p.17). Ereaut and Whiting suggest that:

> this might seem presumptuous and perhaps naïve and create reputational and other risks. Second, DCSF may ultimately seem to be claiming ownership of things for which it cannot be, and did not intend to be, wholly responsible. (p.17)

Whatever the drawbacks and limitations in the way child well-being is defined in government policy in England, Scotland and Wales, there is evidence that it has provided a shared language able to be used positively across disciplines and agencies to develop integrated service planning at the local community level (Aldgate, Chapter 1, this volume; Rose and Rowlands, Chapter 3, this volume). Furthermore, there is evidence of its translation in Scotland into a local, inter-agency model of practice, which is bringing about improvements for children and families and streamlining processes of work within and between agencies (Stradling, MacNeil and Berry 2009).

Within professions, taking a holistic view of children and the development of a shared language for thinking about them has offered a new framework for understanding children's lives and planning how to promote their well-being. This includes explicit consideration being given to the culture, systems and practice within an agency's environment, and the impact these have on children. The value of having a shared perspective and shared language is especially important when professionals become aware that children are not doing as well as they might be expected, and more targeted work is needed with individual children and their families – which may draw in other specialist staff from their own service and staff from other agencies. Munn (Chapter 4, this volume) has demonstrated that the framework can be used to help schools think much more broadly about promoting the well-being of all children by adopting a whole-school approach and addressing issues such as the formal, informal and hidden dimensions of the school curriculum, as well as giving assistance to teachers and other staff when undertaking targeted work with individual children.

Finally, but not least, are the opportunities that child well-being offers to step back and look at the big picture and to think more radically about whether the way in which state services are currently conceived are conducive to achieving the ambitions for children and young people. Jordan, for example, asks searching questions in 'Well-being: The next revolution in children's services?' (2006), about whether the well-being agenda has the potential to reclaim the centrality of relationships in service delivery:

> The well-being agenda (if such a thing exists) could redirect attention to the neglected features of human services – relationships rather than technical expertise – and public policy – coherent contexts for citizenship, rather than a diversity of suppliers. The concept of well-being points service providers to issues about how they give children and young people warm, supportive and consistent adults with whom to explore the world, and an overall system of organisations which help them to make some sense of their experiences of growing up. (p.42)

Jordan concludes by suggesting that:

> The concept of children's well-being is closely related to those of rights, needs, inclusion and material welfare. But it differs by emphasising emotions and experiences rather than claims, skills, deficits or material assets, and by drawing attention to relationships with others rather than to capabilities. (p.46)

Thus the concept of child well-being has the capacity to move us into fundamental, complex and far-reaching debates.

Measuring and comparing well-being: Future directions

There will always be pressures to compare how children are faring in one country in relation to others. And following the UNICEF report there are undoubtedly pressures on the UK and elsewhere to indicate some improvement over time. This, of course, again raises the question about what we understand by well-being and whether there is agreement about the indicators that should be used to measure and monitor it. Whilst comparing progress in one nation or area over time may not be so problematic, measuring across nations (especially when less-developed countries are included) does mean that we are very restricted in the data available for comparison.

The child indicators movement (discussed in detail in Ben-Arieh, Chapter 6, this volume) is relatively new but rapidly expanding. As we have touched upon in earlier chapters, one of the most interesting recent developments in that field has been the growing realisation that we need to include *subjective* accounts along with objective measures as indicators of well-being. This means that children are being consulted as to their views on well-being. Two differing approaches are evident. Using surveys of schoolchildren is the most usual approach – for example, the 'Tellus' online school surveys which aim to 'gather the views of children and young people in Years 6, 8 and 10, on their life, their school and their local area' (Tellus4 2009). The findings from these are intended to inform policy making and to measure progress and performance across the five ECM outcomes at both local and national (England) levels. However, they ask very limited questions and the rationale for the specific questions is unclear. Jonathan Bradshaw, in collaboration with the Children's Society, has been developing a more detailed survey of subjective well-being and the results of this recently completed work are reported in an earlier chapter (Bradshaw *et al.*, Chapter 9, this volume).

A very different approach to subjective well-being is that exemplified by the work of Jan Mason and colleagues in New South Wales. They have directly consulted children in schools about their understanding of well-being. They employed a three-stage qualitative approach involving group and individual interviews along with projects. Based upon the children's responses, they have begun to develop a conceptual framework for understanding children's well-being (Fattore, Mason and Watson 2009). As discussed earlier, they reached the conclusion that the underlying media through which children understood experiences of well-being were children's significant relationships and emotional life. The three overarching dimensions of well-being identified by children were:

- a positive sense of self

- agency-control in everyday life

- security and safety.

This is an example of work where children are shaping our understanding of the concept but also of their *lives*. These children and those who contributed to the research studies and consultations described in the earlier chapter on children's views (McAuley, Morgan and Rose, Chapter 2, this volume) have enriched our adult understanding of their daily lives. Researching children's views on child well-being is as yet at a very early stage but is already raising important issues about how children are involved in the process.

A step beyond that is the suggestion by Ben-Arieh (Chapter 6, this volume) that children should be involved in measuring and monitoring well-being. Ensuring that children are involved effectively and meaningfully will be the challenge, as in their participation in national policy making (Hill *et al.* 2004). Recent work with child researchers (Kellett 2010) would suggest that, with support, children might well be actively designing their own research on well-being in the not too distant future.

References

Aber, L.J. (1997) 'Measuring Child Poverty for Use in Comparative Policy Analysis.' In A. Ben-Arieh and H. Wintersberger (eds) *Monitoring and Measuring the State of Children: Beyond Survival*. Eurosocial Report No. 62. Vienna: European Centre for Social Welfare Policy and Research.

Aber, L.J. and Jones, S. (1997) 'Indicators Of Positive Development in Early Childhood: Improving Concepts and Measures.' In R.M. Hauser, B.V. Brown and W.R. Prosser (eds) *Indicators of Children's Well-Being*. New York: Russell Sage Foundation.

Aber, L.J., Berg, J., Godfrey, E. and Torrente, C. (2010) 'Using Child Indicators to Influence Policy: A Comparative Case Study.' In S.B. Kamerman, S. Phipps and A. Ben-Arieh (eds) *From Child Welfare to Child Well-Being: An International Perspective on Knowledge in the Service of Making Policy*. Dordrecht: Springer.

Aborn, M. (1985) *Statistical Legacies of the Social Indicators Movement*. Paper presented at the annual meeting of the American Statistical Association, Las Vegas, Nevada.

Ainscow, M., Booth, T. and Dyson, A. (2006) *Improving Schools, Developing Inclusion*. London: Routledge.

Alanen, L. (2001) 'Childhood as a Generational Condition.' In L. Alanen and B. Mayall (eds) *Conceptualizing Child–Adult Relations*. London: Falmer

Aldgate, J. (2006) 'Children, Development and Ecology.' In J. Aldgate, D.P.H. Jones, W. Rose and C. Jeffery (eds) *The Developing World of the Child*. London: Jessica Kingsley Publishers.

Aldgate, J. and Jones, D.P.H. (2006) 'The Place of Attachment in Children's Development.' In J. Aldgate, D.P.H. Jones, W. Rose and C. Jeffery (2006) *The Developing World of the Child*. London: Jessica Kingsley Publishers.

Aldgate, J. and McIntosh, J. (2006a) *Looking After the Family – A Study of Children Looked After in Care in Scotland*. Edinburgh: Astron.

Aldgate, J. and McIntosh, J. (2006b) *Time Well Spent: A Study of Well-Being and Children's Daily Activities*. Edinburgh: Astron.

Aldgate, J., Jones, D.P.H., Rose, W. and Jeffery, C. (2006) *The Developing World of the Child*. London: Jessica Kingsley Publishers.

Aldridge, J. and Becker, S. (2003) *Children Who Care for Parents with Mental Illness: The Perspectives of Young Carers, Parents and Professionals*. Bristol: Policy Press.

Alexander, G. and Huberty, T.J. (1993) *Caring for Troubled Children: The Villages Follow-Up Study*. Bloomington, IN: The Villages of Indiana.

Alexander, R. (ed.) (2009) *Children, their World, their Education: Final Report and Recommendations of the Cambridge Primary Review*. Abingdon: Routledge.

Allan, J. (2008) 'Inclusion for All?' In T.G.K. Bryce and W.M Humes (eds) *Scottish Education: Beyond Devolution* (3rd edn). Edinburgh: Edinburgh University Press.

Al-Yaman, F., Bryant, M. and Sargeant, H. (2002) *Australia's Children: Their Health and Well-Being*. Canberra: Australian Institute of Health and Welfare.

Anderson, L., Jacobs, J., Schramm, S. and Splittgerber, F. (2000) 'School transition: beginning of the end or a new beginning?' *International Journal of Educational Research* 33, 325–339.

Andresen, S. and Fegter, S. (in press) 'Children Growing Up in Poverty and Their Ideas on What Constitutes a Good Life.' *Child Indicators Research.*

Andrews, A., Ben-Arieh, A., Carlson, M., Damon, W. *et al.* (Ecology Working Group) (2002) *Ecology of Child Well-Being: Advancing the Science and the Science-Practice Link.* Atlanta, GA: Center for Child Well-Being.

Andrews, A. and Ben-Arieh, A. (1999) 'Measuring and monitoring children's well-being across the world.' *Social Work 44*, 105–155.

Annie E. Casey Foundation, The (2009) *The 2009 KIDS COUNT Data Book: States Profiles of Child Well-Being.* Baltimore, MA: The Annie E. Casey Foundation. Available at www.aecf.org/~/media/Pubs/Other/123/2009KIDSCOUNTDataBook/AEC186_2009_KCDB_FINAL%2072.pdf, accessed on 24 November 2009.

Axford, N. (2009) 'Child well-being through different lenses: Why concept matters.' *Child & Family Social Work 14*, 3, 372–383.

Bannister, J. (1994) *FDCH Congressional Testimony.* Washington, DC: US Congress.

Barnardos Ireland (2008) *Tomorrow's Child.* Dublin: Barnardos.

Barnardos Scotland (2007) *The Index of Wellbeing for Children in Scotland.* Edinburgh: Barnardos.

Bauer, G., Davies, J.K., Pelikan, J., Noack, H., Broesskamp, U. and Hill, C. (on behalf of the EUPHID Consortium) (2003) 'Advancing a theoretical model for public health and health promotion indicator development: Proposal from the EUPHID Consortium.' *European Journal of Public Health 13*, 3, 107–113.

Bauer, R.A. (ed.) (1966) *Social Indicators.* Cambridge, MA: MIT Press.

Ben-Arieh, A. (2000) 'Beyond welfare. Measuring and monitoring the state of children: New trends and domains.' *Social Indicators Research 52*, 3, 235–257.

Ben-Arieh, A. (2002) 'Evaluating the Outcomes of Programs Versus Monitoring Well-Being: A Child-Centered Perspective.' In T. Vecchiato, A.N. Maluccio and C. Canali (eds) *Evaluation in Child and Family Services: Comparative Client and Program Perspective.* New York: Aldine de Gruyter.

Ben-Arieh, A. (2005) 'Where are the children? Children's role in measuring and monitoring their well-being.' *Social Indicators 74*, 3, 573–596.

Ben-Arieh, A. (2006) 'Is the study of the "State of Our Children" changing? Revisiting after five years.' *Children and Youth Services Review 28*, 7, 799–811.

Ben-Arieh, A. (2008) 'The child indicators movement: Past, present and future.' *Child Indicators Research 1*, 3–16.

Ben-Arieh, A. (2010) 'From Child Welfare to Children Well-Being: The Child Indicators Perspective.' In S.B. Kamerman, S. Phipps, and A. Ben-Arieh (eds) *From Child Welfare to Child Well-Being: An International Perspective on Knowledge in the Service of Making Policy.* Dordrecht: Springer.

Ben-Arieh, A. and Frones, I. (2009) *Indicators of Children's Well-Being: Theory and Practice in a Multi-Cultural Perspective.* New York: Springer.

Ben-Arieh, A. and Goerge, R. (2001) 'Beyond the numbers: How do we monitor the state of our children?' *Children and Youth Services Review 23,* 8, 603–631.

Ben-Arieh, A. and Goerge, R. (eds) (2006) *Indicators of Children's Well-Being: Understanding their Role, Usage, and Policy Influence.* Dordrecht: Springer.

Ben-Arieh, A. and Wintersberger, H. (eds) (1997) *Monitoring and Measuring the State of Children: Beyond Survival.* Eurosocial Report No. 62. Vienna: European Centre for Social Welfare Policy and Research.

Ben-Arieh, A., Kaufman, H.N., Andrews, A., Goerge, R., Lee, B.J. and Aber, L.J. (2001) *Measuring and Monitoring Children's Well-Being.* Dordrecht: Kluwer.

Berrick, J.D., Needell, B., Barth. R.B. and Johnson-Reid, M. (1998) *The Tender Years: Toward Developmentally Sensitive Child Welfare Services for Very Young Children.* New York: Oxford University Press.

Bibby, A. and Becker, S. (eds) (2000) *Young Carers in Their Own Words.* London: Calouste Gulbenkian Foundation.

Blatchford, P., Bassett, P., Brown, P., Martin, C., Russell, A. and Webster, R. (2009) *Deployment and Impact of Support Staff Project.* Research Brief 148. London: Department for Children, Schools and Families.

Blome, W.W. (1997) 'What happens to foster kids: Educational experiences of a random sample of foster care youth and a matched group of non-foster care youth.' *Child and Adolescent Social Work Journal 14,* 1, 41–53.

Bosma, H., Stansfeld, S.A. and Marmot, M.G. (1998) 'Job control, personal characteristics, and heart disease.' *Journal of Occupational Health Psychology 3,* 4, 402–409.

Bowlby, J. (1958) 'The nature of the child's tie to its mother.' *International Journal of Psychoanalysis 39,* 350–373.

Boyd, B. (2005) *Primary–Secondary Transition.* London: Hodder Gibson.

Bradshaw, J. (1990) *Child Poverty and Deprivation in the UK.* London: National Children's Bureau.

Bradshaw, J. (ed.) (2002) *The Well-Being of Children in the UK.* London: Save the Children.

Bradshaw, J. (2006) 'The Use of Indicators of Child Well-Being in the United Kingdom and the European Union.' In A. Ben-Arieh and R. Goerge (eds) *Indicators of Children's Well-Being: Understanding Their Role, Usage, and Policy Influence.* Dordrecht: Springer.

Bradshaw, J. and Mayhew, E. (eds) (2005) *The Well-Being of Children in the UK.* London: Save the Children.

Bradshaw, J. and Richardson, D. (2009) 'An index of child well-being in Europe.' *Child Indicators Research 2,* 3, 319–351.

Bradshaw, J., Hoelscher, P. and Richardson, D. (2007) 'An index of child well-being in the European Union.' *Social Indicators Research 80,* 1, 133–177.

Bradshaw, J., Noble, M., Bloor, K., Huby, M. *et al.* (2009) 'A child well-being index at small area level in England.' *Child Indicators Research 2*, 2, 201–219.

Brady, B. and Dolan, P. (2007a) 'Exploring good practice in Irish child and family services: Reflections and considerations' *Practice 19*, 1, 5–18.

Brady, B. and Dolan, P. (2007b) 'Youth mentoring in Ireland: Weighing up the benefits and challenges.' *Youth Studies Ireland*, Issue 2.

Brannen, J., Heptinstall, E. and Bhopal, K. (2000) *Connecting Children: Care and Family Life in Later Childhood.* London: RoutledgeFalmer.

Bronfenbrenner, U. (1979) *The Ecology of Human Development: Experiments by Nature and Design.* Cambridge, MA: Harvard University Press.

Bronfenbrenner, U. and Morris, P. (1998) 'The Bio-Ecological Model of Human Development.' In R.M.V. Lerner, W. Damon and R.M.S. Lerner (eds) *Handbook of Child Psychology, Volume 1: Theoretical Models of Human Development.* Hoboken, NJ: Wiley.

Brooks, A.M. and Hanafin, S. (2005) *An Inventory of Child Well-Being Indicators, National Children's Office.* Dublin: The Stationery Office.

Brooks, F., Van der Sluijs, W., Klemera, E., Morgan, A. *et al.* (2009) *Young People's Health in Great Britain and Ireland: Findings from Health Behaviour in School Aged Children Survey 2006.* Hatfield: University of Herefordshire, CRIPACC (HBSC Publ.)

Brown, B. and Moore, K. (2003) 'Child and Youth Well-Being: The Social Indicators Field.' In R. Lerner, F. Jacobs and J. Wertlieb (eds) *Handbook of Applied Developmental Science: Promoting Positive Child, Adolescent, and Family Development through Research, Policies and Programs.* Thousand Oaks, CA: Sage.

Buehler, C., Orme, J.G., Post, J. and Patterson, D.A. (2000) 'The long-term correlates of family foster care.' *Children and Youth Services Review 22*, 8, 595–625.

Bullock, R., Little, M. and Millham, S. (2001) 'Children's Return from State Care to School.' In S. Jackson (ed.) *Nobody Ever Told Us School Mattered: Raising the Educational Attainments of Children in Care.* London: BAAF.

Burton, P. and Phipps, S. (2010) 'In Children's Voices.' In S.B. Kamerman, S. Phipps and A. Ben-Arieh (eds) *From Child Welfare to Child Well-Being: An International Perspective on Knowledge in the Service of Making Policy.* Dordrecht: Springer.

Canavan, J. Coen, L., Dolan, P. and White, L. (2009) 'Privileging practice: Facing the challenges of integrated working for outcomes for children.' *Children and Society 23*, 5, 377–388.

Cantril, H. (1965) *The Pattern of Human Concerns.* New Brunswick, NJ: Rutgers University Press.

Carpini, M. (2006) *A New Engagement? Political Participation, Civic Life and the Changing American Citizen.* Oxford: Oxford University Press.

Carroll, E. (2002) *The Well-Being of Children: Four Papers Exploring Conceptual, Ethical and Measurement Issues.* Dublin: Irish Youth Foundation.

Casas, F. (2000) 'Quality of Life and the Life Experience of Children.' In E. Verhellen (ed.) *Fifth International Interdisciplinary Course on Children's Rights.* Ghent: University of Ghent.

Casas, F., Figuer, C., González, M., Malo, S., Alsinet, C. and Subarroca, S. (2007) 'The well-being of 12- to 16-year-old adolescents and their parents: Results from 1999 to 2003 Spanish samples.' *Social Indicators Research 83*, 87–115.

Casas, F., González, M., Figuer, C. and Coenders, G. (2004) 'Subjective well-being, values, and goal achievement: The case of planned versus by chance searches on the Internet.' *Social Indicators Research 66*, 123–141.

Casey Family Programs (2003) *Family, Community, Culture: Roots of Permanency – A Conceptual Framework on Permanency from Casey Family Programs.* Seattle, WA: Casey Family Programs

Casey Family Services (1999) *The Road to Independence: Transitioning Youth in Foster Care to Independence.* Shelton, CT: Casey Family Services.

Cassel, J. (1976) 'The contribution of the social environment to host resistance: The Fourth Wade Hampton Frost Lecture.' *American Journal of Epidemiology 104*, 2, 107–123.

Centre for Excellence and Outcomes in Children's Services (C4EO) and Local Government Association (LGA) (2008) *Narrowing the Gap: Final Guidance Year 1.* London: C4EO and LGA. Available at www.c4eo.org.uk/narrowingthegap/files/ntg_final_guidance_year_1_complete.pdf, accessed on 16 June 2010.

C4EO and LGA (2009) *Narrowing the Gap: Final Guidance Year 2. Leadership and Governance.* London: C4EO and LGA. Available at www.c4eo.org.uk/narrowingthegap/files/ntg_final_guidance_year_2_complete.pdf, accessed on 16 June 2010.

Central Statistics Office (2007) *Census 2006.* Dublin: The Stationery Office.

Central Statistics Office (2009a) *Quarterly National Household Survey: Childcare.* Dublin: The Stationery Office.

Central Statistics Office (2009b) *Children and Young People in Ireland.* Dublin: The Stationery Office.

Child Welfare League of America (2003) *Making Children a National Priority: A Framework for Community Action.* Washington, DC: Child Welfare League of America.

Children and Young People's Unit (2001a) *Tomorrow's Future: Building a Strategy for Children and Young People.* London: Children and Young People's Unit.

Children and Young People's Unit (2001b) *Building a Strategy for Children and Young People: Consultation Document.* London: Children and Young People's Unit.

Children's Rights Alliance (2009) *Is the Government Keeping its Promises to Children? Report Card.* Dublin: Children's Rights Alliance.

Clark, A. and Moss, P. (2001) *Listening to Young Children: The Mosaic Approach.* London: National Children's Bureau.

Clarke, L., Bradshaw, J. and Williams, J. (2000) 'Family Diversity and Poverty and the Mental Wellbeing of Young People.' In H. Ryan and J. Bull (eds) *Changing Families, Changing Communities: Researching Health and Well-Being among Children and Young People.* London: Health Development Agency.

Cleaver, H. (2000) *Fostering Family Contact.* London: The Stationery Office.

Cm 4169 (1998) *Modernising Social Services.* London: The Stationery Office.

Cm 5730 (2003) *The Victoria Climbié Inquiry.* London: The Stationery Office.

Cm 5860 (2003) *Every Child Matters.* London: The Stationery Office.

Cm 5861 (2003) *Keeping Children Safe.* London: The Stationery Office.

Cm 7280 (2007) *The Children's Plan.* London: The Stationery Office.

Coleman, J. (2007) 'Emotional Health and Well-Being.' In J. Coleman, L.B Hendry and M. Kloep (eds) *Adolescence and Health.* Chichester: John Wiley.

Coleman, J. (2009) 'Well-being in schools: Empirical measures, or politician's dream?' *Oxford Review of Education 35,* 3, 281–292.

Connors, C. and Stalker, K. (2003) *The Views and Experiences of Disabled Children and Their Siblings: A Positive Outlook.* London: Jessica Kingsley Publishers

Connors, C. and Stalker, K. (2007) 'Children's experiences of disability: Pointers to a social model of childhood disability.' *Disability and Society 22,* 1, 19–33.

Cook, R.J., Fleishman, E. and Grimes, V. (1989) *A National Evaluation of Title IV-E Foster Care Independent Living Programs for Youth* (Phase 2 Final Report, Volume 1). Rockville, MD: Westat, Inc.

Coulton, C., Korbin, J.E. and McDonell, J. (2009) 'Editorial: Indicators of child well-being in the context of small areas.' *Child Indicators Research 2,* 2.

Counterpoint (2008) *Childhood Wellbeing: Qualitative Research Study.* London: DCSF.

Courtney, M. and Dworsky, A. (2005) *Midwest Evaluation of the Adult Functioning of Former Foster Youth: Outcomes at Age 19.* Chicago, IL: University of Chicago, Chapin Hall.

Courtney, M., Piliavin, I., Grogan-Kaylor, A. and Nesmith, A. (2001) 'Foster youth transitions to adulthood: A longitudinal view of youth leaving care.' *Child Welfare 80,* 6, 685–717.

Cummins, R.A. (2009) 'Subjective wellbeing, homeostatically protected mood and depression: A synthesis.' *Journal of Happiness Studies 10,* 6, 1–21.

Cummins, R. and Lau, A. (2006) *Personal Wellbeing Index – Adult* (4th edn). Melbourne: Deakin University.

Currie, C., Gabhainn, S.N., Godeau, E., Roberts, C. *et al.* (2008) *Inequalities in Young People's Health: Health Behaviour in School-Aged Children (HBSC) International Report from the 2005/2006 Survey.* Health Policy for Children and Adolescents, No. 5. Copenhagen: World Health Organization, Regional Office for Europe. Available at www.euro.who. int/eprise/main/WHO/InformationSources/Publications/Catalogue/20080617_1, accessed on 3 June 2009.

Cutrona, C.E. (2000) 'Social Support Principles for Strengthening Families: Messages from America.' In J. Canavan, P. Dolan and J. Pinkerton (eds) *Family Support: Direction from Diversity.* London: Jessica Kingsley Publishers.

Daniel, B. and Wassell, S. (2002) *Assessing and Promoting Resilience in Vulnerable Children,* Workbooks 1, 2 and 3. London: Jessica Kingsley Publishers.

De Lone, R.H. (1979) *Small Futures: Children, Inequality, and the Limits of Liberal Reform.* New York: Harcourt Brace Jovanovich.

Department for Children, Schools and Families (2007) *Guidance on the Duty to Promote Community Cohesion.* Available at http://publications.everychildmatters.gov.uk/default. aspx?PageFunction=productdetails&PageMode=publications&ProductId=DCSF-00598-2007, accessed on 25 June 2010.

Department for Children, Schools and Families (2009a) *The Children's Plan: Two Years On.* London: Department for Children, Schools and Families.

Department for Children, Schools and Families (2009b) *Every Child Matters Programme.* Available at www.dcsf.gov.uk/everychildmatters/about, accessed on 21 September 2009.

Department for Children, Schools and Families (2009c) *Every Child Matters Outcomes Framework.* Available at http://publications.everychildmatters.gov.uk/eOrderingDownload/DCSF-00331-2008.pdf, accessed on 28 November 2009.

Department for Children, Schools and Families (2009d) *Home Page.* Available at www.dcsf.gov.uk, accessed on 9 September 2009.

Department for Children, Schools and Families (2009e) *A School Report Card: Prospectus.* London: Department for Children, Schools and Families.

Department for Children, Schools and Families (2010) personal communication regarding *Every Child Matters.*

Department for Education and Skills (2004a) *Every Child Matters: Change for Children.* London: Department for Education and Skills.

Department for Education and Skills (2004b) *Every Child Matters: Next Steps.* London: Department for Education and Skills.

Department for Work and Pensions (2009) *Opportunity for All.* Available at www.dwp.gov.uk/publications/policy-publications/opportunity-for-all, accessed on 11 December 2009.

Department of Health (2000) *LASSL (2000)3: Consultation of New Guidance for Planning Children's Services.* Available at www.dh.gov.uk/en/Publicationsandstatistics/Lettersandcirculars/Localauthoritysocialservicesletters, accessed on 13 April 2010.

Department of Health (2001) *Co-Ordinated Planning for Vulnerable Children and Young People in England.* London: Department of Health.

Department of Health and Children (2000) *Our Children – Their Lives: The National Children's Strategy.* Dublin: The Stationery Office.

Department of Health, Department for Education and Skills and Home Office (2000) *Framework for the Assessment of Children in Need and Their Families.* London: The Stationery Office.

Department of Social and Family Affairs (2007) *A Social Portrait of Children in Ireland.* Dublin: The Stationery Office.

Diener, E. and Lucas, R.E. (1998) 'Personality and Subjective Well-Being.' In D. Kahneman, E. Diener and N. Schwarz (eds) *Hedonic Psychology: Scientific Perspectives on Enjoyment, Suffering, and Well-Being.* New York: Russell Sage.

Diener, E., Suh, E.M., Lucas, R.E. and Smith, H.L. (1999) 'Subjective well-being: Three decades of progress.' *Psychology Bulletin 125,* 2, 276–302.

Dolan, P. (2008) 'Prospective possibilities for building resilience in children, their families and communities child care.' *Child Care in Practice 14,* 1, 83–91.

Dolan, P. (2010) 'Children's Rights in Ireland: Legacy Issues and Future Prospects.' In D.O. Connell (ed.) *Irish Human Rights Law Review.* Dublin: Clarus Press.

Dyson, A. (2005) 'Philosophy, Politics and Economics? The Story of Inclusive Education in England.' In D. Mitchell (ed.) *Contextualising Inclusive Education.* London: Routledge/Falmer.

Eikemo, T.A., Bambra, C., Judge, K. and Ringdal, K. (2008) 'Welfare state regimes and differences in self-perceived health in Europe: A multilevel analysis.' *Social Science & Medicine 66*, 2281–2295.

Eivers, E., Shiel, G. and Cunningham, R. (2008) *Ready for Tomorrow's World? The Competencies of Irish 15-Year-Olds in PISA 2006: Main Report.* Dublin: Educational Research Centre.

Ereaut, G. and Whiting, R. (2008) *What Do We Mean by 'Wellbeing'? And Why Might It Matter?* Research Report DCSF-RW073. London: Department for Children, Schools and Families.

European Commission (2008) *Child Poverty and Well-Being in the EU: Current Status and Way Forward.* Available at http://ec.europa.eu/employment_social/spsi/docs/social_inclusion/2008/child_poverty_en.pdf, accessed on 11 December 2009.

European Union (2010) *Child Poverty and Child Well-Being in the European Union.* Budapest: TARKI Social Research Institute/Brussels: Applica.

Fattore, T., Mason, J. and Watson, E. (2009) 'When children are asked about their well-being: Towards a framework for guiding policy.' *Child Indicators Research 2*, 1, 57–77.

Federal Interagency Program on Child and Family Statistics (2002) *America's Children: Key National Indicators of Well-Being.* Washington, DC: US Government Printing Office.

Federal Interagency Program on Child and Family Statistics (2009) *America's Children: Key National Indicators of Well-Being.* Washington, DC: US Government Printing Office.

Feldman, G.R. and Elliot, S.S. (1993) 'Capturing the Adolescent Experience.' In G.R. Feldman and S.S. Elliot (eds) *At the Threshold: The Developing Adolescent.* Harvard: Harvard University Press.

Fitzgerald, E. (2004) *Counting Our Children: An Analysis of Official Data Sources on Children and Childhood in Ireland.* Dublin: Children's Research Centre, University of Dublin, Trinity College.

Fixsen, D.L., Naoom, S.F., Blase, K.A., Friedman, R.M. and Wallace, F. (2005) *Implementation Research: A Synthesis of the Literature.* Tampa, FL: University of South Florida, Louis de la Parte Florida Mental Health Institute, The National Implementation Research network.

Flanagan, C. (2001) 'Political Participation/Political Activism.' In J.V. Lerner and R.M. Lerner (eds) *Adolescence in America: An Encyclopedia.* Santa Barbara, CA: ABC-CLIO.

Fonagy, P., Steele, M., Steele, H., Higgit, A. and Target, M. (1994) 'The theory and practice of resilience.' *Journal of Child Psychology and Psychiatry 35*, 231–257.

Frank, C. (2005) 'Young guns: Children in organised armed violence.' *Crime Quarterly 14.* Available at www.issafrica.org, accessed on 1 November 2009.

Frank, J. (1995) *Couldn't Care More: A Study of Young Carers and Their Needs.* London: The Children's Society.

Fraser, S. (2004) 'Situating Empirical Research.' In S. Fraser, V. Lewis, S. Ding, M. Kellet and C. Robinson (eds) *Doing Research with Children and Young People.* London: Sage.

Friedman, M. (2005) *Trying Hard Is Not Good Enough: How to Produce Measurable Improvements for Customers and Communities.* Victoria, BC: Trafford Publishing.

Frones, I. (2007) 'Theorizing indicators.' *Social Indicators Research 83*, 1, 5–23.

Funk, J., Hagan, J. and Schimming, J. (1999) 'Children and electronic games: A comparison of parents' and children's perceptions of children's habits and preferences in a United States sample.' *Psychological Report 85*, 3, 883–888.

Gardner, R. (2003) 'Working Together to Improve Children's Life Chances: The Challenge of Inter-Agency Collaboration.' In J. Weinstein, C. Whittington and T. Leiba (eds) *Collaboration in Social Work Practice.* London: Jessica Kingsley Publishers.

Gilligan, R. (2000) 'Adversity, resilience and young people: The protective value of positive school and spare time experiences.' *Children and Society 14*, 37–47.

Gilligan, R. (2009) *Promoting Resilience: Supporting Children and Young People who are in Care, Adopted or in Need* (2nd edn). London: British Agencies for Adoption and Fostering.

Glisson, C. and Hemmelgarn, A. (1998) 'The effects of organisational climate and inter-organisational co-ordination on the quality and outcomes of children's service systems.' *Child Abuse and Neglect 22*, 5, 402–421.

Goerge, R.M. (1997) 'The Use of Administrative Data in Measuring the State of Children.' In A. Ben-Arieh and H. Wintersberger (eds) *Monitoring and Measuring the State of Children: Beyond Survival.* Eurosocial Report No. 62. Vienna: European Centre for Social Welfare Policy and Research.

Gorin, S. (2004) *Understanding What Children Say: Children's Experiences of Domestic Violence, Parental Substance Misuse and Parental Health Problems.* London: National Children's Bureau.

Gottlieb, D. and Bronstein, P. (1996) 'Parents' perceptions of children's worries in a changing world.' *Journal of Genetic Psychology 157*, 1, 104–118.

Government of Canada (2002) *The Well-Being of Canada's Young Children.* Ottawa: Human Resources Development Canada and Health Canada.

Granger, R.C. (2006) 'Preface.' In A. Ben-Arieh and R. Goerge (eds) *Indicators of Children's Well-Being: Understanding their Role, Usage, and Policy Influence.* Dordrecht: Springer.

Gunter, H. (2007) 'Remodelling the school workforce in England: A study in tyranny.' *Journal for Critical Education Policy Studies 5*, 1, 1–11.

Gutman, L.M. and Feinstein, L. (2008) *Children's Well-Being in Primary School: Pupil and School Effects.* London: Centre for Research on the Wider Benefits of Learning.

Hallam, S. (2009) 'An evaluation of the Social Emotional Aspects of Learning (SEAL) Programme: Promoting positive behaviour, effective learning and well-being in primary school children.' *Oxford Review of Education 35*, 3, 313–330.

Hanafin, S. and Brooks, A.M. (2005a) *Report on the Development of a National Set of Child Well-Being Indicators.* National Children's Office. Dublin: The Stationery Office.

Hanafin, S. and Brooks, A.M. (2005b) *The Delphi Technique: A Methodology to Support the Development of a National Set of Child Well-Being Indicators.* National Children's Office. Dublin: The Stationery Office.

Hanafin, S. and Brooks, A.M. (2009) 'From rhetoric to reality: Challenges in using data to report on a National Set of Child Well-Being Indicators.' *Child Indicators Research 2*, 1, 33–55.

Hanafin, S., Brooks, A.M., Carroll, E., Fitzgerald, E., Nic Gabhainn, S. and Sixsmith, J. (2007) 'Achieving consensus in developing a National Set of Child Well-Being Indicators.' *Social Indicators Research 80*, 1, 79–104.

Hardin, M. (1992) *Establishing a Core of Services for Families Subject to State Intervention.* Washington, DC: American Bar Association.

Hauser, R.M., Brown, B.V. and Prosser, W.R. (eds) (1997) *Indicators of Children's Well-Being.* New York: Russell Sage Foundation.

Her Majesty's Inspectors of Education (HMIe) (2009) *How Good Is Our School? (Version 3).* Edinburgh: HMSO.

Highland Council (2007) *Getting It Right for Every Child: Practice Guidance.* Inverness: Highland Council.

Hill, M., Davis, J., Prout, A. and Tisdall, K. (2004) 'Moving the participation agenda forward.' *Children and Society 18,* 77–96.

Hills, J., Brewer, M., Jenkins, S., Lister, R. *et al.* (2010) *An Anatomy of Economic Inequality in the UK: Report of the National Equality Panel.* London: National Equalities Office.

Hogan, C. (2006) 'How Can We Better Use Whole Population and Outcomes Indicators? A Policymaker's Perspective.' In A. Ben-Arieh and R. Goerge (eds) *Indicators of Children's Well-Being: Understanding Their Role, Usage, and Policy Influence.* Dordrecht: Springer.

Holloway, S.L. and Valentine, G. (2000) *Children's Geographies.* London: Routledge.

Howe, D., Brandon, M. and Schofield, G. (1999) *Attachment Theory, Child Maltreatment and Family Support.* London: Macmillan.

Howes, C. (1999) 'Attachment Relationships in the Context of Multiple Carers.' In U. Cassidy and P.R. Shaver (eds) *Handbook on Attachment – Theory, Research and Clinical Applications.* New York: The Guilford Press.

Hudson, B., Hardy, B., Henwood, M. and Wistow, G. (1999) 'In pursuit of inter-agency collaboration in the public sector: What is the contribution of theory and research?' *Public Management: An International Journal of Research and Theory 1,* 2, 235–260.

Huebner, E.S. (1994) 'Preliminary development and validation of a multidimensional life satisfaction scale for children.' *Psychological Assessment 6,* 2, 149–158.

Huebner, E.S. (1997) 'Life Satisfaction and Happiness.' In G.G. Bear, K.M. Minke and A. Thomas (eds) *Children's Needs II: Development, Problems, and Alternatives.* Bethesda, MD: National Association of School Psychologists.

Huebner, E.S. (2004) 'Research on assessment of life satisfaction of children and adolescents.' *Social Indicators Research, 66,* 3–33.

Husain, F. (2006) 'Cultural Competence, Cultural Sensitivity and Family Support.' In P. Dolan, J. Canavan and J. Pinkerton (eds) *Family Support as a Reflective Practice.* London: Jessica Kingsley Publishers.

Husbands, C., Shreeve, A. and Jones, N.R. (2008) *Accountability and Children's Outcomes in High-Performing Education Systems.* London: DSCF-EPPI-08-08 Research Brief.

International Initiative (2003) *Achieving Results: Policies that Make a Difference for Children, Families and Communities.* London: International Initiative.

Jack, G. and Gill, O. (2003) *The Third Side of the Triangle.* Barkingside: Barnardos.

Jackson, S. (2001) 'The Education of Children in Care.' In S. Jackson (ed.) *Nobody Ever Told Us School Mattered: Raising the Educational Attainments of Children in Care.* London: BAAF.

James, A. and Prout, A. (eds) (1990) *Constructing and Reconstructing Childhood: Contemporary Issues in the Sociological Study of Childhood.* Basingstoke: Falmer Press.

James, A., Jencks, C. and Prout, A. (1998) *Theorising Childhood.* Cambridge: Polity Press.

James, O. (2008) *The Selfish Capitalist.* London: Vermilion.

Jensen, A.M. and Saporiti, A. (1992) *Do Children Count?* Vienna: European Centre for Social Welfare Policy and Research.

Jones, D.P.H. and Ramchandani, P. (1999) *Child Sexual Abuse – Informing Practice from Research.* Oxford: Radcliffe Medical Press.

Jordan, B. (2006) 'Well-being: The next revolution in children's services?' *Journal of Children's Services 1*, 1, 41–50.

Kahn, A.J. (2010) 'From "Child Saving" to "Child Development"?' In S.B. Kamerman, S. Phipps and A. Ben-Arieh (eds) *From Child Welfare to Child Well-Being: An International Perspective on Knowledge in the Service of Policy Making.* Dordrecht: Springer.

Kahneman, D., Diener, E. and Schwarz, N. (eds) (1999) *Well-Being: The Foundations of Hedonic Psychology.* New York: Russell Sage Foundation.

Kamerman, S.B., Phipps, S. and Ben-Arieh, A. (eds) (2010) *From Child Welfare to Child Well-Being: An International Perspective on Knowledge in the Service of Making Policy.* Dordrecht: Springer.

Kellett, M. (2010) *Rethinking Children and Research: Attitudes in Contemporary Society.* London: Continuum.

Kelly, J.G. (1974) 'Towards a Psychology of Healthiness.' Icabod Spencer Lecture, Union College, USA.

Kerman, B., Maluccio, A.N. and Freundlich, M. (eds) (2008) *Achieving Permanence for Older Children and Youth in Foster Care.* New York: Columbia University Press.

Keung, A. (2006) 'The Impact of Life Events on the Subjective Well-Being (SWB) of Young People: Analysis of the British Household Panel Survey.' In W. Ostasiewicz (ed.) *Towards Quality of Life Improvement.* Wrocław: The Publishing House of the Wrocław University of Economics.

Keung, A. (2007) *The Impact of Life Events on the Subjective Well-Being of Young People: Evidence from the British Household Panel Survey.* PhD thesis. York: Department of Social Policy and Social Work, University of York.

Klein, L. (2006) 'Using Indicators of School Readiness to Improve Public Policy for Young Children.' In A. Ben-Arieh and R. Goerge (eds) *Indicators of Children's Well-Being: Understanding their Role, Usage, and Policy Influence.* Dordrecht: Springer.

Kohler, L. and Rigby, M. (2003) 'Indicators of children's development: Considerations when constructing a set of national child health indicators for the European Union.' *Child: Care, Health and Development 29*, 6, 551–558.

Kroger, J. (2004) *Identity in Adolescence: The Balance between Self and Other.* Adolescence and Society Series. London: Routledge.

Lack, N., Zeitlin, J., Krebs, L., Kunzel, W. and Alexander, S. (2003) 'Methodological difficulties in the comparison of indicators of perinatal health across Europe.' *European Journal of Obstetrics and Gynecology and Reproductive Biology 111*, S33–S44.

Land, K. (1975) 'Social Indicators Models: An Overview.' In K. Land and S. Spilerman (eds) *Social Indicators Models.* New York: Russell Sage Foundation.

Land, K. (2000) 'Social Indicators.' In E.F. Borgatta and R.V. Montgomery (eds) *Encyclopedia of Sociology* (rev. edn). New York: Macmillan.

Land, K., Lamb, V.L. and Mustillo, S.K. (2001) 'Child and youth well-being in the United States, 1975–1998: Some findings from a new index.' *Social Indicators Research 56*, 241–320.

Layard, R. (2005) *Happiness: Lessons from a New Science.* London: Penguin.

Layard, R. and Dunn, J. (2009) *A Good Childhood.* London: Penguin.

Lerner, R.M. and Benson, P.L. (eds) (2002) *Developmental Assets and Asset-Building Communities: Implications for Research, Policy and Practice.* Norwell, MA: Kluwer Academic Publishers.

Liebenberg, L. and Ungar, M. (2009) *Researching Resilience.* Toronto: University of Toronto Press.

Lieberson, S. and Waters, M.C. (1989) 'The rise of a new ethnic group: The "unhyphenated American".' *Social Science Research Council Items 43*, 7–10.

Linstone, H.A. and Turoff, M. (eds) (1975) *The Delphi Method Techniques and Applications.* Reading, MA: Addison-Wesley.

Lippman, L. (2004) *Indicators of Child, Family and Community Connections.* Washington, DC: Office of the Assistant Secretary for Planning and Evaluation, US Department of Health and Human Services.

Little, T. (2006) 'Increasing the Impact of Indicators among Legislative Policy Makers.' In A. Ben-Arieh and R. Goerge (eds) *Indicators of Children's Well-Being: Understanding Their Role, Usage, and Policy Influence.* Dordrecht: Springer.

Lohan, J.A. and Murphy, S.A. (2001) 'Parents' perceptions of adolescent sibling grief responses after an adolescent or young adult child's sudden, violent death.' *Omega-Journal of Death and Dying 44*, 3, 195–213.

Lorion, R.P. (2000) 'Theoretical and Evaluation Issues in the Promotion of Wellness and Protection of "Well Enough".' In D. Cicchetti, J. Rappaport, I. Sandler and P. Weissberg (eds) *The Promotion of Wellness in Children and Adolescents.* Washington, DC: Child Welfare League of America.

Lucey, H. and Reay, D. (2000) 'Identities in transition: Anxiety and excitement in the move to secondary school.' *Oxford Review of Education 26*, 191–205.

MacBeath, J., Galton, M., Steward, S., MacBeath, A. and Page, C. (undated) *The Costs of Inclusion: Report Commissioned by the National Union of Teachers.* Cambridge: University of Cambridge.

Maluccio, A. and Pecora, P. (2006) 'Family Foster Care in the USA.' In C. McCauley, P.J. Pecora and W.E. Rose (eds) *Enhancing the Well-Being of Children and Families through Effective Interventions – International Evidence for Practice.* London: Jessica Kingsley Publishers.

Mareš, J. (2006) *Kvalita života u dětí a dospívajících I.* Brno: MSD.

Marmot, M. (chair) (2010) *Fair Society, Healthy Lives: Strategic Review of Health Inequalities in England Post 2010.* London: Department of Health

Marmot, M.G., Bosma, H., Hemingway, H., Brunner, E. and Stansfeld, S. (1997) 'Contribution of job control and other risk factors to social variations in coronary heart disease incidence.' *The Lancet 350*, 9073, 235–239.

McAuley, C. (1996a) *Children in Long-Term Foster Care: Emotional and Social Development.* Aldershot: Avebury.

McAuley, C. (1996b) 'Children's Perspectives on Long-Term Foster Care.' In M. Hill and J. Aldgate (eds) *Child Welfare Services: Developments in Law, Policy, Practice and Research.* London: Jessica Kingsley Publishers.

McAuley, C. (2005) *Pathways and Outcomes: A Ten Year Follow Up Study of Children who have Experienced Care.* Belfast: DHSSPSNI.

McAuley, C. (2006) 'Outcomes of Long-Term Foster Care: Young People's Views.' In D. Iwaniec (ed.) *The Child's Journey through Care: Placement Stability, Care Planning and Achieving Permanency.* Chichester: John Wiley and Sons.

McAuley, C. and Davis, T. (2009) 'Emotional Well-Being and Mental Health of Looked After Children in England.' In C. McAuley, P. Pecora and J. Whittaker (eds) 'High risk youth: Evidence on characteristics, needs and promising interventions.' *Child and Family Social Work, Special Issue, 14,* 2, 147–155.

McAuley, C. , Pecora, P.J. and Rose, W. (eds) (2006) *Enhancing the Well-Being of Children and Families through Effective Interventions: International Evidence for Practice.* London: Jessica Kingsley Publishers.

McDonald, J., Salyers, N. and Shaver, M. (2004) *The Foster Care Straightjacket: Innovation, Federal Financing and Accountability in State Foster Care Reform – A Report by Fostering Results.* Urbana-Champaign, IL: Children and Family Research Center at the School of Social Work, University of Illinois. Available at www.fosteringresults.org/reports/pewreports_03-11-04_straightjacket.pdf, accessed on 24 June 2010.

McGrath, B., Brennan, M.A., Dolan, P. and Barnett, R. (2009) 'Adolescent well-being and supporting contexts: A comparison of adolescents in Ireland and Florida.' *Journal of Community and Applied Social Psychology 19,* 4, 229–320.

Mech, E.V. (2003) *Uncertain Futures: Foster Youth Transition to Adulthood.* Washington, DC: Child Welfare League of America.

Mech, E.V. and Fung, C.C. (1999) 'Placement restrictiveness and educational achievement among emancipated foster youth.' *Research on Social Work Practice 9,* 2, 213–228.

Melton, G. and Limber, S. (1992) 'What Children's Rights Mean to Children: Children's Own Views.' In M. Freeman and P. Veerman (eds) *The Ideologies of Children's Rights.* Dordrecht: Martinus Nijhoff.

Meltzer, H., Corbin, T., Gatward, R., Goodman, R. and Ford, T. (2003) *The Mental Health of Young People Looked After by Local Authorities in England.* London: The Stationery Office.

Miljeteig, P. (1997) 'The International Effort to Monitor Children's Rights.' In A. Ben-Arieh and H. Wintersberger (eds) *Measuring and Monitoring the State of Children – Beyond Survival.* Vienna: European Centre for Social Welfare Policy and Research.

Moore, K.A. (1997) 'Criteria for Indicators of Child Well-Being.' In R.M. Hauser, B.V. Brown and W.R. Prosser (eds) *Indicators of Children's Well-Being.* New York: Russell Sage Foundation.

Moore, K.A., Lippman, L. and Brown, B. (2004) 'Indicators of child well-being: The promise for positive youth development.' *The Annals of the American Academy of Political and Social Science 591,* 125–145.

Moore, K.A., Vandivere, S., Lippman, L., McPhee, C. and Bloch, M. (2007) 'An index of the condition of children: The ideal and a less-than-ideal U.S. example.' *Social Indicators Research 84*, 291–331.

Morgan, R. (2005) *Younger Children's Views on Every Child Matters*. London: Children's Rights Director, Commission for Social Care Inspection.

Morgan, R. (2006a) *About Social Workers*. London: Children's Rights Director, Commission for Social Care Inspection.

Morgan, R. (2006b) *Being a Young Carer*. London: Children's Rights Director, Commission for Social Care Inspection.

Morgan, R. (2006c) *Placements, Decisions and Reviews*. London: Children's Rights Director, Commission for Social Care Inspection.

Morgan, R. (2007a) *Care Matters: Children's Views on the Government Green Paper*. London: Children's Rights Director, Commission for Social Care Inspection.

Morgan, R. (2007b) *Children and Safeguarding*. London: Children's Rights Director, Commission for Social Care Inspection.

Morgan, R. (2008) *Children on Bullying*. London: Children's Rights Director, Ofsted.

Morgan, R. (2009a) *Care and Prejudice*. London: Children's Rights Director, Ofsted.

Morgan, R. (2009b) *Children's Care Monitor 2009*. London: Children's Rights Director, Ofsted

Morgan, R. (2009c) *Children's Messages to the Minister*. London: Children's Rights Director, Ofsted

Morgan, R. (2009d) *Future Rules*. London: Children's Rights Director, Ofsted.

Morgan, R. (2009e) *Keeping in Touch*. London: Children's Rights Director, Ofsted.

Morgan, R. (2009f) *Life in Children's Homes*. London: Children's Rights Director, Ofsted.

Morgan, R. (2009g) *Life in Residential Special Schools*. London: Children's Rights Director, Ofsted.

Morgan, R. (2009h) *Life is Secure Care.* London: Children's Rights Director, Ofsted.

Morgan, R. (2010) *Children on Rights and Responsibilities*. London: Children's Rights Director, Ofsted.

Moss, P. (2002) *From Children's Services to Children's Spaces*. ESRC Seminar series Challenging Social Inclusion, Seminar 1. Edinburgh: University of Edinburgh.

Mullender, A., Hague, G., Imam, U., Kelly, L., Malos, E. and Regan, L. (2002) *Children's Perspectives on Domestic Violence*. London: Jessica Kingsley Publishers.

Munn, P., Sharp, S., Lloyd, G., Macleod, G. *et al.* (2009) *Behaviour in Scottish Schools in 2009*. Edinburgh: Scottish Government.

Munro, E., Stein, M. and Ward, H. (2005) 'Comparing how different social, political and legal frameworks support or inhibit transitions from public care to independence in Europe, Israel, Canada and the United States.' *International Journal of Child and Family Welfare 8*, 197–198.

National Economic and Social Council (2002) *National Progress Indicators for Sustainable Economic, Social and Environmental Development*. Dublin: National Economic and Social Council.

National Economic and Social Council (2009) *Well-Being Matters: A Social Report for Ireland.* Dublin: National Economic and Social Council.

National Research Council and the Institute of Medicine (2009) *Preventing Mental, Emotional and Behavioral Disorders Among Young People: Progress and Possibilities.* Washington, DC: National Research Council and the Institute of Medicine of the National Academies.

National Statistics Board (2009) *Strategy for Statistics 2009–2014.* Dublin: The Stationery Office.

Neff, K.D., Rude, S. and Kirkpatrick, K.L. (2007) 'An examination of self-compassion in relation to positive psychological functioning and personality traits.' *Journal of Research in Personality 41*, 908–916.

Nelson, D. (2009) 'Counting What Counts – Taking Results Seriously for Vulnerable Children and Families.' In The Annie E. Casey Foundation, *The KIDS COUNT Data Book: State Profiles of Child Well-Being.* Baltimore, MD: The Annie E. Casey Foundation. Available at www.aecf.org/~/media/Pubs/Other/123/2009KIDSCOUNTDataBook/AEC186_2009_KCDB_FINAL%2072. pdf, accessed on 24 January 2010.

New Policy Institute (2002) *Poverty Reduction Indicators: A Discussion Paper.* Dublin: Combat Poverty Agency.

Newton, B. and Becker, S. (1996) *Young Carers in Southwark: The Hidden Face of Community Care.* Loughborough: Loughborough University.

NICE (2008) *Promoting Young People's Social and Emotional Well-Being in Secondary Education: Consultation on the Evidence.* London: NICE.

Nic Gabhainn, S. and Sixsmith, J. (2005) *Children's Understanding of Well-Being, National Children's Office.* Dublin: The Stationery Office.

Nic Gabhainn, S., Kelly, C. and Molcho, M. (2007) *HBSC Ireland 2006: National Report of the 2006 Health Behaviour in School-Aged Children in Ireland.* Dublin: Department of Health and Children.

Nic Gabhainn, S., Molcho, M. and Kelly, C. (2009) *Health Behaviour in School-Aged Children (HBSC) Ireland 2006. Middle Childhood Study: Socio-Demographic Patterns in the Health Behaviours, Risk Behaviours, Health Outcomes and Social Contexts of Young People's Health.* Dublin: The Stationery Office.

Niemeijer, D. (2002) 'Developing indicators for environmental policy: Data-driven and theory-driven approaches examined by example.' *Environmental Science and Policy 5*, 91–103.

OECD (2009) *Doing Better for Children.* Available at www.oecd.org/els/social/childwellbeing, accessed on 12 November 2009.

Office of the Minister for Children and Youth Affairs (2006) *State of the Nation's Children: Ireland 2006. Office of the Minister for Children and Youth Affairs.* Dublin: The Stationery Office.

Office of the Minister for Children and Youth Affairs (2007) *The Agenda for Children's Services: A Policy Handbook.* Dublin: The Stationery Office. Available at www.omc.gov. ie/documents/publications/CS_handbook[ENGLISH]lowres.pdf, accessed on 24 June 2010.

Office of the Minister for Children and Youth Affairs (2008) *State of the Nation's Children: Ireland 2008. Office of the Minister for Children and Youth Affairs.* Dublin: The Stationery Office.

O'Hannessian, C.M., Lerner, R.M., Lerner, J.V. and Voneye, A. (1995) 'Discrepancies in adolescents' and parents' perceptions of family functioning and adolescent emotional adjustment.' *Journal of Early Adolescence 15*, 4, 490–516.

O'Hare, W.P. (2008) 'Measuring the impact of child indicators.' *Child Indicators Research 1*, 4, 387–396.

Olk, T. (2004) 'German Children's Welfare between Economy and Ideology.' In A.M. Jensen, A. Ben-Arieh, C. Conti, D. Kutsar, M.N.G. Phádraig and H.W. Nielsen (eds) *Children's Welfare in an Ageing Europe* (Vol. 2). Oslo: Norwegian Centre for Child Research.

Owusu-Bempah, K. (2006) 'Socio-Geneological Connectedness: Knowledge and Identity.' In J. Aldgate, D.P.H. Jones, W. Rose and C. Jeffery (2006) *The Developing World of the Child.* London: Jessica Kingsley Publishers.

Parker, R., Ward, H., Jackson, S., Aldgate, J. and Wedge, P. (1991) *Looking after Children: Assessing Outcomes in Child Care.* London: Her Majesty's Stationery Office.

Parton, N. (2009) 'From Seebohm to Think Family: Reflections on 40 years of policy change of statutory children's social work in England.' *Child and Family Social Work 14*, 1, 69–78.

Pecora, P.J., Kessler, R.C., O'Brien, K., White, C.R. *et al.* (2006) 'Educational and employment outcomes of adults who formerly were placed in foster care: Results from the Northwest Foster Care Alumni Study.' *Child and Youth Services Review 28*, 12, 1459–1481.

Pecora, P.J., Kessler, R.C., Williams, J., O'Brien, K., *et al.* (2005) *Improving Fmaily Foster Care: Findings From the Northwest Foster Care Alumni Study.* Seattle, WA: Casey Family Programes.

Pecora, P.J., Kessler, R.C., Williams, J., Downs, A.C. *et al.* (2010) *What Works in Family Foster Care? Identifying Key Components of Success from an Alumni Follow-Up Study.* Oxford: Oxford University Press.

Pecora, P.J., Whittaker, J.K., Maluccio, A.N., Barth, R.P. and DePanfilis, D. (2009) *The Child Welfare Challenge* (3rd edition). Piscataway, NJ: Aldine-Transaction Books.

Pew Foundation (2008) *Life Chances: The Case for Early Investment in Our Kids.* Available at www.pewtrusts.org/uploadedFiles/American_Prospect_1207_EarlyEdSpecialReport. pdf, accessed on 24 June 2010.

Philip, K. (2003) 'Youth mentoring: The American dream comes to the UK?' *British Journal of Guidance and Counselling 31*, 1, 101–112.

Phipps, S. (2006) 'Using Indicators of Child Well-Being at the International Level.' In A. Ben-Arieh and R.M. Goerge (eds) *Indicators of Children's Well-Being.* Dordrecht: Kluwer.

Pink, B. (2009) 'Maintaining the momentum in Australia: From measures of a nation's progress to measures of a people's progress.' The 3rd OECD World Forum on 'Statistics, Knowledge and Policy: Charting Progress, Building Visions, Improving Life'. Busan, Korea, 27–30 October.

Pinkerton, J. and Dolan, P. (2007) 'Family support, social capital, resilience and adolescent coping.' *Child and Family Social Work 12*, 3, 219–228.

Pithouse, A. (forthcoming) 'Devolution and change since the Children Act 1989: New directions in Wales.' *Journal of Children's Services* (accepted for publication).

Pittman, K. and Irby, M. (1997) 'Promoting Investment in Life Skills for Youth: Beyond Indicators for Survival and Problem Prevention.' In A. Ben-Arieh and H. Wintersberger (eds) *Monitoring and Measuring the State of Children: Beyond Survival*. Eurosocial Report No. 62. Vienna: European Centre for Social Welfare Policy and Research.

Prilleltensky, I. and Nelson, G. (2000) 'Promoting child and family wellness: Priorities for psychological and social interventions.' *Journal of Community and Applied Social Psychology 10*, 85–105.

Prinz, R.J., Snaders, M.R., Shapiro, C.J., Whitaker, D.J. and Lutzker, J.R. (2009) 'Population-based prevention of child maltreatment: The U.S. Triple P System Population Trial.' *Prevention Science 10*, 1–13.

Prout, A. (1997) 'Objective vs. Subjective Indicators or Both? Whose Perspective Counts?' In A. Ben-Arieh and H. Wintersberger (eds) *Monitoring and Measuring The State of Children: Beyond Survival*. Eurosocial Report No. 62. Vienna: European Centre for Social Welfare Policy and Research.

Prout, A. (2003) 'Participation, Policy and Changing Conditions of Childhood.' In C. Hallett and A. Prout (eds) *Hearing the Voices of Children*. London: Falmer/Routledge.

Quilgars, D., Searle, B. and Keung, A. (2005) 'Mental Health and Well-Being.' In J. Bradshaw and E. Mayhew (eds) *The Well-Being of Children in the UK* (2nd edn). London: Save the Children.

Quinton, D. (1994) 'Cultural and Community Influences.' In M. Rutter and D. Hay (eds) *Development through Life: A Handbook for Clinicians*. Oxford: Blackwell Science.

Quinton, D., Rushton, A., Dance, C. and Mayes, D. (1997) 'Contact between children placed away from home and their birth parents: Research issues and evidence.' *Clinical Child Psychology and Psychiatry 2*, 3, 393–413.

Qvortrup, J. (1999) 'The Meaning of Child's Standard of Living.' In A.B. Andrews and N.H. Kaufman (eds) *Implementing the UN Convention on the Rights of the Child: A Standard of Living Adequate for Development*. Westport, CT: Praeger.

Rees, G. and Lee, J. (2005) *Still Running II: Findings from the Second National Survey of Young Runaways*. London: The Children's Society. Available at www.childrenssociety.org.uk/resources/documents/Research/Still_Running_2_Findings_from_the_Second_National_Survey_of_Young_Runaways_3195.html, accessed on 11 December 2009.

Rees, G., Bradshaw, J., Goswami, H. and Keung, A. (2010) *Understanding Children's Well-Being: A National Survey of Young People's Well-Being*. London: The Children's Society.

Rees, G., Francis, L. and Robbins, M. (2005) *Spiritual Health and the Well-Being of Urban Young People*. London: The Commission on Urban Life and Faith.

Reidy, M. and Winje, C. (2002) *Proceedings of the HHS ASPE State Youth Indicators Technical Assistance Workshop for States, Washington DC, April 2002*. Chicago: Chapin Hall Center for Children, University of Chicago.

Resnick, M. (1995) 'Discussant's comments: Indicators of children's well-being.' *Conference Papers* (Vol. 2). Special Report Series. Madison: University of Wisconsin-Madison, Institute for Research on Poverty.

Rhodes, J.E. (2005) 'A Theoretical Model of Youth Mentoring.' In D.L. DuBois and M.A. Karcher (eds) *Handbook of Youth Mentoring.* Thousand Oaks, CA: Sage Press.

Rice, N., Robone, S. and Smith, P.C. (2010) 'International comparison of public sector performance: The use of anchoring vignettes to adjust self-reported data.' *Evaluation 16*, 81–101.

Richardson, D. (2010) 'Regional Case Studies – Child Well-Being in Europe.' In S.B. Kamerman, S. Phipps and A. Ben-Arieh (eds) *From Child Welfare to Child Well-Being: An International Perspective on Knowledge in the Service of Policy Making.* Dordrecht: Springer.

Richardson, D., Hoelscher, P. and Bradshaw, J. (2008) 'Child well-being in Central and Eastern European countries (CEE) and the Commonwealth of Independent States (CIS).' *Child Indicators Research 1*, 211–250.

Rigby, M. and Kohler, L. (eds) (2002) *Child Health Indicators of Life and Development.* Luxembourg: European Commission.

Rose, W. and Aldgate, J. (2000) 'Knowledge underpinning the Assessment Framework.' In Department of Health, *Assessing Children in Need and their Families: Practice Guidance.* London: The Stationery Office.

Ross, T. and Vandivere, S. (2009) *Indicators for Child Maltreatment Prevention Programs.* Washington, DC: Child Trends.

Rowe, G. and Wright, G. (1999) 'The Delphi technique as a forecasting tool: Issues and analysis.' *International Journal of Forecasting 15*, 353–375.

Rowe, J. and Lambert, L. (1973) *Children Who Wait.* London: BAAF.

Russell, J.A. (2003) 'Core affect and the psychological construction of emotion.' *Psychological Review 110*, 1, 145–172.

Rutter, M. (1985) 'Resilience in the face of adversity: Protective factors and resistance to psychiatric disorder.' *British Journal of Psychiatry 147*, 598–611.

Santos-Pais, M. (1999) *A Human Rights Conceptual Framework for UNICEF.* UNICEF Innocenti Essay 9. Florence: UNICEF Innocenti Research Centre.

Sauli, H. (1997) 'Using Databases for Monitoring the Socioeconomic State of Children.' In A. Ben-Arieh and H. Wintersberger (eds) *Monitoring and Measuring the State of Children: Beyond Survival.* Eurosocial Report No. 62. Vienna: European Centre for Social Welfare Policy and Research.

Schaffer, H.R. (1996) *Social Development.* Oxford: Blackwell.

Scott, J. and Hill, M. (2006) *The Health of Looked After and Accommodated Children.* Edinburgh: Social Work Inspection Agency.

Scottish Executive (2001) *For Scotland's Children.* Edinburgh: Scottish Executive.

Scottish Executive (2002) *It's Everyone's Job to Make Sure I'm Alright: The Child Protection Audit and Review.* Edinburgh: Scottish Executive.

Scottish Executive (2003) *Improving Health in Scotland – The Challenge.* Edinburgh: Scottish Executive.

Scottish Executive (2004) *Protecting Children and Young People: The Charter.* Edinburgh: Scottish Executive.

Scottish Executive (2005) *Getting It Right for Every Child.* Edinburgh: Scottish Executive.

Scottish Executive (2006) *Getting It Right for Every Child – Proposals for Action: Consultation with Children and Young People.* Edinburgh: Scottish Executive.

Scottish Government (2007) *Sustainable Development and Wellbeing.* Presentation from the Scottish Government Greener Directorate, Edinburgh.

Scottish Government (2008) *A Guide to Getting it Right for Every Child.* Edinburgh: Scottish Government.

Scottish Government (2009) *A Curriculum for Excellence: Health and Wellbeing Experiences and Outcomes.* Edinburgh: Scottish Government

Scottish Government (2010) *A Guide to Implementing* Getting it Right for Every Child*: Messages from Pathfinders and Learning Partners.* Edinburgh: Scottish Executive.

Scottish Government and COSLA (2007) *Single Outcome Agreement between Central Government and Local Authorities.* Edinburgh: Scottish Government.

Seligman, M.E.P., Ernst, R.M., Gillham, J., Reivich, K. and Linkins, M. (2009) 'Positive education: Positive psychology and classroom interventions.' *Oxford Review of Education 35,* 3, 293–311.

Sen, A. (1997) *On Economic Inequality.* Oxford: Oxford University Press.

Shaw, C. (1998) *Remember My Messages: The Experiences and Views of 2000 Children in Public Care.* London: BAAF.

Shek, D.T.L. (1998) 'A longitudinal study of Hong Kong adolescents' and parents' perceptions of family functioning and well-being.' *Journal of Genetic Psychology 159,* 4, 389–403.

Shonkoff, J. and Phillips, D. (2000) *From Neurons to Neighborhoods: The Science of Early Childhood Development.* Washington, DC: National Research Council and Institute of Medicine.

Sinclair, I. (2005) *Fostering Now: Messages from Research.* London: Jessica Kingsley Publishers.

Sinclair, I., Wilson, K. and Gibbs, I. (2005) *Foster Placements: Why They Succeed and Why They Fail.* London: Jessica Kingsley Publishers.

Sinclair, R. (2004) 'Participation in practice: Making it meaningful, effective and sustainable.' *Children and Society 18,* 106–118.

Skuse, T. and Ward, H. (2003) *Outcomes for Looked-After children: Children's Views of Care and Accommodation.* Interim report. London: Department of Health.

Skuse, T. and Ward, H. (forthcoming) *Listening to Children's Views of Care and Accommodation.* London: Jessica Kingsley Publishers.

Social Exclusion Unit (1998) *Truancy and Social Exclusion.* London: Social Exclusion Unit.

Stalker, K. and Connors, C. (2004) 'Children's perceptions of their disabled siblings: "She's different but it's normal for us."' *Children and Society 18,* 218–230.

Steele, M. (2003) *Attachment Theory and Research: Recent Advances and Implications for Adoption and Foster Care.* Paper given at the President's Interdisciplinary Conference, Dartington Hall.

Steer, A. (2009) *Review of Pupil Behaviour: Interim Report 4*. London: Department for Children, Schools and Families. Available at www.dcsf.gov.uk/behaviourandattendance/uploads, accessed on 15 September 2009.

Stevens, K., Dickson, M., Poland, M. and Prasad, R. (2005) *Focus on Families: Reinforcing the Importance of Family. Families with Dependent Children – Successful Outcomes Project. Report on Literature Review and Focus Groups*. Wellington: Families Commission. Available at www.familiescommission.govt.nz/sites/default/files/downloads/focus-on-families.pdf, accessed on 24 June 2010.

Stradling, B., MacNeil, M. and Berry, H. (2009) 'Changing Professional Practice and Culture to Get It Right for Every Child.' *An Evaluation Overview of the Development and Early Implementation Phases of 'Getting It Right for Every Child' in Highland 2006–2009*. Edinburgh: University of Edinburgh.

Sweeting, H. (2001) 'Our family, whose perspective? An investigation of children's family life and health.' *Journal of Adolescence 24*, 2, 229–250.

Tarki/Applica (2010) *Child Poverty and Child Well-Being in the European Union*. Draft report for the European Commission DG Employment, Social Affairs and Equal Opportunities. Available at www.tarki.hu/en/news/2009/items/20091126_en.html, accessed on 28 November 2009.

Teitler, J. and Ben-Arieh, A. (2006) 'So Where Should the Research Go? Some Possible Directions and their Research Implications.' In A. Ben-Arieh and R. Goerge (eds) *Indicators of Children's Well-Being: Understanding Their Role, Usage, and Policy Influence*. Dordrecht: Springer.

Tellus3 (2008) *Tellus3 National Report*. Available at www.nationalschool.gov.uk/policyhub/news_item/tellus_ofsted08.asp, accessed on 11 December 2009.

Tellus4 (2009) *Local Authorities Information – Further Information about the Survey*. Available at www.tellussurvey.org.uk/LAInformation.aspx, accessed on 28 November 2009.

Thomas, C. (1999) *Female Forms: Experiencing and Understanding Disability*. Buckingham: Open University Press.

Thomas, N. and O'Kane, C. (1999a) 'Children's participation in reviews and planning meetings when they are "looked after" in middle childhood.' *Child and Family Social Work 4*, 221–230.

Thomas, N. and O'Kane, C. (1999b) 'Experiences of decision-making in middle childhood: The example of children "looked after" by local authorities.' *Childhood 6*, 369–387.

Thomas, N. and O'Kane, C. (2000) 'Discovering what children think: Connections between research and practice.' *British Journal of Social Work 30*, 819–835.

Tierney, J., Grossman, J. and Resch, N. (1995) *Making a Difference: An Impact Study of Big Brothers Big Sisters of America*. Philadelphia, PA: Public/Private Ventures.

Tisdall, K. and Davis, J. (2004) 'Making a difference? Bringing children's and young people's views into policy-making.' *Children and Society 18*, 131–142.

Torsheim, T., Currie, C., Boyce, W. and Samdal, O. (2006) 'Country material distribution and adolescents' perceived health: Multilevel study of adolescents in 27 countries.' *Journal of Epidemiology and Community Health 60*, 156–161.

Trewin, D. (2006) *Improving Statistics on Children and Youth: An Information Development Plan*. Canberra: Australian Bureau of Statistics.

UNESCO (in press) *Global Strategy on Youth 2009–2013*. Geneva: United Nations Education Science and Cultural Organisation.

UNESCO (2010) 'UNESCO's social and human sciences strategy for 2010-2011.' *Social and Human Sciences at UNESCO: Special issue 2001-2010.* Available at http://unesdoc.unesco.org/images/0018/001874/187407E.pdf#2, accessed on 25 June 2010.

Ungar, M. (2008) 'Resilience across cultures.' *British Journal of Social Work 38*, 2, 218–235.

UNICEF (2005) *The State of the World's Children*. New York: UNICEF.

UNICEF (2007) *Child Poverty in Perspective: An Overview of Child Well-Being in Rich Countries*. Innocenti Report Card 7. Florence: UNICEF.

UNICEF (2008) *The State of the World's Children*. New York: UNICEF.

UNICEF (2009) *Convention on the Rights of the Child*. Available at www2.ohchr.org/english/law/crc.htm, accessed on 11 December 2009.

United Nations (1989) *UN Convention on the Rights of the Child*. Geneva: United Nations.

US Census Bureau (2008) *American Indian and Alaskan Native Policy of the US Census Bureau*. Available at http://factfinder.census.gov/home/aian/Appendix-F.pdf, accessed on 20 April 2010.

US Department of Health and Human Services (2003) *The AFCARS Report – Preliminary FY2001 Estimates as of March 2003*, 8, 1–7. Washington, DC: US Government Printing Office.

US Department of Health and Human Services (2006) *Child and Family Services Reviews Procedures Manual* (Working Draft). Available at www.acf.hhs.gov/programs/cb/cwmonitoring/tools_guide/proce_manual.htm, accessed on 17 January 2010.

US Department of Health and Human Services (2009) *Child Maltreatment 2007*. Washington, DC: US Government Printing Office.

US Government Accountability Office (2004) *Child and Family Services Reviews: Better Use of Data and Improved Guidance Could Enhance HHS's Oversight of State Performance* (No. GAO-04-333). Washington, DC: US Government Printing Office. Available at www.gao.gov/new.items/d04333.pdf, accessed on 24 January 2010.

Van Ijzendoorn, M.H. and Sagi, A. (1999) 'Cross-Cultural Patterns of Attachment: Universal and Contextual Dimensions.' In J. Cassidy and P.R. Shaver (eds) *Handbook on Attachment – Theory, Research and Clinical Applications*. New York: The Guilford Press.

Vincent, C. (2009) *Child Death and Serious Case Review Processes in the UK*. Research Briefing 5. Edinburgh: Centre for Policy Learning in Child Protection.

Ward, H. (ed.) (1995) *Looking after Children: Research into Practice*. London: Her Majesty's Stationery Office.

Warnock, M. (2005) *Special Educational Needs: A New Look*. Impact No. 11. London: The Philosophy of Education Society.

Welsh Assembly Government (2004) *Children and Young People: Rights to Action*. Cardiff: Welsh Assembly Government.

Welsh Assembly Government (2007) *Rights in Action: Implementing Children and Young People's Rights in Wales*. Cardiff: Welsh Assembly Government.

Welsh Assembly Government (2008) *The Children's Monitor: Children's and Young People's Well-Being Monitor for Wales*. Cardiff: Welsh Assembly Government.

White, C.R., Havalchak, K., Jackson, L.J., O'Brien, K. and Pecora, P.J. (2007) *Mental Health, Ethnicity, Sexuality and Spirituality among Youth in Foster Care: Findings from the Casey Field Office Mental Health Study*. Seattle, WA: Casey Family Programs.

Whittaker, J.K. (2009) 'Evidence-based intervention and services for high-risk youth: A North American perspective on the challenges of integration for policy, practice and research.' *Child and Family Social Work 14*, 2, 166–177.

Wilkinson, R.G. (2005) *The Impact of Inequality*. Abingdon: Routledge.

Wilkinson, R. and Pickett, K. (2009) *The Spirit Level: Why More Equal Societies Almost Always Do Better*. London: Allan Lane.

Wistow, G. (2002) 'The Future Aims and Objectives of Social Care.' In L. Kendall and L. Harker (eds) *From Welfare to Wellbeing: The Future of Social Care*. London: Institute for Public Policy Research.

Woods, J., Hammersley-Fletcher, L. and Cole, M. (2009) 'Teaching assistants in schools – some reflections on their changing roles.' Paper presented at the annual conference of the British Educational Research Association, University of Manchester, 2–5 September.

Wulczyn, F., Barth, R.P., Yuan, Y.T., Harden, B. and Landsverk, J. (2005a) *Beyond Common Sense: Child Welfare, Child Well-Being and the Evidence for Policy Reform*. Somerset, NJ: Aldine Transaction.

Wulczyn, F.H., Orlebeke, B. and Mitchell-Herzfeld, S. (2005b) *Improving Public Child Welfare Agency Performance in the Context of the Federal Child and Family Services Reviews*. Chicago: Chapin Hall at the University of Chicago. Available at www.chapinhall. org/research/report/improving-public-child-welfare-agency-performance-context-federal-child-and-family-s, accessed on 24 January 2010.

Wulczyn, F.H., Orlebeke, B. and Haight, J. (2009) *Finding the Return on Investment: A Framework for Monitoring Local Child Welfare Agencies*. Chicago: Chapin Hall at the University of Chicago. Available at www.chapinhall.org/sites/default/files/Finding_Return_On_Investment_07_20_09.pdf, accessed on 4 January 2010.

Youniss, J., Bales, S., Christmas-Best, V., Diversi, M., McLaughlin, M. and Silbereisen, R. (2002) 'Youth civic engagement in the twenty-first century.' *Journal of Research on Adolescence 12*, 1, 121–148.

Zill, N., Sigal, H. and Brim, O.G. (1982) 'Development of Childhood Social Indicators.' In E. Zigler, S.L. Kagan and E. Klugman (eds) *America's Unfinished Business: Child and Family Policy*. New York: Cambridge University Press.

Zimmerman, R.B. (1982) *Foster Care in Retrospect*. Studies in Social Welfare, Volume 14. New Orleans, LA: Tulane University Press.

List of Contributors

Jane Aldgate OBE is Professor of Social Care at The Open University and is an Honorary Professorial Fellow at the University of Edinburgh. She has researched a wide range of child welfare issues, including family support services, child protection and services for looked after children. Jane is a qualified social worker. She is currently seconded to the Scottish Government as a professional advisor on the *Getting It Right for Every Child* programme.

Asher Ben-Arieh PhD is Head of the Joseph J. Schwartz MA Program at the Paul Baerwald School of Social Work and Social Welfare, The Hebrew University of Jerusalem. He is also Editor in Chief of the *Child Indicators Research* journal and the *Child Well-Being: Research and Indicators* Springer Book Series. He is also Co-Chair of the International Society for Child Indicators (ISCI).

Jonathan Bradshaw CBE, FBA is Professor of Social Policy at the University of York. In recent years his research has focused on international comparisons of child poverty, child benefit packages and child well-being. He has also published three studies of the state of child well-being in the UK and is working on a fourth to be published in 2011 by Policy Press.

Anne-Marie Brooks is a Senior Research Officer, Department of Health and Children, Dublin. She is a co-author of Ireland's biennial State of the Nations Children Report.

Pat Dolan is Joint Founder and Director of the Child and Family Research Centre, National University of Ireland, Galway, and also holds the UNESCO Chair in Children, Youth and Civic Engagement. Throughout his career he has had an active interest in family support and community-based interventions to support adolescents. More recently his focus has been on civic engagement and youth mentoring.

Haridhan Goswami PhD is Statistical Researcher at The Children's Society, UK. His research interests include issues of inter-group relations, particularly prejudice and discrimination, children's well-being and quantitative research methods.

Sinead Hanafin PhD is Head of Research, Department of Health and Children, Dublin. She has been the lead author of the State of the Nation's Children Report which has been published every two years since 2006 by the Office of the Minister for Children and Youth Affairs, Ireland.

Markell Harrison-Jackson is a Special Education Specialist, Pinal County Education Service Agency, US.

Antonia Keung PhD is a Research Fellow in the Department of Social Policy and Social Work, University of York. Her research interests focus on children's well-being and outcomes. Her recent research also looked at social exclusion of young people, and the costing of 16–18-year-olds not in education, employment or training (NEET) in England.

Sylda Langford is the former Director General, Office of the Minister for Children and Youth Affairs, Dublin. She is now an Adjunct Professor in the School of Applied Social Studies, University College Dublin.

Colette McAuley is Professor of Social Work in the School of Applied Social Science at University College Dublin. Prior to that, she was the Founding Director of the Child Well-Being Research Centre at the University of Southampton. The Centre was based upon an interdisciplinary collaboration between the Schools of Social Sciences and Education and developed a strong alliance with the Child Health Research Group.

Roger Morgan OBE is Children's Rights Director for England. He was previously a research fellow, social services manager and local authority chief inspector and worked at the Department of Health. He initiated Paired Reading and authored the original National Minimum Standards for Residential Care.

Pamela Munn OBE is Emeritus Professor of Curriculum Research at the University of Edinburgh. She is a former Dean of the School of Education and Past President of the British Educational Research Association. She led the Scottish Anti-Bullying Network.

Peter Pecora PhD is Managing Director of Research, Casey Family Programs, and Professor of Social Work at the University of Washington, Seattle. He has led a series of significant research programmes on children in foster care and alumni. He has focused specifically on their educational attainment and mental health needs with a view to influencing policy and practice development.

Gwyther Rees is Director of Research for The Children's Society – a children's charity in England – and manages the charity's programme of research on children's well-being, which is undertaken in collaboration with the University of York.

Wendy Rose OBE is Senior Research Fellow at The Open University. She was previously a senior civil servant advising on children's policy in England. She works on national and international research and development projects that aim to improve outcomes for children, and is currently seconded to the Scottish Government as a professional adviser to the *Getting It Right for Every Child* programme.

John Rowlands OBE is a Visiting Fellow at the Institute of Education, Thomas Coram Research Unit, University of London. He was formerly an advisor to the UK government on children's social care.

Subject Index

Author Index